How to Reach Japan by Subway

HOW TO REACH JAPAN BY SUBWAY

America's Fascination with Japanese Culture, 1945–1965

MEGHAN WARNER METTLER

UNIVERSITY OF NEBRASKA PRESS | LINCOLN AND LONDON

Portions of this book originally appeared as
"Gimcracks, Dollar Blouses, and Transistors: American
Reactions to Imported Japanese Products, 1945–1964"
in *Pacific Historical Review* 79, no. 2 (2010): 202–30.

"Buddhism Now and Zen" by Felicia
Lamport originally appeared in *Scrap Irony*
(Boston: Houghton Mifflin, 1961).

Library of Congress Control Number: 2017041405

Set in Sabon Next by Mikala R Kolander.
Designed by N. Putens.

For Peter

CONTENTS

ILLUSTRATIONS

ACKNOWLEDGMENTS

This project would not have been possible without the professional, financial, and moral support of various individuals and institutions. Providing invaluable help in locating resources were Robin Everly and Nancy Luria at the National Arboretum library, Peter Haskel at the First Zen Institute, Pat Jonas and Betty Scholtz at the Brooklyn Botanic Garden, Abby Lester at the Sarah Lawrence College archives, and the staffs of the Japan Societies of Washington DC and Northern California. I would also like to thank Allie Uyehara of Ikebana International, who not only answered a number of my questions and directed me toward materials of interest, but also attended and provided feedback on my presentation on ikebana at the 2009 Society for Historians of American Foreign Relations conference. Fellow university of Iowa alumnus David Tucker passed along a hefty stack of photocopied materials from his own project on Japanese architecture, and Chiaki Sakai at the University of Iowa library offered many helpful suggestions as the project unfurled at the dissertation stage. For aiding me in my research in Kyoto, I would like to thank Prof. Masumi Izumi at Doshisha University and the students in her seminar for their input on my work, Steve Ring for helping me navigate the Ryosen-an library, and Mitsue Fujita for her recollections of Ruth Fuller Sasaki. Most of all, domo arigatoo gozaimasu to Dr. Sohken

Togami who aided me immensely in both his roles as retired professor of sociology and practicing zen priest, chauffeured me around Kyoto, and served as an incredibly generous host to a poor American researcher with a limited knowledge of Japanese. Finally, generous financial support for this project was provided by the Matstushita International Foundation and The Center for Asian Pacific Studies at the University of Iowa.

Since this project began life as a graduate dissertation, I owe a large debt to advisers and colleagues at the University of Iowa and beyond. Stephen Vlastos proved to be an unfailing source of sage advice and thoughtful criticism in his role as dissertation advisor. Other UI faculty members—Linda Kerber, Paul Kramer, Michaela Hoenicke-Moore, and Nick Yablon—took the time to read drafts and offer insightful suggestions, and the late Ken Cmiel first launched me on this path of academic inquiry at the professional level and taught me how to think like a historian without losing my sense of humor. Also thanks to my fellow graduate students to who offered insight and various kinds of support along the way, in particular Matti Conn, Gabi von Roedern, Jeroen Laemmers, Josh Cochran, Jake Altman, Jake Hall, Brian and Angela Miller Keysor, John McKerley, Jo Butterfield, Mandy Trevors, and John and Annie Liss. Thanks also to the history faculty at Towson University, where I served as a lecturer. Feedback on my work from the faculty reading seminar was incredibly helpful, especially suggestions from Ronn Pineo and Kimberly Katz. Special thanks also to Mike Masatsugu and Akim Reinhardt for moral support as well as feedback on my academic work. I was also privileged over the years to receive valuable feedback from other historians in my field, at conferences and other venues, including Naoko Shibusawa, Sayuri Guthrie Shimizu, Jennifer Miller, Shuji Otsuka, Marlene Mayo, Drew McKevitt, and Meredith Oda.

Finally, there is my husband, Matt, foolish enough to marry a fellow scholar with expertise in mid-twentieth-century America. While this situation may have led to some professional compromises, it also has allowed him to offer valuable insight and feedback, above and beyond the coaching and support offered by most spouses. Thanks to him for sticking with me for various moves around the country trying to maintain my place in academia that eventually led to this book. And last but least only in stature, Peter Alexander Mettler was delivered mere months before this manuscript and only has the vaguest inkling what Mommy is typing behind him while she wears him, but he has already boosted my morale inordinately, if not providing initiative to complete this project sooner rather than later. If someday he reads this book and is able to learn a thing or two, he will confirm this entire endeavor was worth it.

INTRODUCTION

"The Gentleman in Gilbert and Sullivan who confessed that he did *not* 'long for all one sees that's Japanese' would find himself in the minority today." So began a March 1960 article in the *New York Times* Sunday magazine written by Donald Keene: author, translator, Columbia professor, and one of the United States' foremost authorities on Japan. He continued, "Almost any mention of Japan will bring exclamations of delight even at hardened cocktail parties, and rare is the home that lacks one or two 'oriental' touches." A "craze" was occurring, he observed, that "dwarfed" all prior American interest in Japan and its culture. He noted the prevalence of hibachi stoves, cochin lanterns, and shoji screens in American living rooms. New Japanese restaurants were opening throughout the country, and popular histories of Japan rivaled books on the Civil War in sales.[1] Indeed, in the twenty years following World War II, Japan loomed large in the personal tastes and leisure pursuits of the *Times'* main readership of upper-middle-class white Americans.

Importation of foreign cultures was, of course, nothing new to the United States by the mid-twentieth century; since colonial times Americans had purchased fine porcelain from China, copied clothing styles from France, and studied German literature.[2] All of these cases, including the "Japan craze," were about more than simply consuming products, fashions, or ideas; they were imbedded in the context of foreign relations, among government officials and diplomats, and in the minds of average citizens as well. Yet this particular instance of fascination is notable in part because it appears so unlikely on several fronts. As a newly crowned superpower and the unquestioned leader of the "free" capitalist world following World War II, the United States seemed in a better position to extend its cultural influence outward than to borrow from other nations. For the most part this was indeed the case, as the American military and corporations made their influence known around the globe.[3] Yet it was in the midst of such "Coca-colonization" (as Reinhold Wagnleitner has dubbed it), and therefore against the grain of hegemony, that Americans adopted many aspects of Japan's culture, a nation over which the United States exercised strong political influence. Moreover, only a decade before this "Japan craze" began in earnest, the United States and Japan had been engaged in one of the most destructive, brutal, and racially charged military conflicts in human history. The same consumers who were purchasing bonsai trees and shoji screens in the 1950s had recently sacrificed personal resources—and at times, loved ones—toward defeating a Japanese enemy portrayed as brutal and subhuman by the U.S. government and popular media.

How did Americans come to embrace a recent enemy with such enthusiasm? How did the hierarchical relationship between the two nations affect this cultural exchange? What does the phenomenon reveal about how Americans perceived the nation of Japan, both nations' positions in the world, and their own international role as U.S. citizens? This book seeks to explore all of these questions, within the contexts of foreign relations and American middle-class society during the postwar "Age of Affluence." I examine as case studies Americans' fascination with samurai films, *ikebana* flower arranging, bonsai cultivation, *sho-in* architecture, and Zen Buddhism. Each serves to illustrate how American consumers' adoption of Japanese culture as a fascinating alternative to their own reinforced Japan's friendly yet subordinate position toward the United States during the era of occupation and the early Cold War.

Historians John Dower and Naoko Shibusawa have each already deftly demonstrated how American images of Japan altered significantly in the wake of World War II to transform a threatening enemy into a welcome and compliant ally.[4] In the midst of World War II, not only did American propaganda depict Japanese people as monkeys, rats, and vermin to an extent that Germans and Italians never were, but news stories also included accounts of U.S. soldiers collecting ears and teeth as trophies from dead Japanese soldiers. Meanwhile, the U.S. government interred more than 100,000 Japanese Americans who they presumed would be more loyal to their race than their nation.[5] Nor did there seem to be much appreciation for Japanese culture when *Life* magazine described the tea ceremony as "asinine," claiming it was "evolved from the Chinese who have long since forgotten it. . . . Japanese life is full of similar nonsense."[6] Yet much of that hatred and suspicion seemed to evaporate immediately following Japan's surrender, when the United States took the lead in Japan's postwar military occupation. The U.S. goal was to ensure Japan's political and economic stabilization, avoiding a scenario resembling the collapse of post–World War I Germany. The U.S. military and State Department embarked on a project not only to remake Japan but to do so in a more democratic vein. In addition to providing direct economic aid, they helped craft a new constitution that extended voting rights—most significantly toward women—and distributed wealth more equitably via land reform and the breaking up of monopolistic corporations. But in the midst of this project of stabilization and reform, Cold War tensions between the United States and the USSR increased, and occupation authorities began to see a new goal for a reconstructed Japan: serving as a "bastion of freedom" in the Pacific. Policymakers envisioned Japan as a model of republican government and capitalist free enterprise for the entire region that would act as a preferable trading partner over communist China and the Soviet Union.

As part of their efforts, the State Department sought to transform Japan's public reputation quickly from a menacing and brutish war machine into a softer, friendlier nation. In a democracy like the United States, leaders can lose their positions due to unpopular policies, and some degree of consent of the governed is therefore required for any declared foreign policy program. In this case, the American electorate had to be sold on accepting their old enemy as a new ally. But trading a new set of flattering images for the ugly and grotesque portrait of old did not mean placing Japan on equal footing with the United States. Commentators referred to Japan as the "junior partner" in the new binational relationship, and while a friendly Japan was certainly preferable to the mad brute of the war years, the new image often carried with it implications of weakness, dependence, and ultimately inferiority. One of the most effective methods for carrying out this makeover involved emphasizing images of gentle women and children over the threatening Japanese soldier. Building off assumed hierarchies of race and gender, by extension the entire nation of Japan began to appear more appealing to Americans as meek and subordinate.

Official policymakers were well aware that they could not succeed in remaking Japan's image without the efforts of private tastemakers, like the popular press and cultural institutions, helping to broadcast their ideas to a wider audience. The State Department, White House, and armed forces all issued official statements that attempted to humanize Japanese people. These communications employed a range of rhetoric casting the Japanese first as pathetic victims, then as a compliant people, eager to learn the ways of democracy. In addition to government press releases and public statements, policymakers hoped members of the American public would take their own personal interest in Japanese culture to solidify the idea that the Japanese were in fact peace-loving people. As one Portland, Maine, columnist explained in 1954, "Foreign policies and 'white papers' are often couched in phrases that the public does not grasp. But when we hear the music, see the dancing, view the home décor, fashions, and other attitudes of daily living in Japan, and find them agreeable and understandable, that is carrying national policy to its destination."[7] More accessible to the American public, cultural programs could provide an effective means to cement the new alliance between the people of both nations.

It should be noted that such a cultural strategy was not limited to American views of Japan. At the same time that Americans were enjoying Japanese traditions, they learned about other important allies by taking up French cooking or studying German architectural design. Or they sported leis at luau-themed barbeques to promote solidarity with the newly annexed state of Hawai'i.[8] The Japanese themselves even engaged in their own share of foreign cultural consumption in the 1930s and '40s, strengthening ties throughout their fledgling empire. They studied, admired, and purchased pottery from Korea, Manchuria, and Okinawa, treating them as products of antique cultures more pure and honest than modern Japan's. Casting their countries of origin as admirable but backward, this craze for colonial handicrafts served a purpose eerily similar to the postwar American Japanese trend, helping consolidate the Pacific colonies' status as Japan's friendly junior partners.[9]

In creating its new portrayal and understanding of Japan, American political and cultural leaders at times fell into patterns similar to those theorized by literary scholar Edward Said in his renowned study, *Orientalism*. In 1978 he described a process whereby self-proclaimed experts on the Middle East created an image of the region and its inhabitants that was uniform, timeless, and inherently inferior to Europe. In producing such depictions, Orientalists often relied on previous European scholarship more heavily than any input from actual middle easterners, building a paradigm in which Oriental people had a tendency to appear childlike, feminized, overly emotional, and superstitious. More recently, in applying the model of Orientalism to twentieth-century U.S. foreign policy, scholars like Melani McAlister and Christian Klein found Said's framework flawed in several crucial respects. To begin with, Said tended to overlook differences in motives, interests, and backgrounds among Orientalists themselves, creating the simplified impression that Western scholars consistently described the East in uniform terms. His work thus ignores nuances and diversity across European writers, and at times he has been accused of performing a kind of Orientalist reduction on the Orientalists. In actuality, significant variations did exist among nineteenth-century Middle East experts, let alone Americans who interpreted Asian culture in the twentieth century. Not only that, but American policymakers after World War II actually took pains to distinguish themselves from earlier imperialists. Out to create Cold War alliances more than exploit colonies for resources, they attempted to appear more sensitive, benevolent, egalitarian, and less racist than their European counterparts. Their underlying goal was more often to build affinity with the people of Asia than to belittle them or create distance. In Klein's words, U.S. actions in the region functioned according to a "principle of international integration rather than . . . territorial imperialism," leading to "an ideology of global integration rather than one of racial difference." It is primarily for these reasons that McAlister urges U.S. historians to keep Orientalism "in its place." While its specifics might not be fully applicable, she argues, the fundamental model does provide a broadly useful framework for understanding Americans' perceptions of Asia since the fall of imperialism by describing the practice of westerners viewing the East through a distorted lens to promote their own interests.[10]

In addition, cultural scholar Anne McClintock built off Said's work to offer a theoretical model that proves even more applicable to U.S. overseas involvement in her study *Imperial Leather*. Expanding on *Orientalism*'s essential premise that colonial powers rhetorically constructed mythologized perceptions of their colonized territories, she frames that construction in the metaphor of home and family. Nineteenth-century Europeans often cast themselves in the role of rational, masculine father figures, with their colonial subjects depicted as more feminine or childlike in their racial backwardness. By emphasizing familial relations, this particular theory allows for more flexibility by promoting affinity as well as dominance, and is thereby applicable to twentieth-century U.S. actions. Americans cast themselves as more benevolent and caring fathers than their European counterparts, yet nevertheless remained in the seemingly natural role of male adult superiority. Also useful to American perceptions of Japan after World War II is McClintock's concept of "anachronistic space," that is, geographical territories in which time appears to stand still. To reinforce the depiction of colonial subjects as juvenile and feminine (at a time when women were often considered as naïve as children), imperial Europeans mapped out colonial territories as places whose inhabitants were inherently primitive and underdeveloped.

"Prehistoric, atavistic, and irrational," these lands were "inherently out of place in the historical time of modernity." Bound by tradition and a backward worldview, the people of such regions were presumed to be locked in a perpetual past. They would never advance to catch up with the dynamic West, at least not without direct aid and guidance from the West itself.[11]

It was in this spirit that many mid-twentieth-century American "Japan hands" (as the State Department's Japan experts were known throughout the U.S. government) approached Japanese culture, treating it as continuous and unchanging. They presumed that the way Japanese people thought and behaved in the 1950s was the same as they had thought and behaved in the twelfth century, always according to the same timeless patterns. Sociologist Ruth Benedict's 1945 study, *The Chrysanthemum and the Sword*, provides an excellent example of this type of thinking. While the book did not sell many copies in its own time, having been commissioned by the Office of War Information, it was nevertheless greatly influential in government circles. Without having visited Japan herself, Benedict surmised through reading and speaking with other American scholars that Japanese culture had two primary facets remaining constant across time. Both stressed the value of self-restraint, which she interpreted as the core of the unchanging Japanese mind-set. The first was a highly disciplined military ethic that encouraged near fanatical devotion to the emperor (the sword), the second a sense of spirituality that appreciated harmony and the serene contemplation of nature, inspiring minimalist art forms like *haiku* poetry and brush painting (the chrysanthemum). Notably, almost all of the cultural forms she cites achieved their greatest popularity in Japan before the late nineteenth century, when the nation experienced a republican political revolution and subsequent rapid industrialization. Yet she uses these examples of tradition to explain Japanese thoughts and attitudes in the 1940s as if they remained as relevant as they had ever been, and Japan itself was frozen in time with its culture and values staying perpetually constant despite drastic historical change.[12]

Influenced by such logic, U.S. policymakers did their best to discourage the influence of the militaristic sword, both among the Japanese people and in the American media, and built instead on the foundation of more peaceful and sedate traditions. In doing so, they had at their disposal substantial historical precedent, since this was not the first time Americans would cultivate a taste for the more quaint aspects of Japanese culture. In 1853 American naval commodore Matthew Perry "opened" Japan to the world after years of state-enforced isolationism. As the country began to industrialize in the late nineteenth century and expand its presence on the world stage, American consumers developed a newfound interest in its traditions. Japanese pavilions at a series of international exhibitions (i.e., world's fairs) and the popular travelogues of Lafcadio Hearn and Isabella Bird all helped further this wave of *japonisme*. Wealthy Americans decorated their sitting rooms in an "oriental flavor" incorporating paper lanterns and *kakemono* calligraphy scrolls. Japan-America Societies opened in New York and California, hosting public events and sponsoring art exhibits and theater performances. A lively trade arose in woodblock prints, incidentally launching the career of a young art dealer named Frank Lloyd Wright. Women's advice magazines praised Japanese art for its simplicity and honesty and claimed it could encourage the qualities of humility and personal restraint. Japanese traditions appealed to American consumers both as exotic exports from a country newly rediscovered and as a culture that could reflect and reinforce their own middle-class values. It was this type of popular interest in Japan that the U.S. government hoped to recultivate in the mid-twentieth century.[13]

Following World War II, the first group of Americans to help spread interest in Japan's culture were those stationed there. Managing such a massive undertaking of reconstruction and reform as the occupation required a sprawling bureaucracy of government workers from policy writers to secretaries and clerks, as well as military servicemen to maintain order. Additionally, private international humanitarian organizations like the Red Cross maintained a presence in postwar Japan as well. Even after the occupation ended in 1952, the string of military bases throughout the archipelago hosted large numbers of staff members. All told, hundreds of thousands of Americans found themselves temporarily living in Japan between 1945 and 1960.[14] During the occupation, the most common form of interaction with the native population occurred between GIs and Japanese women as they engaged in various forms of sexual and romantic relationships from prostitution to marriage.[15] But rank-and-file servicemen experienced their surroundings in other ways, too, such as visiting tourist sites on their time off or shopping and sending home souvenirs. Officers' wives and children also possessed ample spare time to interact with Japanese servants, shopkeepers, and playmates, and to take classes in traditional Japanese arts, like ikebana flower arranging and bonsai cultivation.[16]

Beginning in the mid-1950s, returning service personnel presented Japanese traditions to the American public, often with the help of privately funded art and cultural institutions. Influential Japan enthusiasts like John D. Rockefeller III at Japan Society, Museum of Modern Art director Arthur Drexler, and George Avery, head of the Brooklyn Botanic Garden, created exhibits that placed Japanese art, architecture, and horticulture on display for a wide variety of tourists visiting New York City. They also sold books on Japanese design in their gift shops and offered classes on how Americans could create their own Japanese handicrafts. In organizing such displays, museum directors were assisted by like-minded institution heads and practitioners from Japan, many of whom began their own campaigns to educate the American public. Bonsai master Yuji Yoshimura went on a speaking tour, accomplished Japanese garden designer Osamu Mori published books, and public intellectual D. T. Suzuki became the most famous proponent of Zen Buddhism in the United States. Allowing actual Japanese to speak for their own culture is one respect in which postwar Americans differed from earlier Orientalists. However, direct input from Japanese nationals did not necessarily translate into an alternative, less-reductive image of their country, as most Japanese spokesmen tended to promote the same cultural interpretations as their American counterparts. Seeing Japan's image broadcast around the world in any kind of flattering light appealed to many patriotic Japanese, and some proved willing to advance Orientalist assumptions about themselves in the service of bolstering their nation's (or their own) reputation abroad.

Americans who never had the chance to visit Japan or attend these exhibits could still encounter Japanese culture indirectly in mass-circulation newspapers and magazines. Throughout the 1950s and early 1960s, many periodicals aimed at an upper-middle-class readership, including the *New York Times*, *Vogue*, the *New Yorker*, and the *Saturday Review*, carried articles discussing the various Japanese art forms making their way to the United States via returning military service personnel or put on display by museums and cultural organizations. With a wide circulation (the *Times* reached a large subscribership beyond New York City), these publications helped spread the Japan craze to millions of readers. In doing so, they inevitably served as mediators for their readers, interpreting rather than simply presenting Japanese culture. Most frequently, as dispensers of advice and self-appointed heralds of good taste, magazines promoted Japanese culture as fashionable or intellectually stimulating, creating the impression that Japanese traditions were, somewhat paradoxically, influencing the latest fashions in mainstream American culture.

Beyond popularizing Japanese culture, experts and tastemakers established a concept of what it was and what it meant, and for the most part they seemed to arrive at a basic consensus on their portrayal of Japan. Some borrowed a word directly from the Japanese language to describe what they understood to be its essence. By 1960, "shibui" emerged as shorthand for a particular graceful, minimalist Japanese aesthetic. Often translated among postwar American commentators as "tastefully austere" or "beautifully imperfect," in 1950s Japan it actually held a range of possible meanings, from implying a bitter flavor or acquired taste to suggesting refinement and elegance.[17] Today it is most frequently used by young people to describe aging yet still handsome male celebrities.[18] But when the term first appeared in English in designer Jiro Harada's 1936 book, *The Lesson of Japanese Architecture*, he defined it as "beauty in simplicity." Harada claimed that the word was "difficult to translate" and that it stood for "quiet, delicate and refined taste, the beauty that does not show on the surface, austerity in art without severity. . . . it is opposed to anything which is gaudy, crude or ostentatious." Arthur Drexler resurrected the word nineteen years later and defined it as "an austere taste informed with a certain pleasurable melancholy."[19] It was soon adopted by other writers, including the editors of *House Beautiful* magazine, whose September 1960 issue featured articles entitled "How to Be Shibui with American Things" and "New Home Furnishings with the Shibui Concept of Beauty." Advertisers eventually embraced the word as well, and by 1964 "shibui" had become the brand or model name for a variety of products including ceramic tile, interior wall paint, fiberglass dinner trays, "Wunda-Weve" nylon carpet, and women's undergarments.[20]

In its postwar American context, the "shibui" aesthetic primarily helped reinforce the "chrysanthemum" image of Japan. Americans came to understand through promotional materials that ikebana, bonsai, and Japanese homes and gardens all adhered to a timeless appreciation for simplicity and reflected spiritual qualities, including an appreciation of nature. Many further believed that the philosophy of Zen Buddhism underlay all of these art forms and promoted quietude and restraint through its serene approach to life. In claiming that Japan's culture, and by extension its inhabitants, were fundamentally and inherently peaceable, these "shibui" traditions furthered foreign policy goals. But they simultaneously held a personal appeal for many American consumers that had nothing to do with foreign policy. Appearing to stem directly from an ancient civilization that embraced a foreign set of values, white Americans believed Japanese culture provided a system of alternative aesthetics and beliefs from which they could usefully borrow. For instance, homeowners could balance the cheap and disposable feeling of mass-produced gadgets scattered about their living room by displaying a hand-cultivated, timelessly beautiful bonsai on the bookshelf, or they could find respite from the hurried pace of contemporary American life through Zen meditation. At the same time, many cultural institutions and journalists posited that these traditions followed aesthetic patterns of minimalism and abstraction similar to modern art, then popular among members of the upper middle class in North America and Europe. Ikebana and sho-in architecture employed clean, simple lines, while intellectual movements of the time held a moral relativism akin to Zen beliefs. Americans were thus able to embrace shibui culture because it appeared both foreign and familiar, ancient and modern, distinctly Other, but sharing the same values as Western designers and intellectuals.

This image of Japanese culture as undeniably foreign yet still recognizable coincided perfectly with the way policymakers wanted the American public to view the people of Japan as well. To most white Americans, the Japanese populace belonged to a distinct race, differentiated even from other Asians, and their differences went beyond physical appearance to include unique tastes and habits. The precise characteristics ascribed to them vacillated over generations between their appearing backward, genteel, artistic, and disciplined. During the war, Americans most frequently viewed the Japanese as ignorant and duplicitous at best, maniacal and sadistic at worst. But in the dramatic about-face that accompanied the war's end, occupation authorities argued that under U.S. influence the Japanese could become reliable allies by copying American values of democracy and entrepreneurship. While superficial differences would persist, the Japanese race would essentially acquire a more honest and egalitarian approach to the world that was familiar to the average American.[21] This attempt to blur lines of racial difference was furthered by a wider reluctance on the part of most American commentators to utilize the concept of race at all in the postwar era. Many avoided even using the word "race," most likely in efforts to distance both themselves and their readers from the Nazis' heavily racialized rhetoric. But, of course, circumventing the term did not make the concept disappear. Instead, many speechwriters and journalists replaced the notion of racial difference with cultural difference. "Culture" was able to do the same fundamental work as race when treated as so ingrained in a particular people as to be deterministic. Instead of claiming that Africans, South Americans, or Asians behaved in a certain manner because of their biological race, Americans could attribute inherent differences to the influence of quaint, exotic, or retrograde traditions. On a fundamental level, the study of foreign cultures became the study of the race cloaked in a new and softer guise.[22] Thus while the mainstream American media no longer referred to "the Japanese race," Japanese people remained subject to a new framework of stereotypes based on culture, which scholars and other commentators discussed as inborn and unchanging.

Now that the concept of culture carried the heavy weight of determining the worldview and personality traits of an entire race, almost anything Americans assumed about Japanese culture and traditions would apply to all Japanese people by extension. A 1961 Gallup poll revealed that the most common adjectives respondents used to describe Japanese people were "artistic" and "practical," just like traditional Japanese arts that combined beauty and utility. Also ranking high was "hardworking," such as those who skillfully produced such handicrafts. All three characterizations outranked the previous belief that the Japanese were "sly," suggesting that positive race-based stereotypes had indeed succeeded in replacing earlier negative ones. At the same time, an equally small number of respondents characterized Japanese people as "progressive," that is, most Americans surveyed felt they were backward-looking and beholden to tradition.[23] As a more benign understanding of the nation of Japan and its culture took hold, Americans soon thought of the Japanese people themselves as shibui.

At the same time that this new image of Japan allowed Americans to hold race-based assumptions without appearing to be racist, it created a highly gendered image of Japan as well. Just as the Japanese people seemed to transform from sly to artistic overnight, their culture changed from threateningly hyper masculine to serenely feminine. In *America's Geisha Ally*, Naoko Shibusawa illustrates how such a transition was achieved. As Japan moved from enemy to ally, she explains, the country needed to appear less threatening and more welcoming to incoming occupiers. Therefore, images of accommodating and appealing women and children replaced the fanatical kamikaze pilot as the most common figure representing Japan in American media. Building on the supposedly natural hierarchy of male dominance, as well as assumptions that women are inherently submissive, the feminization of Japan helped cast the nation in its new role of subordinate partner and helpmeet. Press coverage of the "Hiroshima Maidens," a charity project providing plastic surgery to female atomic bomb victims, helped to solidify this new image. So too did Hollywood films like *Geisha Boy*, *My Geisha*, and the adaptation of James Michener's novel *Sayonara*, all of which featured Japanese female love interests and few adult male Japanese characters.[24] Shibui art forms furthered this process. While none of the traditional Japanese arts promoted in the United States were necessarily considered "women's work" in Japan, American promoters attributed supposedly feminine virtues to them, including passivity, restraint, and subtle beauty. Not only did Americans see more female Japanese faces during this era; they came to view Japanese culture as fundamentally female as well.

As a consequence, even if unintended by American policymakers, such Japanese arts attracted equal, if not greater, numbers of American women as they did men. While gender stereotypes of the time led many Americans to assume that women's involvement in diplomatic relations was minimal to nonexistent, this new form of cultural exchange endowed typically female pursuits like interior decorating and flower arranging with new meaning, allowing women to participate in furthering an important international alliance. Indeed, this book introduces a large cast of American female historical actors who conscientiously worked in various capacities to promote the cause of United States–Japanese friendship. Some, like Ikebana International founder Ellen Gordon Allen, ran binational organizations that promoted cross-cultural exchange. Military wives taught their American friends about the arts and traditions they encountered living in Japan, while homemakers did their part as consumers to purchase and display Japan-inspired furnishings. Even under the seemingly strict gender codes of the postwar era, these women, consciously or not, were doing their part to promote American appreciation for their new ally.

Yet Japanese arts were neither strictly the purview of women nor entirely feminine. Samurai movies and Zen Buddhism both included undeniably "manly" elements like swordplay and tough-minded stoicism. Because associating such traits with Japan could disrupt the image of the nation as peace-loving and eager to accept U.S. aid, such masculine attributes often lost their menace when they appeared as safely contained in Japan's distant past. Samurai who fought with swords in movies—as opposed to, say, contemporary protestors of the U.S.-Japan security agreement—carried out their violence in costume dramas depicting a long ago, less enlightened feudal era. Zen monks who went without food and sleep during periods of rigorous meditation did not appear nearly as threatening as the soldiers who reportedly practiced similar levels of self-denial during the war. Instead, as relics of a bygone era, the holy men's extreme religious devotion appeared more curious than sinister. In cases where Japanese culture resisted feminization, U.S. interpreters aged it instead. Cultural scholar Jane Naomi Iwamura has identified the trope of the "Oriental Monk." Rendered passive and compliant by both his age and spiritual convictions, he echoed the accommodating attitude of the geisha as he welcomed westerners to learn from his ancient wisdom, making Asians appear more appealing while simultaneously reinforcing racial hierarchy.[25] Extending this character as a symbol for the entire nation, Japan resembled a weakened old man whose days of strength lay behind him, unable to compete with the modern, virile United States.

This aging of Japanese culture—the assumption that the country was governed by traditions that linked the present directly to a timeless past—is the most salient feature of the "shibui" phenomenon, helping to shape its racial and gendered assumptions. Admiring Japanese culture on several fronts, and at times upholding it as more spiritual or intellectual than America's commercial culture, postwar Japan enthusiasts nevertheless treated Japan as an anachronistic space, acting as if the nation had contributed little to the arts and sciences since ancient times. Many came to treat Japanese arts as if they had sprung fully developed out the mysterious mists of time, remaining essentially unchanged into the present era. In actuality, all of these practices had been subject to processes of adjustment and revision over the span of centuries in Japan. Bonsai growers had added new cultivation techniques to their repertoire, a plethora of new ikebana styles had emerged, each suited to the taste of its own time, and since the turn of the twentieth century, Japanese homeowners had begun decorating their houses with Western-style furnishings. The exact version of Zen Buddhism that some Americans came to believe underlay all other Japanese arts was in fact an ideology formulated in the late nineteenth century to win the admiration of Europeans and Americans during the Meiji reform era. In fact, the notion that the Japanese people held an inherent love of nature was a concept largely furthered by Japan's militarist government to promote national solidarity when mobilizing for war in the 1930s.[26]

Despite the alterations and recent origins of these "traditions," many self-appointed experts and authorities on Japan in the postwar United States sought to revive what they perceived as pristine artifacts of Japan's prouder past. In their view, an encroaching modernity threatened to sully and corrupt Japan's ties to its traditional cultural roots. In his 1964 autobiography, film star Charlie Chaplin, who had by then become an ardent Japan enthusiast, wrote that the Japanese "people's appreciation of those simple moments in life—so characteristic of their culture—a lingering look at a moonbeam, a pilgrimage to view cherry blossoms, the quiet meditation of the tea ceremony—seems destined to disappear in the smog of western enterprise."[27] Perfectly preserved, Japanese culture was considered artistic, humble, subdued, and intriguingly exotic; the noise, ugliness, and stresses of the modern world where most Americans spent their lives could only soil such a harmonious setting.

As a consequence, American Japan enthusiasts tended to seek out art forms that in actuality held little relevance in contemporary Japan. By the 1950s most Japanese considered bonsai a hobby that old men took up in retirement, and they avoided Zen for its co-optation by the wartime military. Indeed, most mid-twentieth-century Japanese people confronted the same stresses and ugliness as their American counterparts. In 1960 Arthur Koestler, a Hungarian-British essayist, published *The Lotus and the Robot*, in which he criticized Japan enthusiasts for focusing exclusively on the staid traditions of the past. His own travelogue paints a far busier, more hectic, and confused picture of the nation, filled with harried bureaucrats, agonizingly competitive students, and tranquilizer-popping housewives. Instead of traditional hobbies like bonsai and ikebana, the most popular forms of entertainment among modern Japanese consumers included listening to jazz in neon-lit nightclubs and gambling at *pachinko* parlors filled with the flashing lights and ringing bells of rows of gambling machines. Even traditional Japanese culture itself, Keene pointed out in his article, included gaily colored pottery and Buddhist temples practically dripping with lavish ornaments, hardly examples of minimalist restraint.[28]

Time would prove that these other facets of Japanese life and culture could not remain entirely hidden from Americans' view. Commercial goods imported from Japan at the time were often mass-produced and inexpensive, far more the products of an industrialized society than a traditionally artistic one. The Beat Movement of disaffected young artists attempted to infuse Zen with a sense of jazzy spontaneity. But undoubtedly the biggest example of unrefined, unrestrained Japanese culture ever to reach U.S. shores was Godzilla, who first appeared on American movie screens in 1956. Standing fifty meters tall and breathing atomic fire as he trampled Tokyo beneath his mammoth scaly feet, he was anything but subdued and elegant. Even so, he could do little to damage the concept of Japan as ancient and serene. Godzilla was promoted like any other science fiction monster, and few Americans realized he was Japanese until they actually saw the movie. Moreover, given that his appeal lay more in the base human fascination with destruction and violence than with a particular Eastern aesthetic, he would go on to become a universal icon who defied classification. Originating in Japan, yet not seeming to belong entirely to any nation, he never really bore the weight of teaching Americans the true essence of Japanese culture.

But such transnational figures were rare in the popular culture landscape. While both the positive and negative aspects of American commercial culture quickly went global, Americans could selectively accept only those elements of Japanese culture that they labeled as particularly characteristic of a quaint and foreign culture. By interpreting Japanese traditions exclusively as serene, subtle, and timeless, the promoters of shibui arts succeeded in creating an image of Japan as a peaceful nation, capable of serving as a trustworthy American ally. Perhaps unintentionally, they cast it as a bastion of elegance as well as freedom, providing Americans with cultural forms that supposedly combined the minimalism of modernist aesthetics with ancient Eastern wisdom and spirituality. In the process they successfully remade the image of Japan to replace the race-fueled hatreds of war by trading one set of stereotypes for another. In the end, they created a flattering yet distorted image of Japan: as a country that was worthy of admiration and emulation, but harmlessly locked in a subdued and tasteful past.

CHAPTER I

HUMBLE LEADERS OF THE FREE WORLD

Historical Context of the Shibui Aesthetic

While it is unlikely that many American Japan enthusiasts in the 1950s would overtly state they loved Japanese culture because the State Department encouraged it, they might claim they were promoting international understanding and furthering ties between the United States and Japan. But they were even more likely to argue they loved ikebana, bonsai, sho-in architecture, rock gardening, or Kurosawa's films for their beauty and craftsmanship. Like most historical actors who cannot see the full landscape of their era while standing within it, most followers of the shibui trend remained unaware of how the complex contours of global politics and international hierarchies were shaping their personal tastes or decisions as consumers.

Nevertheless, all of these occupation personnel, museum directors, magazine editors, and suburban homeowners were indeed part of a larger historical context. When World War II ended, the United States emerged not just as an Allied victor but ultimately as the world's most powerful nation in terms of military and economic might. The stated goal of most U.S. policymakers, as well as many concerned middle-class citizens, was to wield such power benevolently, to uplift and improve all nations to ensure a more lasting peace than they had found in the first half of the twentieth century. While internationalist ideology encouraged the consumption of Japanese culture from across the globe, within the United States that appreciation was shaped by America's socioeconomic structure, especially the notion of status hierarchy. In touting the shibui aesthetic's resemblance to fashionable modern art, wide-circulating publications conveyed to their middle-class readership that America's wealthy elite appreciated Japanese traditions. Such press coverage lent Japanese culture a degree of social cachet and gave some consumers yet another reason to embrace it. Finally there were those Americans who seemed caught between these overseas and domestic contexts. Japanese Americans were often viewed as perpetually foreign, with some white Americans assuming they held the potential to serve as intermediaries between the two cultures. But questions arose over whether this was a role that all members of the Japanese American community would willingly embrace.

The International Context: Cultural Exchange and Japan's Rehabilitation

When Japan surrendered to the Allied Powers on August 15, 1945, plans had already been set in motion for a postwar occupation program. After essentially excluding the USSR and marginalizing Great Britain and Australia, the United States emerged as the clear leader of the operation. But rebuilding Japan was not the United States' only postwar project. Troops were simultaneously stationed in Germany, Austria, and Italy, reestablishing order in those former enemy nations as well. The fledgling United Nations was also taking shape under American auspices that summer in New York City. Within several years, the Marshall Plan would offer financial aid to help war-torn Western Europe rebuild its economies and infrastructure. Each of these projects was part of a larger optimistic goal popular among the allied victors at the time: to prevent future war by promoting political and economic stability worldwide, and providing a forum in which nations could resolve their differences without the use of military force. It soon became clear that cultural exchange would play a significant role in these endeavors, under the theory that nations who mutually understand each other will be less likely to engage in conflict. As self-appointed leaders of this new postwar order, Americans inside and outside the government saw themselves as possessing both the means and the responsibility to promote peace and understanding around the globe.

Finding themselves in the newfound position of a global superpower, policymakers and concerned citizens alike sought to put a benign face on U.S. global hegemony, warmly embracing other nations while they exercised power and influence over them. Many were influenced by Wendell Willke's best-selling 1943 travelogue *One World*, in which the former liberal Republican presidential candidate toured the Soviet Union and Asia and put forward his vision for a postwar world order that emphasized human commonality. The book was so popular by the war's end that the term "One World-ism" entered American rhetoric to describe this new mindset. Christina Klein offers a more precise term for this line of thinking as a "global imaginary of integration." In contrast to the contemporary rhetoric of containment, which was premised on division by depicting the Soviet Union and other communist nations as perpetually threatening to the United States, this worldview called on Americans to find sympathy with other "free peoples" across the globe. Indeed, as the 1940s became the 1950s and Cold War tensions rose, this strategy grew in strength as it was deployed to cement ties with other allied and nonaligned nations. The subsequent drive to expand economic markets and free trade, spreading strength and prosperity among capitalist nations (not least the United States), further encouraged such an integrationist model. Over the several decades following World War II, Americans came to conceive of their nation as "less a free-standing, armed defender of the world and more a member of a community bound through emotional bonds." The global imaginary of integration "served as a way for Americans to affirm themselves as a global yet non-imperial power." Unlike the exploitative Europeans of earlier generations, Americans would take a more egalitarian and empathetic approach toward the regions of the world they nonetheless dominated.[1]

Such a conceptual framework was bolstered by cultural projects—in the world of fine arts as well as popular culture—aimed to capture and promote a spirit of universal unity and cooperation. The 1955 traveling photography exhibit *The Family of Man* featured images from around the world of people engaging in similar life activities, such as schooling, weddings, and funerals. More famously, Disneyland's *It's a Small World* attraction opened in 1964 in a similar spirit. Both placed images of people from various countries on display for an audience of everyday Americans, often depicting their subjects in traditional clothing and native settings to demonstrate that despite superficial differences, everyone across the globe experiences the same basic human emotions. Meanwhile, forms of popular entertainment, including magazine articles, movies, and Broadway musicals, carried stories meant to expose Americans to foreign cultures and evoke sympathy with foreign peoples. The federal government created international exchange programs, including the Fulbright Program in 1945 and the Foreign Leader Program in 1948. The latter sponsored visits by foreign politicians and journalists to the United States, while the former welcomes scholars from around the world, as well as sending American students and academics abroad.[2]

But no matter how friendly the United States appeared to the rest of the world, it remained undeniable that they were at the top of the international hierarchy. When helping to found the United Nations, Eleanor Roosevelt spoke of a "hub and spoke system," envisioning the United States as the undisputed center of a new global network promoting peace and democracy, with all other like-minded nations revolving around the outside.[3] This America-centric attitude quickly became apparent in many U.S. outreach programs. A 1953 study by the State Department's Advisory Commission on Educational Exchange discovered that foreign students visiting the United States typically found their American classmates far more eager to tout the strengths of their own national character than to learn about foreign perspectives. Politicians and journalists sponsored by the Foreign Visitors Program tended to be selected on the basis of how sympathetic they might be toward the United States and its overseas goals, rather than what unique insight they could bring to bear on American policy. While exchange clearly was occurring, communication remained lopsided, as America's central position bred a form of chauvinism that promoted the American Way.[4]

The U.S. occupation of Japan reflected this wider strategy of promoting global cultural understanding with the caveat of American superiority. In 1950 the State Department sponsored a commission to assess the state of U.S./Japanese cultural exchange, led by John D. Rockefeller III. With the conclusion of the study, he proclaimed, in typically "One World-ist" language:

> The interchange of culture in this broad sense is a means of helping to bring people of different countries closer together in their appreciation and understanding of each other and each other's way of life.... Just as it would be considered folly to let political and economic relations between countries drift, so it is wasteful and even dangerous to let the cultural aspects go unanalyzed and undirected. In any country the attitude of its citizens toward another nation is a powerful factor in the forming of international policies.[5]

In other words, a lasting peace could only be achieved between the United States and Japan if the two nations' citizens understood each other on a fundamental level. Rockefeller advocated the establishment of academic exchanges, information centers, and institutes to translate literature. His intention was that this flow of ideas and information would occur equally in both directions, employing the metaphor of a "two-way street," with Americans learning as much about the Japanese as the other way around.[6] Ambassador John Foster Dulles later agreed, telling the British ambassador to Japan in 1951 that he wanted to "set up an attraction" with Japan through the exchange of culture, scholars, and scientific knowledge. Such actions would be "indispensable to keep Japan over a long period in association with us," avoiding the temptation to develop a close trade relationship with China "as long as [mainland China] remains Communist and they are in a position to open attractive markets." However, he also stated that the U.S. government had no official plans to sponsor such exchanges and that they would be carried out on an informal basis, supposedly by universities and private cultural institutions.[7]

For its part, the Japanese government had a fairly long-standing tradition of direct involvement in spreading its national culture overseas. Ever since its victories in the Sino-Japanese and Russo-Japanese wars at the turn of the century, Japan had been trying to find a louder voice on the international stage. According to historian Jessamyn Abel, even after the Japanese withdrew from the League of Nations in 1933 to pursue a more aggressive imperialist policy, they continued to embrace a spirit of internationalism. In 1934 the Foreign Ministry established the Kokusai Bunka Shinkokai, translated as the Society for International Cultural Relations. In addition to publishing books and pamphlets in various languages and promoting exhibits of Japanese culture, by 1940 the KBS was dispatching experts in traditional Japanese arts throughout their fledgling empire to teach classes and indoctrinate their colonial subjects with a new, shared cultural identity. After 1945 the organization remained largely intact and made a relatively easy transition from belligerent to peaceful purposes. The structure of the cultural exchange programs remained the same, but their ideology shifted to depict Japan as a nation of rich traditions that approached the rest of the world in a spirit of cooperation and peace. Throughout the 1950s they published pamphlets, manuals, and "coffee table" books in English that were distributed in the United States, and sponsored exhibits and performances at American museums. The organization still exists today promoting similar rhetoric, having changed its name to the Japan Foundation in 1972.[8]

Yet while the institutional framework was certainly in place for Americans to learn about Japanese culture—to borrow a remark from historian John Dower—what emerged instead of mutual exchange was a "two-way street [that] amounted to a multilane highway on the U.S. side, and a single lane on the other."[9] The stubborn constraints of U.S. chauvinism applied here as well, and as Japan became the recipient of much American education and counsel, often tied to financial aid or sponsorship, Japanese voices had to struggle to make Americans listen to them. Rockefeller himself did not always treat Japanese as equals, publicly expressing doubts that they were capable of grasping democracy without American tutelage.[10]

Such beliefs in both the superiority of American culture and the inherent ignorance of the Japanese people were common among American occupation leaders within the Supreme Command of the Allied Powers (SCAP). Historians such as Shibusawa, as well as Michael Schaller and others, have shown how policymakers were able to swiftly transform Japan from enemy to ally by taking a condescending attitude toward its people.[11] Despite the fact that Japan had recently proven itself fully industrialized and capable of waging modern technological warfare, SCAP leadership subscribed to the Orientalist notion that the Japanese had lost the war, at least in part, due to an unenlightened worldview. Japan specialists within the State Department claimed that the nation's inherent emphasis on self-discipline and repression was to blame in leading the country to wage war in the first place. They argued that an aggressive mind-set premised on "the way of the samurai" had created an overly militant outlook that allowed leaders to impulsively plunge the nation into a war they could not possibly win. U.S. observers further reasoned that Japan's cultural emphasis on hierarchy discouraged the public from protesting such foolhardy decisions; cowed into submission, they allowed the fanatical leadership to proceed. According to occupation authorities, it was imperative to replace such antiquated values of both aggression and submission with more rational and egalitarian American values in order to prevent future Japanese violence.[12]

The occupation therefore involved numerous reform programs that sought to change the roots of Japanese society down to the ways people conceived of themselves and their leadership. Led by the same policymakers who had crafted Roosevelt's New Deal legislation, now working for the State or War/Defense Departments, new programs instituted in occupied Japan attempted to undo hierarchical ways of thinking along with status differentials between landowners and tenants, business owners and employees, and husbands and wives. Tenant farmers received free land after a SCAP decree broke up vast estates. Massive corporate conglomerates known as *zaibatsu* were dissolved and reduced into smaller independent companies. Women were granted the right to vote for the first time, and informational campaigns encouraged husbands to show more respect toward their wives and children. In essence, the U.S. military paradoxically imposed democracy and equality on the occupied Japanese populace via government dictate to the people. In 1947 SCAP did "reverse course" somewhat, to use the State Department's own terminology, with the new goal of strengthening Japan as an economic Cold War ally. Zaibatsu were permitted to regain their lost holdings, and a communist purge occurred throughout the government and labor union leadership. Nevertheless, the occupation's underlying goals had been firmly established, with the United States reforming Japanese society according to its democratic ideals, eradicating what SCAP perceived as backward hierarchical traditions, and overhauling the Japanese mind-set.

Best embodying this role of reformer by decree was Gen. Douglas MacArthur, the individual to whom the title of Supreme Commander or SCAP was also frequently applied. Rarely leaving his headquarters in Tokyo's requisitioned Dai Ichi hotel, or even interacting directly with Japanese citizens, he ran the occupation much like a benevolent dictator. Working through legions of American bureaucrats, he would hand down edicts to the Japanese government, expecting them to comply without hesitation, in some respects following the machinations of an autocracy more than a democracy. Toward the occupation's end, he bore the brunt of much criticism from the Japanese press for comparing the nation to "a boy of twelve" in his May 5, 1951, testimony before the U.S. Senate. When taken out of context, this four-word phrase appeared to be a simple insult directed toward the Japanese populace he had been effectively governing for five years. But when viewed in light of his entire testimony, his characterization is more complex in its attempt to commend the Japanese for the progress they had made since the war's end, albeit in a highly condescending way. Referring to the occupation as "a tuitionary period," he contrasted the Japanese people to more rigid and conservative Germans and argued that the former were "susceptible to following new models, new ideas. You can implant basic concepts there. They were still close enough to origin to be elastic and acceptable to new concepts."[13] In essence, he was describing them as apt pupils, and indeed a year earlier, diplomat George Kennan had criticized SCAP for taking a "school-masterish and smug attitude" toward the occupation.[14] If his perception was accurate, this approach to the Japanese as open-minded students eager to embrace American values began at the top.

At its opposite end, the Japanese and American publics alike were led to believe that the United States had won the war due to the superiority of its culture and values over the benighted worldview that had led Japan astray. Numerous accounts of the occupation in the U.S. press emphasized the pathetic circumstances of Japanese women and children devastated by the war, while simultaneously proclaiming their eagerness for American aid and reform. An oft-photographed scene from the immediate postwar years was Japanese children swarming U.S. jeeps, eager to receive chocolates and chewing gum from GIs. But it wasn't just small handouts that the Japanese longed for. According to accounts by both U.S. government and outside observers, they desperately wished to reform themselves and their culture according to American ideals. In her 1949 book on the occupation, Red Cross worker Lucy Herndon Crockett described a national craze for American culture and the concept of democracy. She described the typical Japanese man as "grasping at the now extended hand that so recently knocked him down, and striving, with wildly varying results, to model himself after concepts that must run contrary to every one of his deeply ingrained feudal instincts."[15] Crockett depicted a typical Japanese man as longing to abandon his old misguided culture and learn important lessons from the victors. In such depictions, the Japanese appeared infantilized as students, a role which simultaneously humanized them and cast Americans above them as knowledgeable, benevolent teachers.[16]

In actuality, this particular interpretation of postwar relations, wherein friendly Japanese learned eagerly from their American tutors, fell far short of the truth. In his short story "American *Hijiki*," Nosaka Akiyuki remembered being one of those children clamoring around American jeeps asking for candy and gum. But his gratitude was mixed with large doses of humiliation and confusion (chewing gum does little to ease the pain of starvation).[17] Indeed, while the United States and Japan have remained official allies since the surrender, resentment toward American hegemony has continuously simmered among significant sectors of the Japanese populace. After Japan regained its autonomy in 1952, the United States left a network of military bases throughout the nation whose presence Japanese protestors resented on several fronts. Not only did they lead to the emergence of vice districts catering to American servicemen, but many Japanese exhausted by World War II also worried that such military installations might implicate their nation in a future conflict with the nearby Soviet Union or China. Moreover, these bases could potentially house the expanding U.S. supply of nuclear weapons, an understandable sore spot for many Japanese citizens. Relations over this particular issue deteriorated further in 1955 when the Japanese fishing boat *Lucky Dragon No. 5* absorbed fallout from nearby U.S. nuclear testing. These tensions culminated in 1960 with the renegotiation of the bilateral Security Treaty. The revised agreement made more explicit the United States' obligation to defend Japan, but also turned former Japanese military bases over to U.S. control and threatened to entangle Japan in future regional military conflicts, requiring the nation to help support security in the Far East. Protests led by unions and university students broke out across the country in response. Some turned violent, including the storming of the parliamentary diet building by Japan Socialist Party members that left 482 protestors and 536 police injured, as well as one student trampled to death.[18]

But much of this resentment, resistance, or any form of Japanese anger tended to be ignored or brushed aside in American representations of Japan's culture. While Japanese leftists took to the streets, American experts, tastemakers, and consumers continued to focus on the nation's traditional art forms that projected beauty, delicacy, and quietude. The protests may have made news headlines, but they did not affect in any way advertisements for Japanese-inspired home furnishings or articles promoting bonsai cultivation. By the mid-1950s, cultural exchange between the United States and Japan had grown lopsided in such a way that while America promoted or imposed all aspects of its value system and commercial culture on Japanese citizens, Americans had the luxury of being selective as to what aspects of Japanese life and culture they chose to care about. Such a relationship emerged due to the power imbalance between the two nations, but this sense of inequality was not something many American Japan enthusiasts reflected upon too heavily as they helped to rebuild friendship between the two nations. In fact, it was part of their integrationist worldview that allowed them to take on the role of a superior but benevolent nation reaching out to other inferior but fascinating and friendly people. Casting only passing glances at the ugly tensions and protests, followers of the shibui trend kept their eyes planted on a much more pleasant image of a beautiful, peaceful, traditional Japan.

The Domestic Context: Socioeconomic Class and Modernist Taste

While the appreciation for certain Japanese traditions proved to be geographically widespread, it did not occur evenly throughout all demographic sectors of the American population. Gender was not always much of a factor, with women and men seeming to enjoy Japanese-inspired art and hobbies in equal numbers, but class and race certainly were. For the most part, working-class Americans, unless they served in postwar Japan with the U.S. military, largely ignored the trend, preferring to embrace familiar Western aesthetics. At a time when deeply ingrained societal racism hindered many racial minorities from achieving middle-class status, the Japanese culture trend remained almost exclusively a white phenomenon, with a few Japanese American exceptions discussed below. Fractures even appeared within the broadly defined postwar middle class, as finer lines of difference became apparent in terms of how affluent upper-middle-class consumers treated and used Japanese traditions, in comparison with suburbanites of more modest income.

As the prosperous echelons of U.S. society expanded their ranks in the 1950s, those who were wealthy and "well-off" felt an increasing need to distance themselves from those who were merely comfortable. Practices of consumption and the concept of fashion acquired new significance, in which Japanese culture would play a role. In *Distinction: A Social Critique of the Judgment of Taste*, sociologist Pierre Bourdieu argues that the privileged classes are able to maintain their status by creating standards of taste, built on such seemingly mundane choices as the selection of "houses, furniture, paintings, books, cars, spirits, cigarettes, perfume [and] clothes." Those with the influence and power to do so invest each selection with a perceived value in terms of where it falls "between the beautiful and the ugly, the distinguished and the vulgar."[19] In other words, to gain acceptance in the dominant socioeconomic class, a consumer must purchase the "correct" furniture, books, and clothing, or run the risk of being considered ignorant or uncouth, someone who does not deserve entry into elite circles. Those possessions, leisure activities, and general habits that would mark someone as a person of "good taste" are imbued with what Bourdieu terms "cultural capital." Just as financial capital can help a business owner find economic success, so too can purchasing and displaying the right products and enjoying the right hobbies help assure a consumer high social standing. As they reached the United States, most Japanese imports described as shibui proved to carry a good degree of cultural capital for those who appreciated them.

Despite the fact that Bourdieu's ideas were not published until the 1980s, contemporary cultural observers in the 1950s did formulate their own theories of how consumer choices contributed to social distinction. The most widely read of these was sociologist Vance Packard, who in his best-selling study *The Status Seekers* demonstrated how the things Americans purchased, wore, displayed, and enjoyed could determine their position in a complex socioeconomic hierarchy. One 1959 *Look* magazine cartoon nicely captured many readers' reaction to the book. A respectable-looking wife sets down her copy to ask her husband, "Are we in the uppermost upper part of the lower middle class, or the mid-lower part of the upper middle class?"[20] Most journalists and other commentators at the time simplified this complex scale of taste by using the shorthand terms "highbrow" and "lowbrow," with an emerging "middlebrow" culture in between.

In a 1949 *Harper's* magazine article, managing editor Russel Lynes provided a useful model for his readers to understand what these terms meant and how they functioned in relation to one another. He divided the population into four groups according to taste: highbrow, upper middlebrow, lower middlebrow, and lowbrow. Highbrows were not necessarily the wealthiest members of the population, but possessed the most of what Bourdieu would later term "cultural capital." Typically university professors or artists, they held themselves above the fray of commercial culture and claimed to consume for the sake of self-improvement over materialistic concerns. At the other end of the spectrum, lowbrows were working-class Americans who knew what they liked and didn't seem to care about the latest fashions or what rich people thought of their personal taste. In the middle echelons, upper middlebrows were usually wealthy professionals who cared deeply about commercial viability and strove constantly to be on the cutting edge of fashion. Lower middlebrows were stereotypical suburban white-collar families who followed their lead. Hardly innovative themselves, they kept abreast of trends in order to appear sophisticated and retain some level of social status. In a move that seemed to prove Lynes's point about the trickle-down effects of culture, the lower middlebrow *Life* magazine later boiled down these ideas into a graphic chart laying out which forms of consumption each group enjoyed. For example, under "Entertainment," ballet was considered highbrow, theater upper middlebrow, Hollywood musicals lower middlebrow, and western movies lowbrow. When consuming alcohol, highbrows enjoyed a glass of red wine, upper middlebrows a dry martini, lower middlebrows bourbon and ginger ale, and lowbrows, a glass of beer.[21] It was within the upper echelons of this hierarchy that most Japanese imports could be found, with a few Godzilla-like exceptions.

At the time, highbrows and upper middlebrows displayed a penchant for contemporary art and intellectual developments labeled "modern," to which Japanese aesthetics would be frequently compared. This term has since become problematic for historians in that it has been overused to mean many things in different contexts. In this case, I use it to refer to a specific aesthetic and scholarly movement that began in Europe in the late nineteenth century, rose to prominence in the United States in the 1930s, and found fairly widespread acceptance by the 1950s. Modernist aesthetics sought to cast aside previous assumptions about beauty by prioritizing functionality and efficiency and avoiding any ornamentation that appeared excessive or unnecessary. They expressed a minimalist ethos that American cultural critics and art promoters would discover in traditional Japanese aesthetics as well. Modern art reduced the meticulous detail of realistic figures to their abstract forms. Modern office layouts were organized, standardized, and sparsely decorated, wasting as little space as possible to increase productivity. According to one 1953 home economics textbook, "The spirit of modern furniture is basically one of simplicity, impersonality, and adjustability." Americans came to appreciate this style not just for its sense of streamlined efficiency but also for the fact that it followed the latest developments in design. The same textbook claimed that modern design "suits the people who are pioneers at heart." Therefore, a consumer who appreciated modernism could project the message that they were both practically minded and at the cutting edge of fashion.[22]

However, many observers were simultaneously beginning to take issue with modernism's "impersonality," which could appear soulless and inhuman. They appreciated its functionality, but also feared that it could promote mechanization, automatization, and disposability. In 1957 industrial designer George Nelson complained that the style had become too rigid and that some "polite expressions that tried for warmth [had] achieved only blankness."[23] In response, many "highbrows" tried to bring the human touch back into what they consumed, as well as ensure it was of the highest quality, even if doing so required more time, money, and effort. They rejected mass-produced items in favor of those that were handcrafted, including perhaps Japanese art and ceramics. They appreciated challenging literature and sought out intelligent films that were rarely screened in main street theaters, including foreign films. Speaking of such consumers in his popular study of postwar America, *The Lonely Crowd,* sociologist David Riesman explained, "Any leisure that looks easy is suspect, and craftsmanship does not look easy." He added that hobbies involving folk arts and other pre-industrial practices provided an opportunity for many of his subjects to build appropriate levels of character.[24]

Japanese culture offered a potential welcome solution to the problem of modernism's impersonality; it followed the same clean aesthetics as modern design, but its rootedness in seemingly timeless premodern tradition lent it a more human touch. Many upper middlebrow tastemakers noted that Japanese art followed the same simplified abstraction and graceful lines as modernism, an unsurprising comparison given that early American modern artists, like Mary Cassatt, had in fact taken inspiration from

Japanese prints. American art critics noted similarities between Japanese sho-in architecture and European Bauhaus designs in that neither one used much ornamentation. In contrast to earlier baroque and Gilded Age designs that were awash in accents and decoration, modern buildings and sho-in architecture derived beauty from their functional facades and interiors that did little to embellish the building's basic structure. Experts on Zen Buddhism admired its relativist stance toward morality, in keeping with popular modernist philosophies like existentialism. Yet while they held much in common with Western modernism, Japanese traditions' long history prevented them from being entirely "modern" in the sense of being new. Interpreting Japanese arts as inherently preindustrial, Americans felt they required a certain level of honest hard work and embodied an appreciation of nature that was "culturally" (which should be read as racially) inherent to the Japanese people. Bonsai cultivation was a hobby requiring meticulous care, and proper Zen study demanded years of meditation and personal contemplation. Traditional Japanese houses integrated a view of the garden in their design, while ikebana and bonsai worked directly with natural materials. This paradoxical quality of being simultaneously modern and premodern, familiar yet foreign, lies at the heart of the shibui concept.

However, the term began to stray from this original intent with the appearance of "Shibui" brand dinner trays and brassieres, which functioned like similar mass-produced American goods, but were adorned with floral and bamboo motifs or Japanese characters. In such cases, shibui connoted the superficial appearance of Japanese style, without necessarily duplicating its supposedly spiritual, preindustrial qualities. This type of marketing was a consequence of the cultural capital that Japanese culture had come to acquire. Once Japanese arts were touted as chic, American consumers wanting to appear more sophisticated eagerly climbed on the bandwagon and copied fashionable Japanese designs. This is not to say that these consumers were simply aping their wealthier counterparts. Many "lower middlebrow" suburbanites likely held a sincere appreciation for modern design and desire for more spiritual depth, but lacked the money and leisure time to invest in experiencing and appreciating Japanese culture to the same extent as the "highbrows." More accessible versions of Japanese traditions held a strong appeal for Japan enthusiasts who didn't have the time to grow their own bonsai from a seed or the financial resources to participate in Zen meditation retreats. Instead they could employ horticultural shortcuts to create easier bonsai or learn about Zen from a mass-market paperback philosophy book. New kinds of furniture also emerged, which lent the suburban living room a Japanese flair, yet were still sturdy and practical enough to hold up under the wear and tear of family use. Durable plastic replaced the traditional rice paper in shoji screens, and hibachi stoves exchanged coal fires for electric heating coils. As imported Japanese cultural forms attracted wider audiences, they often became adapted and updated in significant ways.

Some Japan experts, mainly from the upper middlebrow ranks, denounced such practices for diluting Japanese traditions. They complained about mass-produced bonsai or worried that too few American Zen enthusiasts were making the effort to correctly practice the religion, accusing them of dilettantism and disrespect. One could not plug a hibachi into a wall outlet or create a respectable bonsai in a Saturday afternoon and remain authentic. By altering these forms in ways more suited to their own lives, American consumers appeared to be playing fast and loose with centuries-old artifacts and practices. Less overtly, such altered versions of Japanese culture also appeared troubling to status-conscious affluent Americans in that they undermined the authority of self-appointed Japan experts to define what was indeed "shibui." Many American consumers who embraced these adapted forms didn't necessarily care about the challenging aspects of modern art, enjoying Japanese aesthetics on their own terms for their exotic appeal. They purchased furniture with Oriental accents or admired bonsai for its novelty rather than for its spiritual qualities. Instead of seeming familiar in form and exotic in function, some of these lower middlebrow adaptations were exotic in appearance and Americanized in their use, exactly the opposite of how experts thought consumers should properly appreciate Japanese culture.

Yet adaptation and adjustment needed to occur for widespread cultural importation. Left preserved in a more strictly authentic form, few Japanese traditions would have found a niche in twentieth-century U.S. life. Why, for instance, would any suburban mother want to put paper screens in her home only to have her children quickly tear them to pieces? By constructing shoji out of new materials, Americans were updating them to suit the needs of their time, a process of adjustment and revision that most Japanese arts and lifestyles had been undergoing for centuries before gaining popularity in the United States. By adapting Japanese culture without apologizing or preserving it in a pure form, American manufacturers and consumers liberated these imports somewhat from their Orientalist sense of timelessness. In this respect, these "lower middlebrows" actually embraced Japanese arts in a more authentic way than elite experts, making them objects of everyday use, as opposed to preserved and rarefied museum pieces.

In the end, even if significant numbers of American suburbanites failed to completely stick to the script while incorporating Japanese culture into their lives, they still reinforced the same general message about Japan: that its traditions embodied a particularly Oriental sense of subtle beauty and love of nature. Even if they grew bonsai from a kit because they were intrigued by its superficial appearance, they still appreciated it as delicate and graceful in a way American houseplants could never be. Those who kept Zen paperbacks on their nightstand might not have meditated on a regular basis, but still felt the religion offered a serene alternative spiritual outlook on life. Differences arose in exactly how Americans appreciated Japanese culture according to their income levels, adding new layers of complexity in terms of how and why particular individuals interpreted and consumed the concept of "shibui," but these varying contours never did threaten the basic peace-loving image of Japan that Americans were encouraged to accept during the postwar era.

Japanese Americans: Between Two Cultures

Most media coverage of the "Japan craze," as well as the majority of Japan enthusiasts themselves, depicted the phenomenon in terms of white Americans engaging with Japanese arts to learn about a foreign culture. But lest this study fall into the same presumption, it cannot overlook the presence of more than 120,000 people of Japanese descent living in the United States at this time who brought their own experience to bear on the trend. In the postwar era, many white Americans presumed Japanese Americans to be the perfect natural conduits for disseminating Japanese culture; personifying a bridge between the two nations, they held the potential to serve as the physical embodiment of cross-cultural understanding. Yet at the same time, most of the cultural institutions discussed here preferred to establish ties directly with Japan, bypassing Japanese-American expertise. Moreover, most Japanese Americans tended to view their newfound cultural bridge role ambivalently. While many appreciated and took advantage of the more positive stereotypes the trend encouraged regarding the "Japanese race," especially as they experienced decreased discrimination in employment and housing, few Japanese Americans seemed eager to promote traditional art forms directly. For the *Issei*—that is, first-generation immigrants to the United States who were born in Japan—such cultural practices were simply their way of life, which they never considered to be exotic or intriguing. Meanwhile, most second-generation *Nisei*, having grown up in the United States, were far more familiar with mainstream white American culture than Japanese traditions, and by midcentury most felt assimilated into white society. Moreover, while both groups were able to parlay the general interest in Japanese culture by white Americans to their advantage, such gains were inevitably tainted by skepticism cultivated over a long history of racial discrimination.

Japanese immigrants had been living in the United States since the 1890s, when Meiji government reforms allowed widespread emigration from Japan for the first time in centuries. By 1900, most were living on the West Coast, centered around the major metropolitan areas of San Francisco, Los Angeles, and Seattle. In 1907 the so-called Gentleman's Agreement between the U.S. and Japanese governments allowed Nisei to attend white schools in exchange for severe restrictions on Japanese immigration to the United States. Such regulations ensured that few unskilled Japanese laborers made the journey across the Pacific in the twentieth century, meaning that Japanese American urban communities would be composed mostly of financially stable working-class families. During these years many Japanese Americans would find work as tenant farmers, because racism excluded them from higher paying professions and nativist state laws prohibited Issei from owning real estate. Later, the Immigration Act of 1924 all but ended Japanese immigration by banning foreigners "ineligible for citizenship," which, under immigration policy of the time, basically referred to Asians. By the 1940s this left the Japanese American community with an oddly shaped demographic pattern that included many older Issei who immigrated before the 1920s, a large number of Nisei then in their teens and twenties, a handful of infant members of the third generation, and few people in between.[25]

The blanket mistreatment of all Japanese Americans during World War II by the U.S. government understandably left many of them reluctant to fully trust white Americans by the 1950s. When the Japanese navy bombed Pearl Harbor on December 7, 1941, many Japanese Americans knew that their future in the United States had become uncertain. All Nisei were American citizens by virtue of their birth, so at first some only feared for the safety of their parents who retained Japanese citizenship. In doing so, they underestimated the racist tendencies of many influential white Americans to consider Asians as perpetual outsiders, assuming they would remain more loyal to their race than to their nation. The first round of internment measures were indeed directed against noncitizen Issei active in pro-Japanese groups; in the week following December 7, 1941, about 1,500 were arrested and sent to camps. But in the ensuing months, all Japanese Americans regardless of birth or citizenship would be subject to surveillance, warrantless searches, and local curfews. Then, in February 1942, President Roosevelt signed Executive Order 9066 calling for the removal of all Americans of Japanese descent from the West Coast into concentration camps, allegedly for their own protection. Over the next three months families were rounded up, one neighborhood at a time, and sent to assembly centers near their homes, from which they were later moved to more permanent relocation camps in the country's interior.

While the Supreme Court upheld the practice of internment on the grounds of military necessity, it was clear even to observers at the time that

FIG. 1. Los Angeles. Japanese American evacuation from West Coast areas under U.S. Army war emergency order. Waiting with their luggage at the old Santa Fe station for a train to take them to Owens Valley in April 1942. Library of Congress Prints and Photographs Division, LC-DIG-fsa-8a31172.

the decision was based on racial discrimination. Neither German nor Italian Americans were treated in a similar manner, as contemporary stereotypes suggested that Asian immigrants were less capable of assimilating into American society than Europeans.[26] But the War Relocation Authority, the federal bureau established to oversee the camps, denied charges of racism and sought to prove that their mission was humane and benevolent, nothing like Germany's ghettoization of Jews. Overall conditions in the camps were livable—in an oft-cited statistic, more people were born in them than died—but barely comfortable. Families of five or more were forced to share hastily constructed two-bedroom cabins. Three square meals were served daily, but consisted mostly of army rations, often including food unfamiliar to Issei diets. Internees felt like they were perpetually standing in line: for mealtimes, mail call, or to use communal bath and latrine facilities. When they left their homes, most were allowed to carry only one suitcase and forced to abandon the rest of their property. When the war was over, those who did return to the West Coast found their houses and businesses sold or looted, and they were forced to completely rebuild. While American concentration camps were a far cry from their Nazi counterparts, they nevertheless imposed massive disruption in the lives of tens of thousands of citizens, based solely on their racial origins.[27]

The WRA was ordered to dismantle the Japanese internment camps in December 1944, after the Supreme Court found them unconstitutional, and some Japanese Americans returned to their old lives on the West Coast, but not all.[28] The previous year, the agency had initiated steps to release some internees, deciding that Japanese who proved themselves sufficiently loyal should be allowed to go free. Young Nisei men were permitted to fight in the army, but exclusively on the European front, where army leadership could feel confident they would not defect. All other internees were subject to a loyalty questionnaire in an attempt to determine who could be trusted to be released from the camps. Those who passed were given the option to relocate to the Midwest, where authorities assumed they would be unable to serve as spies across the Pacific. Most participants in this early resettlement program were Nisei well assimilated to American life before the war; few practiced Japanese customs or were literate in the Japanese language. While the WRA established resettlement centers in most major cities in the Midwest and New York City, the most popular resettlement destination was Chicago, a city that for the first time would play host to a substantial Japanese American community. In the last several years of the war, aid organizations sprang up to assist Japanese Americans with job placement and securing housing, establishing an ethnic presence in the middle of the country that had not existed before.[29]

After the war ended and Japanese Americans had either begun life in a new city or attempted to reconstruct the one they left behind, the attitudes of white Americans toward them remained ambivalent but on the whole much more tolerant than they had been previously. The sudden postwar about-face that occurred toward the nation of Japan itself seemed to reflect back on Japanese Americans; as the shibui phenomenon made

Japanese culture appear more noble and appealing, so too did the people who supposedly practiced it. Over time, whites living on the West Coast in particular began to contrast Japanese people with the most denigrated racial group in the country at the time: African Americans. Historians Charlotte Brooks and Scott Kurashige have both demonstrated that white homeowners in postwar California appeared more willing to rent or sell to Japanese families than to blacks, presuming them to be more respectable and less troublesome. Such beliefs stemmed in part from Japanese Americans' seemingly innate ability to overcome adversity through the trauma of internment, but also from the presumed value their culture placed on stoicism and serenity. Once Japanese American people themselves were seen to take on admirable qualities like humility and restraint, they were better able to scale the socioeconomic ladder. Leaving tenant farming behind, they created improved lives for themselves in the postwar suburbs alongside whites and planted the seeds of what would be known as the Asian "model minority" in subsequent decades.[30]

But while Japanese Americans used the newfound appreciation for their culture to break through some barriers of prejudice, many white Americans still found it difficult to embrace a former "enemy race" as friends and fully accept them as equals. In 1964, on the usually progressive television show *The Twilight Zone*, a young George Takei portrayed a Nisei whose father had helped guide planes at Pearl Harbor toward their targets, despite the fact that no evidence of such collaboration on the part of any Japanese American exists. In other ways as well the episode provides examples of white ambivalence toward Japanese Americans. While Takei's character appears polite and competent and comports himself like a respectable middle-class Californian, by the end of the episode he becomes possessed by the ghost of a Japanese army officer through a "samurai sword" discovered in a white army veteran's attic. The episode's horror derives from the Nisei's inability to overcome his racial roots, no matter how hard he tries to assimilate. But its script also alludes to the idea that Japanese Americans had become more accepted in white society than they had been in the past. The white veteran calls the Nisei a "dirty Jap," but does so as he proclaims in confused frustration, "First you're an ape, now all of a sudden you're some kind of cultured people. I've been pushed and pulled this way and that, until I hate everybody!"[31] While the new fascination with Japanese culture helped ease discrimination toward Japanese Americans, many would continue to encounter prejudice from white Americans, even as they were able to participate in postwar affluence.

Within this complex context, most Japanese Americans used their more positive postwar reputation to their advantage whenever they could, but there is little evidence that many of them helped further the shibui image of Japan directly. In 1946 a team of sociologists from the University of California conducted a series of interviews with Chicago-area Nisei transplants. Evidence from this study suggests that the majority would have avoided the Japan craze for a variety of reasons. Many Nisei claimed they wanted to leave the world of their parents behind them. For some, this meant assimilating into white society, and for others, it meant creating a distinctive Japanese American subculture. But to none of the interviewees did it mean embracing or promoting the culture of Japan. Yet at the same time, the Chicago Resettlers Committee, a welfare organization composed largely of Nisei, did stage displays of Japanese music and dancing at museums, YMCAs, and other community centers around the city.[32] In addition, interviews conducted with Issei by the Japanese American Citizens League in the 1990s reveal that some first-generation immigrants who had practiced traditional Japanese arts before the war continued their hobbies of ikebana, bonsai, or gardening while interred, at times giving lessons to fellow internees to help them all alleviate the tedium of camp life.[33] However, few made efforts to teach these same skills later to whites. Upon release, most Issei moved in the opposite direction from assimilationist members of the second generation, withdrawing further into their older ethnic enclaves, now even more distrustful of white America and its government than they had been in the past.[34] Neither generation seemed fully committed to spreading knowledge about specific traditional arts, at least not on a communitywide level.

Yet there were exceptions to these general tendencies, and some Japanese Americans proved not only willing but eager to further the popularity of Japanese culture. After resettling eastward, Frank Okamura and Mary Takahashi both made profitable careers of teaching bonsai and ikebana, respectively. In Los Angeles, a group of Little Tokyo businessmen resurrected the neighborhood's Nisei Week festival. Whereas the event began in the 1930s as an effort to preserve Japanese heritage among the American-born second generation, in the 1950s its primary purpose transformed to become a showcase for traditional culture to a newly interested white clientele. San Francisco's Japanese Cultural and Trade Center, constructed in the 1960s, involved the collaboration of a handful of Japanese architects and businessmen eager to promote Japanese traditions—as well as sell Japanese products—to an American audience.[35] It is of course hard to discern the personal motives of these individuals who decided to actively accept the role of bridge between Japan and the United States. On some level, they were proud of their heritage and flattered that it had found a wider audience, but it cannot be denied that participating in the phenomenon often proved lucrative for Japanese Americans as well. Not only did the Nisei Festival and Japan Center draw more customers looking to purchase shibui objects, but Okamura and Takahashi also enjoyed local renown in their own rights. It is difficult to know to what extent Japanese Americans who shared their love of Japanese culture with a larger audience did so out of shrewdness and personal gain as much as a desire to further international friendship. Considering the population as a whole, it appears few Japanese Americans stepped forward to help enlighten whites through their culture, but many nevertheless used the situation to their best advantage, making what gains they could in a society that remained racist, even as that racism became more benign.

It was against this backdrop that samurai films, bonsai, ikebana, Japanese architecture, rock gardens, Zen Buddhism, and giant monsters arrived in the United States. The situation was complicated on the receiving end by the large-scale diversity of the American population. Those most welcoming of these cultural imports were often narrowly defined as white and affluent, but even this categorization proves overly general, as Americans from different socioeconomic backgrounds adopted Japanese culture in different ways. Meanwhile, people of Japanese descent could hardly be ignored as part of the American population in this situation. But the group that might appear to some most likely to step to the fore in this cultural exchange often remained on the sidelines, even if they did benefit from an improved reputation.

While the demographic picture within the United States proved very complex indeed, the image that white middle-class Americans formed in their minds about Japan was fairly straightforward. According to their understanding of the postwar international situation, Japan had charged foolishly into an unwinnable war due to its population's antiquated, unenlightened mind-set. It was now the project of the United States to replace their dangerous, outdated beliefs with the superior, progressive concept of democracy. But for true friendship to be solidified between two nations that had so recently been at war, cultural interest and exchange would have to be mutual. To prove the benevolence of their intentions, Americans had to honor the Japanese by taking at least a selective interest in their traditions as well. This was the initial impetus for middle-class America's postwar love of Japan: solidifying international bonds by embracing the best—that is, the most beautiful, artistic, and appropriately nonthreatening—facets of Japanese culture.

CHAPTER 2

SAMURAI AT THE SURE SEATERS

1950s "Highbrow" Japanese Movies in the United States

During the years of the occupation from 1945 through 1952, Americans most commonly encountered Japan in their everyday lives through news stories about the success of U.S. efforts in restoring and rehabilitating their former enemy. It would take several years of Japanese economic recovery before direct cultural exports would find their way to American shores. Japanese movies were the first of these exports, reaching U.S. audiences beginning in the last several years of the occupation. Prior to the war, plenty of Japanese films had been playing in Japantown theaters in West Coast cities, but few were translated and circulated among a wider English-speaking audience. Once the war ended, a number of factors across the international film landscape led to an unprecedented appreciation for Japanese cinema among upper-middle-class white Americans.

The first Japanese movie to arrive in the United States was Akira Kurosawa's *Rashomon* in 1951.[1] Two other critically celebrated films followed three years later: Kenji Mizoguchi's *Ugetsu* and Teinosuke Kinugasa's *Gate of Hell*. Slightly predating widespread interest in arts like ikebana and bonsai, these movies provided many Americans with their first postwar glimpse into Japanese culture. Shown primarily in exclusive art house theater settings, critics and upper-middle-class audiences hailed these early imports as refined and sophisticated. While all three movies featured samurai and swordplay, U.S. commentators drew little attention to themes of violence or "the way of the sword" that might invoke Japan's militarist past. Instead, they emphasized the films' seemingly feminine qualities, like graceful photographic composition and measured pacing that supposedly stemmed from an inherent Japanese artistic sensibility exemplified in media like brush painting and haiku. Through such a focused lens, these early 1950s critics implied that Japan's success in movie making was due to the influence of the refined arts of its past, as opposed to individual directors' skilled mastery of a modern medium.

It took relatively little time for these three movies to solidify from an American perspective the notion of what a Japanese film should be: an artistic piece of cinema that was subtle in theme and composition and as such stood in marked contrast to commercialized, melodramatic Hollywood fare. Meanwhile, Japanese movie producers interpreted these films' success in the opposite way, reasoning that samurai movies appealed to American viewers because they resembled Hollywood westerns. Studio heads adopted the strategy of exporting more movies that supposedly reflected American tastes, only to find them rejected by critics who preferred their films be more distinctively "foreign." Often embracing "highbrow" values, critics wanted the Japanese industry to serve as a counterweight to their own popular culture, striving toward timeless high art principles rather than twentieth-century commercial concerns.

Japanese Movies Arrive at the American Art House

Subtitled versions of Japanese films began appearing in American theaters in the early 1950s due to thawed relations between the two nations as well as widespread interest in Japan sparked by the occupation. These movies were also part of a wider trend of increasing numbers of foreign films screened in the United States. During the silent era foreign films had been fairly common, but when movies began to talk, translation became an obstacle to overcome. From the 1930s onward, Americans viewed Hollywood products almost exclusively. Meanwhile, the U.S. film industry grew to become the world's largest; by 1940 eight major American studios accounted for 65 percent of the movies seen across the globe.[2] During World War II, international trade outside of military arms and equipment essentially ground to a halt, including motion pictures. After normalcy returned, U.S. dominance of global markets continued to grow, as wartime devastation hampered other nations' output, and the United States coerced many European countries into signing trade agreements favorable to American films.

Yet foreign movies did return to U.S. screens in the postwar era, in numbers far surpassing those from immediately before the war. Imported films formed 5 percent of the American market in 1954. Six years later, that figure had jumped to 25 percent.[3] Domestically, several factors contributed to this change. One was the *Paramount* Supreme Court decision of 1948, which declared the Hollywood studio system in violation of federal antitrust laws and consequently threw the industry into turmoil. Once studios were no longer able to reap inflated profits by monopolizing theater chains—that is, allowing their theaters to show only their movies and all of their movies— many decided to cut back production and focus on quality over quantity. The result was a drastic reduction in "grade B" features, the type of small budget movies that were affordable to many independent "neighborhood" theaters. Left with little domestic product, theater owners began to set their sights abroad, since imported movies were often far less expensive to rent than first-run American films.[4]

At the same time, a major barrier to foreign film exhibition was removed, as the Hays censorship code gradually died out over the course of the 1950s. The code restricted the content of Hollywood films by denying its seal of approval to any movie that did not meet its high moral standards. Any film that included sexually suggestive nudity, or even sexually suggestive conversation, would not be granted a seal. Nor would any film that displayed excessive violence, revealed procedures for committing a successful crime, or did not punish those who broke the law before the closing credits. The code included other more specific proscriptions as well, such as rules prohibiting animal cruelty, expression of antipatriotic sentiments, and overly negative depictions of foreigners (to avoid international tensions when films were exported). Since standards of censorship have always varied across international borders, and few foreign producers consulted with the Motion Picture Association of America's (MPAA) censorship office in making their films, distributors constantly faced headaches trying to sell films that failed to obtain a code seal. All of that began to change the year after *Rashomon* premiered. In the case of *Burstyn v. Wilson*, the Supreme Court declared that the motion picture in question, an Italian film called *The Miracle*, was not a commercial product but a work of art, and as such, to censor it would be a violation of free speech. Although the MPAA technically continued to adhere to the code until the early 1960s, its authority began to erode significantly following the ruling.[5]

Yet even with their easier access and rise in popularity, foreign films were still considered to have only a niche appeal. In the 1950s, theaters showing major first-run releases would rarely exhibit foreign films, assuming they would not perform well in terms of ticket sales, since these movies forced audiences to overcome issues of language and cultural translation.[6] But a haven for foreign movies did emerge in the art house, a type of upscale movie theater that proliferated throughout the United States following World War II. Most of these theaters were small, with a seating capacity of 300 to 750, and advertised that they specialized in intelligent films for the more mature movie viewer. By 1952 more than four hundred art houses had opened in major metropolitan centers and college towns, and by 1958 the number of art house theaters nationwide had doubled, including some chains that catered to rural areas.[7] Many art house owners courted a "lost audience" of sophisticated adults. Louis Sher, the owner of a midwestern chain of art houses, stated, "Lately, we've got a very definite impression that commercial theaters have deteriorated to the point where they no longer served my purpose—which was to relax. . . . Double features and kids thundering up and down the aisles, popcorn stands going full blast, all these things tend to discourage adults from attending the commercial theater." Most theaters sought to create a haven for such mature patrons in their design and amenities, offering coffee instead of popcorn, displaying fine art exhibits instead of movie posters in their lobbies, and barring children from attending. Over time, art houses tended to take on what

Nation's Business magazine referred to as "a subtle snob appeal." Attending one, most middle-class Americans felt, could make them appear intelligent and sophisticated, bolstering their personal status.[8]

Many art house patrons sought them out to view different kinds of movies from what Hollywood typically offered. The main purpose of the major American movie studios has always been to make money more than art, and in the 1950s that frequently entailed turning a profit by aiming for a kind of safe middle ground. Producers shied away from content that might confuse, shock, or alienate the average filmgoer. It further seemed that the major studios were de-prioritizing content in favor of spectacle, as they attempted to fend off the new threat of television. To convince patrons that it was still worth their while to leave their living rooms, Hollywood offered Technicolor extravaganzas with enormous casts, filmed in new widescreen techniques like "CinemaScope" or "VistaVision." Finally, content became even safer and more banal as the film industry emerged from the Red Scare of the late 1940s badly scathed. After screenwriters, producers, and stars were called to testify before the House Un-American Activities Committee in 1947, studios not only blacklisted suspected communist employees but also turned down any film proposals that could be labeled suspiciously leftist. Consequentially, most movies were left defanged in terms of offering any kind of thoughtful commentary on complex or relevant social issues.[9]

Foreign studios, often heavily subsidized by national governments, did not worry nearly as deeply about profits or the pressures of McCarthyism. As such, they were more open to taking artistic and thematic risks and could offer thought-provoking alternatives to typical Hollywood extravaganzas. This circumstance helps explain why by 1960, foreign films made up about 80 percent of art house offerings. Like many highbrow pursuits, these movies required extra effort, in this case reading subtitles and engaging with unfamiliar cultures and situations. But in doing so, they rewarded their viewers' efforts by providing a more fulfilling artistic cinematic experience than what they could find at larger theaters.[10]

Most art house owners discovered new foreign films to exhibit by following developments at European film festivals, institutions that expanded rapidly in number and scope during the postwar era. The first major recurring film festival was held in Venice in 1932, and soon it fell under the influence of Mussolini's fascist regime. In response, Great Britain, France, and the United States collaborated to open a competing festival in Cannes in the south of France, but its inaugural was postponed by the war until 1946. From that point onward, other festivals appeared throughout Europe. Many, including those in Locarno, Edinburgh, Brussels, and Oberhausen, were established in an attempt to promote European movies in the face of increasing competition from Hollywood. Others were founded with Cold War motivations in mind, including the U.S. funded festival in West Berlin and Karlovy Vary and Moscow festivals sponsored by the Soviet Union. Whatever their initial intent, by the 1950s these festivals had become a fixture in the global cinema industry, forming an established network through which films could gain international recognition. Older festivals especially, like Venice and Cannes, earned a respected reputation among filmmakers and critics and lent a great deal of prestige to the films they endorsed.[11]

Through the Venice Film Festival in particular, English-speaking American audiences gained their first postwar exposure to Japanese cinema. Despite the fact that Japan was home to one of the world's largest film industries, westerners knew little about Japanese movies in 1950. The festival organizers decided to remedy that situation, and they sent an invitation to Japan to submit an entry. Previously, Japanese filmmakers had taken little interest in European festivals, and studio heads had a hard time agreeing on a suitable candidate on short notice. *Rashomon* was not even among the finalists they considered; its producers at the Daiei film company had found the film utterly confusing, and most Japanese critics had panned it. Instead, Guilliana Stramigioli, head of Italiafilm in Japan, submitted the film outside of Japan's official entries. When *Rashomon* won first prize at the Venice Film Festival, the news probably came as a bigger shock to filmmakers in its home country than anywhere else.[12] Once they recovered, Japanese industry heads quickly realized that they had succeeded in breaking into a vast and potentially profitable international market.[13]

One of the reasons Japanese producers initially disliked *Rashomon* was

FIG. 2. Still from the film *Rashomon*, 1950. Directed by Akira Kurosawa, produced by Daiei Studios.

that its storytelling format was unusual for its time and confused some viewers.[14] (The plot device has perhaps become now almost cliché, having been employed by numerous television writers since the 1950s.) The plot revolves around the murder of a samurai in a dense forest glen in twelfth-century Japan and four witnesses who offer their own versions of what took place, with each story contradicting the others. The accounts are framed by a conversation between three men seeking shelter from a downpour at Kyoto's Rashomon gate. The samurai's wife, a bandit the couple encounter, and the victim himself (through the aid of a medium), each recount the murder in such a way that they act according to the tenets of their own code of honor. But then one of the men discussing the trial at the gate reluctantly reveals that he too had witnessed the entire incident, and in his version no one appears stoic, courageous, or morally upstanding. While this final portrayal including each character's flawed actions appears to be closest to the truth, after the woodcutter finishes his account, his companion forces him to admit that he had stolen an expensive dagger from the crime scene, thus throwing his reliability into doubt as well.[15] The full truth remains hidden, and it appears that no one can be trusted because humans perpetually lie to everyone, including themselves.

After the movie's unexpected success in Venice, the American studio RKO distributed *Rashomon* in the United States. Like most foreign films at the time, it debuted in a New York art house, in this instance on Christmas night 1951. The film's premiere marked not only the first showing of a Japanese movie to an English-speaking American audience in almost fifteen years, but also the reopening of the Little Carnegie Theater following an extensive renovation project, thus warranting a degree of fanfare, including coverage on both local radio and Voice of America Japan. *Rashomon* next opened in Washington DC on February 25, 1952—at another gala event involving American and Japanese dignitaries—and in other U.S. cities soon thereafter.[16] The movie did well at the box office by art house standards and won the National Board of Review's award for best foreign film, an Oscar for best foreign film, and a Screen Directors Guild Award, as well as a nomination for a Film Critics' Award.[17]

After it disappeared from first-run theaters, *Rashomon* continued to play in other venues throughout the decade. Local American film festivals exhibited the movie, as did art museums and public lecture series. It also proved popular as a 16mm print, a format that enabled organizations like churches, schools, and clubs to show films on noncommercial projectors. In the late 1950s, *Rashomon* was revived through the emerging repertory film movement, wherein theaters devoted themselves entirely to showing older movies considered part of cinema's classic canon.[18] The story and its innovative plot device also found their way to other media, encouraged by the film's success. A translation of the Japanese short story collection that had inspired the film's script was released in American bookstores in 1952, also to critical acclaim. Broadway producers Fay and Michael Kanin bought the rights to the story and adapted it as a play that premiered in 1959, to mixed reviews and moderate success. The play was in turn adapted into a Hollywood movie entitled *The Outrage*, which moved the story to the Old West and starred Paul Newman as the now Mexican bandit. Perhaps the film's most unusual tribute was the "Rashomon" model men's cufflinks, part of the Swank Company's 1959 "Oriental Dynasty" line.[19]

Rashomon had succeeded in becoming "the most famous Japanese movie ever made,"[20] and indeed it was the best-known Japanese art house movie of the decade. But other films would soon establish their own reputations among critics and art house patrons. The next to arrive was *Ugetsu*. Set in Japan's "Warring States Period" (the mid-fifteenth through early seventeenth centuries), it sought to illustrate the toll these ongoing battles took on ordinary people. Genjuro the potter goes to town to sell his goods, leaving behind his wife, Miyagi, and taking along his neighbor Tobei and his wife, Ohama. Tobei and Ohama are separated and embark on adventures that grant Tobei samurai status and leave Ohama working in a brothel. Genjuro, meanwhile, becomes involved in a lurid affair with a mysterious noblewoman who is later revealed to be a ghost. He eventually returns home exhausted to find his wife cooking dinner, but is informed by the village headman the next morning that soldiers had killed Miyagi while Genjuro was away, and that the woman in his home is in fact another ghost. Tobei and Ohama, once reunited, also return to the village. The three fire up their kiln and begin their simple lives again, somewhat the worse and much wiser for their journey.

After the film received the Silver Lion award for best director at the 1953 Venice Film Festival, the owners of Plaza Theater in Manhattan imported the movie with the help of independent distributor Edward Harrison. *Ugetsu's* premiere took place on September 7, 1954, as part of an event sponsored by New York's Japan Society and attended by several Japanese dignitaries. Ambassador Sadao Iguchi introduced the screening with a speech commending American audiences for welcoming Japanese cinema. Within the next week, the film brought in near record box office returns for the Plaza. *Ugetsu* soon appeared on critical yearly "Ten Best" lists for both the *Saturday Review* and *Time* magazine (as did *Gate of Hell*). On the heels of such acclaim, the movie spread to other art houses throughout the country during the following year. As the decade progressed, like *Rashomon, Ugetsu* found new audiences at film festivals and repertory theaters. About a decade after its U.S. release, Art Blakey's Jazz Messengers paid the movie homage by borrowing its name for the title of their Japan-themed bebop album.[21]

While *Ugetsu* enjoyed a favorable reputation among discerning filmgoers, *Gate of Hell*, the next Japanese film to arrive in America, proved more capable of transforming critical prestige into box office earnings. Part of its broad appeal lay in the fact that it was the first color film ever produced in Japan and, as such, offered a more vivid visual spectacle. The movie's plot, in contrast, was dull and featured rather one-dimensional characters. The short-tempered samurai Moritoh falls in love with the Lady Kesa when he is asked to protect her in the course of a battle. When the war is over, his lord offers to reward him for his loyalty and bravery, and Moritoh asks to marry Kesa. The only problem is that Kesa is already married to an upstanding samurai named Wataru. Moritoh then spends most of the film trying to force his affections on the devoted Kesa. Eventually she appears to relent after he threatens to harm her family and agrees to a plot to slay her husband and run away with Moritoh. Unbeknownst to him, however, Kesa hides in Wataru's bed, and after murdering her instead, Moritoh flees to a monastery in despair.

Gate of Hell followed a similar path to the United States as its predecessors. After winning the Grand Prize at the 1954 Cannes Film Festival, *Ugetsu*'s Edward Harrison again handled distribution in the United States. *Gate of Hell* also received a New York gala premiere sponsored by Japan Society, this time at the Guild Theater, and soon went on to win a plethora of film awards, including a National Board of Review Award, the MPDAA's Joseph Burstyn Award, a Critic's Choice Award, a New York Film Critics' Circle Award, and a Photographic Society of America Award. The movie also won an Academy Award for best foreign film, and some critics felt it was cheated out of a nomination in the category of best color photography.[22] Over the course of the next year, the film became the most lucrative Japanese movie shown in America to date. It was typical practice for many art houses to continue playing the same film until it was no longer profitable, no matter how long the run, so the Guild screened *Gate of Hell* for more than ten months, continuously setting new box office records for the theater. In the meantime, *Gate of Hell* proved profitable in Los Angeles, Washington, San Francisco, and Chicago.[23] Once a film was retired from first-run theaters, industry standards required that second-run houses wait thirty-five days before showing the film themselves. True to form, about a month after *Gate of Hell* closed at the Guild, it reopened in other venues across New York City. A similar phenomenon took place in Chicago; after opening for an extended run at the Loop Theater in February, *Gate of Hell* was screened in second-run theaters throughout the region starting in July. By May 1955 the film had reached the list of top ten grossing movies nationwide, a feat rarely accomplished by a foreign film.[24]

Critical Response to the Newly Popular Japanese Cinema

American criticism of most foreign films during the postwar era tended to be based on the assumption that every nation's film industry held its own distinctive characteristics. Critics viewed Hollywood as the standard, with the national cinema of every other country differing from that norm in its own particular way. At the time, American film critics and scholars often traded in overgeneralizations, such as Italian films were starkly realist, French films treated sex lightly, and British films dealt frankly with the problems of the urban poor.[25] As they were incorporated into this standard system, Japanese films gained a reputation for artistic visual composition and measured pacing that critics interpreted more as products of a timeless line of Japanese tradition than the works of individual contemporary artists. While Akira Kurosawa is well known today as a prominent director with his own personal style and Kenji Mizoguchi continues to be heralded by film scholars, in the 1950s both directors were relatively unknown to the American public and film critics alike, and as such, *Rashomon*, *Ugetsu*, and *Gate of Hell* were frequently lumped together. As the first three movies to arrive in the postwar United States from Japan, they became examples of a unified national school of "Japanese Film."

In truth these three films did share a number of similarities. They all fit the specific genre of costume dramas set in feudal times, and all three were produced at Daiei Studios by Masaichi Nagata. As such, they had some coincidental overlap in production personnel; *Rashomon* and *Ugetsu* shared the same cinematographer, Kazuo Miyagawa, and the same musical composer, Fumio Hayasaka, and actress Machiko Kyo played a noblewoman in all three films (the wife in *Rashomon*, Lady Wakasa in *Ugetsu*, and Lady Kesa in *Gate of Hell*). But were these shared traits significant enough to treat all three movies simply as products of the same national style? Considerable differences existed between the films as well, which many American critics tended to gloss over. While Akira Kurosawa voiced his admiration for Kenji Mizoguchi on numerous occasions, the two directors remained very different kinds of filmmakers.[26] In Japan, Mizoguchi had a reputation for portraying the tragic lives of long-suffering women, of which Miyagi and Ohama provide excellent examples. Despite the complex multidimensional character offered by the wife in *Rashomon*, Kurosawa was best known for his depictions of strong and independent male heroes. Moreover, Mizoguchi established a "one scene, one shot" method of filming in which he relied on camera movements instead of cutting, a technique that he employed in *Ugetsu*. Kurosawa, in stark contrast, relied heavily on the quick cut, and *Rashomon* in particular contains the highest average number of shots per minute of any of his films.[27]

Gate of Hell is perhaps the biggest outlier. Ever since their initial production, *Rashomon* and *Ugetsu* have been hailed by film scholars around the world as masterpieces of cinema. However, *Gate of Hell*, the most commercially successful of the three in its own time, has now been largely forgotten. Donald Richie, an American film critic who moved to Japan in the 1950s and later established himself as the United States' preeminent expert on Japanese cinema, referred to the movie in his 2001 guide to Japanese film as "weak." He called it "a period play made into limp film with flaccid performances. . . . If anyone paid attention to this film it was because of [cinematographer] Sugiyama Kohei's superlative color photography."[28] *Gate of Hell* was simply a poorer quality film and one that, like Hollywood spectaculars, prioritized visual dazzle over intellectual elements. Overall, it seemed to have little in common with the other two films, save that its production studio and setting were both in Japan. Yet for American critics, these shared national origins were enough to consider the film of a piece with the superior fast-paced *Rashomon* and slow-tempoed *Ugetsu*.

Once it was established that all Japanese films fit into the same national mold, reviewers sought to uncover the core elements of this Japanese Cinema. Since art house patrons often placed more weight on critical acclaim than the general public, critics' interpretations of these films carried even more influence than they would for mainstream movies. The primary trait most reviews emphasized above all was that these films were unmistakably foreign and Other. *Time* referred to *Rashomon*'s "peculiarly Oriental flavor," and described *Ugetsu* as "wholly Oriental in its lidded introspection" and "a descent into the grey and moaning hell of an Oriental soul." The *Nation*'s Robert Hatch elaborated on this characterization, positing that a Japanese film "presents an exciting problem to the Western observer. Not only must he try to grasp the impulse behind the deeds of people with whose reactions and habits of logic he is unacquainted, not only must he respond to excerpts from a culture that is almost entirely closed to him; he must try to gauge how much of what seems to him savage, archaic or exotic would seem so also to an Oriental spectator." While Hatch's statement is a rather evenhanded assessment based in cultural relativism, other critics were not as sympathetic. Bosley Crowther, the eminent *New York Times* critic, wrote that both *Rashomon* and *Ugetsu* were "so different in their concepts and structures from the general characteristics of American films that the average patron of pictures is sure to find them as baffling as their speech." By far the worst offender in this respect was John McCarten of the *New Yorker*, a critic whom Richie described as "dislik[ing] because disliking is easy and because their publications encourage it." In his review of *Rashomon*, McCarten ridiculed the movie, reviving several well-worn stereotypes of Asian deviousness in the process. He claimed that the film was "a lot more simple-minded than any product of the mysterious East has any right to be" and that it "subjected [audiences] to a series of inscrutable variations on a Japanese theme," employing an adjective frequently applied to supposedly duplicitous Asians in the past. He even described one character as "right out of 'Fu-Manchu," referring to British dime novelist Sax Rohmer's infamous Chinese villain from the turn of the century.[29]

While McCarten took the most overtly racist tone of any film critic, he was not alone in his mockery of some of the films' foreign aspects. There is no way to deny that foreign movies contain some elements that American viewers would find unfamiliar, and many journalists must have felt themselves in the position that Hatch described. For instance, the way in which women's kimonos fit them tightly at the knees in the feudal Japanese style would make the movements of many Japanese actresses appear unnatural to Western audiences.[30] Concepts of beauty could also appear different, as demonstrated by a *New York Times* reader who wrote in to ask about Machiko Kyo's painted eyebrows in *Ugetsu*, which she ineloquently referred to as "forehead smudges." McCarten and Crowther in particular were put off by the supernatural elements in *Rashomon* and *Ugetsu*, which they felt were too fantastic for American viewers to swallow. However, Robert Bingham of the *Reporter* pointed out in response that the theme of falling in love with ghosts is hardly unknown in Western literature.[31]

A criticism many reviewers made of the films' foreignness was that Japanese acting was exaggerated and overly emotional. McCarten described the style in *Rashomon* as "wheezing, grunting, gurgling, and falling down," and in *Ugetsu* as "more writhing and tumbling than has been seen since the Keystone Cops turned in their badges." The *New Republic* similarly warned its readers that the actors in *Rashomon* "howl and spit, they leap in the air, beat the shrubbery, rend their garments, roll on the ground, foam at the mouth, and scratch their fleas." Bingham also wrote of *Gate of Hell*, "It's hard not to laugh at the passionate lovers who grunt and groan and fall on their faces." The acting in these movies is, in fact, often more emotionally expressive than the "method acting" techniques popular in Hollywood at the time, but these descriptions create the impression that the characters are in the constant grip of epileptic fits.[32] Furthermore, critics were too quick to mark this as an inherent Japanese trait. Japanese critics similarly found *Rashomon*'s acting overly emotional, and in encouraging such a style, Kurosawa was drawing not upon Japanese traditional theater for inspiration but Hollywood movies of the silent era.[33] If these three films did employ unusual acting styles, it was due to the individual choices of their directors more than any inherent Asian characteristics.

But this notion that all three movies were the homogeneous product of a single national style could also work in their favor, especially when reviewers drew linkages between these contemporary films and seemingly timeless traditional Japanese art. Admittedly, some commentators did find similarities in these films' aesthetics and modernism, much in the same way that architects and ikebana enthusiasts did for their respective arts. Designer Aline Saarinen included *Ugetsu*, along with the works of Joan Miro and Alexander Calder, as an example of "the modern" in a 1954 *New York Times Magazine* article, and Parker Tyler of New York's Cinema 16 film society favorably compared *Rashomon*'s complex viewpoints to one of Picasso's cubist paintings.[34] However, critics who wrote for mainstream publications were far more likely to find connections with much older examples of uniquely Japanese culture. *Newsweek* claimed that *Rashomon*'s sets "recall the historic glories of Japanese art" in their "traditional simplification of the image," and that *Ugetsu* contained scenes "which reach back to Japanese painting for their effect." Of the same film, *Time* posited "the moviegoer has the sense of living in a classic Japanese watercolor or of walking in a world that is really a giant pearl," and its review of *Gate of Hell* claimed that actress Machiko Kyo "moves like a figure wooed to life from an antique fan." Arthur Knight of the *Saturday Review* also compared *Gate of Hell* to a Japanese painting, adding, "Its delicacy, its subtlety provide an almost startling contrast to our Hollywood-conditioned concepts of color in films," due to Japan's "centuries of accumulated wisdom in the psychology and philosophy of color." Even McCarten made a reference to the traditional art of ikebana in comparing *Ugestu* to "the flower arrangements, and all that."[35]

Also common were comparisons to traditional theater. Knight was one critic who sought to defend *Gate of Hell*'s acting style, and he did so by uncovering its roots in kabuki. Hatch made the same argument, writing that actor Kazuo Hasegawa, who played Moritoh, "grimaces like a devil mask and moves with the abrupt square grace of a kabuki dancer, which he once was." *Newsweek* further pointed out that *Gate of Hell*'s director, Teinosuke Kinugasa, was also an actor in the kabuki theater earlier in his career.[36] In response to such comparisons, Donald Richie and his colleague Joseph Anderson published an essay in *Film Quarterly* in 1958, entitled "Traditional Theater and the Film in Japan: The Influence of Kabuki, Noh, and Other Forms on Film Content and Style." Their first sentence flatly stated, "Well, to be brief, there isn't any. All of the parallels ... are forced; all the pigeonholes are wrongly labeled; all the conclusions, so carefully jumped at, are as false as the assumptions on which they are based." They went on to argue that older Japanese dramatic forms had little to offer a modern transnational medium like film. Furthermore, they pointed out that around 90 percent of contemporary Japanese people had never attended a kabuki performance, and thus kabuki acting on screen would appear as strange to them as to the typical American moviegoer.[37] The fact that so many critics insisted on such connections reveals their eagerness to essentialize these movies as stemming from an ancient Asian tradition, when in fact they were as innovative as any twentieth-century films anywhere in the world.

Even when they weren't making direct comparisons to traditional Japanese arts, critics added to the impression that these films reflected an ancient past in more subtle ways as well. They highlighted elements with universal appeal that filmgoers of any national background would appreciate; yet the strengths they pointed to often remained characteristically "Japanese." Western observers have singled out the Japanese people for creating stunning visual art—especially depicting nature—since the *ukio-e* print craze of the turn of the century. In similar fashion, many critics commended *Rashomon* and *Ugetsu* for their compositional skill, especially in regard to Miyagawa's photography. Bosley Crowther found the camera work in *Rashomon* "expressive beyond words." *Newsweek* claimed that "the genius of [*Ugetsu*] rests on the superb photography" and praised *Rashomon's* skilled cinematography, which the reviewer attributed to "the legendary esthetic powers of the Japanese." Even McCarten had to admit of the latter film, "The workings of the Japanese mind are odd, but I should add that the workings of the Japanese cameramen who made the film are ingenious and aesthetic. Some of the shots of the bleak, rush-grown country are undeniably fascinating."[38]

In this regard, many reviews of *Gate of Hell* chose to focus on its use of color, as Robert Hatch called it "the best movie color we have ever seen." Some were explicit in crediting uniquely Japanese artistic skills for the film's praiseworthy photography. *Time* established a contrast between traditional Japan and modern Hollywood by claiming that *Gate of Hell* captured "the mood of those monstrous feudal murals of Nippon" as opposed to American movies that "scorched" audiences' eyeballs with "so many Technicolored prairie fires." Crowther practically gushed over the film's visual style: "No subtle pictorial compositions, no color patterns and harmonies to compare with those in this picture have ever been seen by this writer on a movie screen." He then attributed this remarkable quality to "an intelligence" with regard to color "that embraces the whole tradition of Japanese culture and art."[39]

Despite critics' tendencies to examine these films as the endpoint of a specifically Japanese artistic tradition, there are indeed many easily discernible universal elements in all three of these movies, especially in terms of theme. Each movie depicts the horrors of war, including references to death, pain, and loss that undoubtedly resonated with people in the wake of World War II all over the world. In particular, *Rashomon*'s contemplation of the nature of truth echoed contemporary debates over moral relativism by modernist intellectuals, which some critics did indeed acknowledge. *Newsweek* noted the film was "deeply based on moral ambiguities" and that its plot made "for the richest kind of psychological texture."[40] But even in this case, critics continued to doubt that such universal reflection made these movies any less Japanese. Crowther questioned whether *Rashomon*'s themes had any relevance to American audiences or if "its dismal cynicism . . . reflect[s] a current disposition in Japan." Knight added, "The 'humanism' [Japanese] directors have adopted is perhaps, by our standards, still highly formalized and ritualistic." *Newsweek* stated most straightforwardly, "The symbolism behind the simple plot of [*Gate of Hell*] is universal, although it wears peculiarly Japanese clothing."[41] Even as they aimed to tackle issues that carried relevant weight for all industrialized nations recovering from war, American critics nevertheless insisted these films were fundamentally different from U.S. movies, perpetually marked by the foreign national tradition that created them.

By the mid-1950s, these critics appear to have formulated a general understanding of what made a Japanese film different from the films of any other nation, including (perhaps especially) the United States. Overall, they praised these movies more often than they offered negative criticism. However, the films' value often derived from the fact that, unlike Hollywood movies, they drew on a rich vein of Japanese tradition with centuries' worth of wisdom regarding subtle visual aesthetics. The acting in the movies might have appeared odd, but their camera work was as well composed as a nineteenth-century Hiroshige print. They might attempt to contribute to debates on modern intellectual themes, but they did so with a Japanese voice. In the end, minor flaws related to strange plots or acting styles might not really matter as, according to *Newsweek*, "the genius" of these films "rests with the superb photography which transforms the acting, the story, and the background into a flow of insistently haunting images."[42] Ignoring Richie's warning against drawing such direct lines between the past and the present, and seeming to forget that cinema is an inherently modern medium, critics were able to transform these twentieth-century movies into artifacts of a timeless Eastern artistic tradition that stood out as completely separate from typical Hollywood movies.

The Japanese Film Industry Responds to Its Newfound Success

As emblems of Japanese Cinema, *Rashomon*, *Ugetsu*, and *Gate of Hell* did not garner praise and esteem overseas only for themselves but for the entire Japanese industry. In 1954 *Time* and *Life* both ran feature stories on Japanese studios, with *Life* proclaiming that Hollywood producers would "find much to learn and to follow in the Japanese films' unsurpassed use of color and their clear, delicately composed pictorial images." Soon thereafter, *Time*'s year in review observed, "Two pictures from Japan outweighed, in many reviewers' scales, the rest of the world's product put together." In 1955 the

New York Times remarked, "Lately Italy" (then heralded for its neorealist "renaissance") "seems to be yielding leadership among foreign filmmakers to Japan."[43] Japanese movie executives happily accepted such compliments, and seeing an opportunity to capitalize on American critics' essentializing tendencies, they tried to take advantage of their new reputation.

Following on the heels of their first three successful movies, Daiei Studios became the top earning company of any kind in Tokyo, followed in second and third place by Toho and Nikkatsu studios. As the industry expanded, increasing numbers of Japanese movies were screened in the United States, with Japanese film exports jumping 19 percent between 1955 and 1956.[44] The first all-Japanese film festival in the United States was held at UCLA in 1956, followed a year later by a much larger event in Manhattan.[45] In August 1960 the Toho studios opened the Toho La Brea theater in Los Angeles. Located several blocks south of the famous "Miracle Mile," it was the first theater in a predominately white neighborhood to show only Japanese films. The studio expanded to a second franchise in New York three years later, suggesting the LA theater was indeed financially successful, but it is unclear how many patrons were white English-speaking Americans as opposed to Issei.[46]

Nevertheless, heads of other Japanese studios became similarly invested in marketing their films abroad. The first and most famous of these was Daiei's Masaichi Nagata, producer of *Rashomon*, *Ugetsu*, and *Gate of Hell*, who was dubbed the "Daryl Zanuck of Japan" by members of the American film industry. He quickly became a star in his own right, winning a special achievement award from the Foreign Press Association of Hollywood (a precursor to the Golden Globes) before *Ugetsu*'s American premiere. He made several tours of the United States with the American press in tow, especially in 1955, when he was accompanied by Machiko Kyo.[47] Apparently unaware that Nagata had initially hated *Rashomon*, American journalists hailed him as the genius promoter who first introduced Japanese cinema to the United States. He gained a favorable reputation as a savvy business-man with an eye for the overseas market and a mission to ensure that his nation's movies were appreciated across the globe.

After Nagata's successes of 1954, other producers began to follow his lead, courting American distributors for their movies. However, studios remained selective about which films they exported, painfully aware that in the contemporary climate of film criticism, one bad picture could ruin the reputation of the nation's industry. Richie and Anderson estimated that of the entire film output for Japan in 1959, only about 5 percent were considered "high quality," and of those, only a fraction were ever shown abroad.[48] However, as would become apparent by the late 1950s, Japanese producers and American critics did not always see eye to eye on what made a picture "high quality." American critics knew that foreign cinema did not have a widespread appeal in the United States and was largely limited to the discerning art house palate. Therefore, they appraised Japanese movies on artistic merits that would appeal specifically to this group. Japanese studio heads, in contrast, wanted to compete directly with Hollywood and break into the American mainstream movie market. They followed Hollywood producers' lead in aiming for the middle as far as content was concerned, promoting films they thought would speak to the average American.

This discrepancy was compounded by the fact that many Japanese producers seemed to misinterpret *Rashomon*'s American success. Almost as soon as it won the grand prize Golden Lion at Venice, Japanese critics began claiming that the film's appeal lay in its inherent "Western-ness," a charge that Kurosawa denounced but that continues to haunt discussion of his work.[49] Studio executives reasoned that Americans appreciated *Ugetsu* and *Gate of Hell*, as well as *Rashomon*, because they were historical dramas featuring depictions of thrilling duels and alienated masculine figures in a manner similar to Hollywood's "Old West" genre.[50] Thus they began exporting samurai movies to such an extent that in 1959, Kurosawa himself complained that this genre was "all the West has seen and continues to see of Japanese cinema."[51] Conversely, there appeared to be a consensus across the industry that foreign audiences wouldn't enjoy any movie that was "overly Japanese." For example, they refused to export the films of Yasujiro Ozu, who is today considered by many film scholars to be one of Japan's greatest directors, because they felt his movies depicted modern life in a particularly Japanese style. If indeed American audiences appreciated Japanese movies for their foreign distinctiveness, as many U.S. critics suggested, this perhaps was a missed opportunity for Japanese studio executives.[52]

In addition to carefully selecting which films to send abroad, producers created films specifically for export overseas, and *Gate of Hell* was in fact the first example of such a project. Despite U.S. critics' attempts to categorize the film as part of a long-standing Japanese artistic tradition that included *Rashomon* and *Ugetsu*, *Gate of Hell* was designed with modern commercial interests in mind to an extent that the other two films were not. The use of color photography that American critics had attributed to a timeless Japanese aesthetic sensibility was actually based on American techniques. Before production began, Daiei Studios sent color technicians to Warner Brothers as well as to several European studios to learn how to create visual effects that would appeal to Western tastes. Similarly, the film's allegedly Japanese aesthetic style was created by an art director whose brother had an established career in Hollywood.[53] The film's feudal setting and inclusion of many traditional Japanese art forms was a calculated effort on the part of the studio to attract American audiences by playing up its foreign origin. Throughout the movie, viewers witnessed traditional dances, koto playing, and samurai sporting competitions set against antique temples, gardens, and picturesque natural landscapes of Japan. At times the movie almost resembles a travelogue whose sole purpose is to exhibit a country's attractive and exotic scenery and customs. Judging from the positive response to the film, it appears this overall strategy of appearing familiar in style yet intriguingly foreign in content worked. Crowther found that *Gate of Hell* was "not as fantastic as *Ugetsu* . . . or as strange and complex as . . . *Rashomon*." Critic John McCarten softened his tone in his review, admitting that it was a quality film, without resorting to the race-baiting winks and rib pokes he employed in describing earlier Japanese movies.[54] Given the movie's large box office receipts, it is evident it attracted viewers beyond the circle of regular art house patrons, making it the commercial success its producers were aiming for.

After such techniques proved successful, some producers tried to take them even further and create movies along the lines of the Hollywood spectaculars so popular at the time, like Cecil B. DeMille's *The Ten Commandments* (1956) or 20th Century Fox's *The Robe* (Henry Koster, 1953). In 1959 Toho Studios began production on the epic *The Three Treasures*, which portrayed Japan's mythical beginnings. Nagata also tried his hand with *Buddha*, a retelling of the life of the spiritual leader featuring a massive budget and a cast of thousands. However, as foreign films in the United States they were denied the wide distribution that most American spectaculars enjoyed, and they failed to impress art house patrons because they were so imitative of Hollywood. Stuck in a kind of Catch-22, they flopped on the U.S. market. Other attempts involved collaborations with American or European studios, but these often proved unprofitable as well, at times failing even before shooting was completed.[55]

In the end, few of the Japanese studios' efforts to make and export more "Western" (in several senses of the word) movies paid off, possibly because they misunderstood their films' appeal to the niche American market that appreciated them. Japanese producers assumed it was the violent action and John Wayne–like heroes in these movies that Americans enjoyed. Instead, in an era when Americans were willfully trying to forget Japan's recent violent past, U.S. critics emphasized the movies' more feminine-seeming attributes of beautiful, well composed cinematography and sedate, graceful pacing. In addition to miscalculating the movies' gendered appeal, Japanese producers also misjudged the class distinction associated with foreign films in the United States. The "lowbrow" moviegoers who most seemed to enjoy the western genre rarely frequented art houses. Meanwhile, upper-middle-class art house patrons claimed to prioritize artistic photography and intellectually challenging themes over the action and excitement offered by most Hollywood westerns. Audiences for foreign films enjoyed them not because they looked similar to American movies but because they wanted them to provide something different.

As such, when American critics thought Japanese movies felt too familiar, they were not impressed. In 1955 *Time* gave a negative review to *The Impostor* (Tatsuo Osone), declaring that the film "has the look of a grade A Hollywood costume adventure that was shot with an almond-eyed camera."[56]

Bosley Crowther had a similar opinion of the movie, as well as *The Samurai* (Hiroshi Inagaki, 1956), which he dismissed by writing, "Its drama is largely a conglomeration of contemporary Japanese romantic clichés, very much on the order of the conventional situations that occur in Hollywood western films." He made similar comments about several later Kurosawa period films when they premiered in New York, including *The Hidden Fortress* (1962) and *Yojimbo* (1962).[57]

One final notable case in point is *Seven Samurai* (1956). While considered by many movie fans today to be Kurosawa's masterpiece, at the time of its initial U.S. release the film remained largely unappreciated. Columbia Studios had only one copy of the film to circulate, meaning it played for just one week in New York and received no critical attention at all during its brief subsequent run in Chicago. It did not win any awards, nor was it nominated for a best foreign film Oscar. While Crowther stated that he enjoyed *Seven Samurai* overall, he found it lacking in the essential Japanese qualities that he felt had made *Rashomon* such an excellent movie. Instead, he argued, "Mr. Kurosawa is telling a story that has been told a hundred times (or maybe more) in a setting of sagebrush and with sheriffs instead of samurai."[58] Perhaps fittingly, most Americans did not even hear about the film until 1960, when director John Sturges remade it as *The Magnificent Seven*. At the time of *Seven Samurai*'s release, it failed to conform to American critics' expectations of Japanese films: that they should reflect an artistic Japan and offer something different and better than the usual Hollywood product, that they should be more shibui than spectacular.

Several subsequent feudal dramas did prove successful in the United States, both at the box office and on the awards circuit, including *The Samurai* and *The Rickshaw Man* (also directed by Inagaki, 1960), but few other Japanese art house movies would do much to distinguish themselves later in the decade. Beginning as early as 1955, American film journalists reported that Japan's showing at international festivals was declining.[59] If the *New York Times* truly was the bellwether for newspaper critics across the country, most found the Japanese films screened in the late 1950s to be decidedly disappointing, often in their seeming imitation of American movies. To take one example, in 1959 Crowther scathingly referred to *The Human Condition* (Masaki Kobayashi) as "turgid and tedious as drama" and concluded that "there is nothing in its substance, its theme or the prison-camp melodramatics that you might not see in a cheap American film."[60] Even subsequent films by Kurosawa and Mizoguchi failed to impress, as he derided *The Men Who Tread on the Tiger's Tail* (Kurosawa, 1960) and *Throne of Blood* (Kurosawa, 1962),[61] and found *Yang Kwei-Fei* (Mizoguchi, 1956) tedious and *Street of Shame* (Mizoguchi, 1959) mediocre.[62] The prestige of Japanese cinema in the United States had reached its peak with *Gate of Hell*.

By the early 1960s, Japanese studios were facing a deep financial crisis as they encountered increasing competition from television, and both the quantity and quality of their output began to diminish.[63] But as most film scholars today respect and appreciate *Yojimbo*, *Street of Shame*, and especially *Seven Samurai*, perhaps a bigger factor was the interpretation most critics formed of Japanese Cinema, as opposed to that of any other nation, reflecting a subdued, restrained, often-feminine artistic sensibility. These qualities held the potential to counteract both Japan's militarist reputation of the recent past and the perceived banality of contemporary American popular culture. According to this characterization of Japanese movies, even when the Japanese appeared to master a decidedly twentieth-century medium, they did so thanks to the quiet artistry of timeless tradition, not individual directors' competency in a new art form that reflected Japan's complex contemporary reality.

CHAPTER 3

FRIENDSHIP THROUGH FLOWERS

Americans' Appreciation of Ikebana and Bonsai

While many Americans encountered Japanese culture from the familiar surroundings of their local movie theater, hundreds of thousands of U.S. military personnel and their families were experiencing life in Japan firsthand. The U.S. occupation required not only a large contingent of peacekeeping troops but also the presence of a vast military bureaucracy, as well as the assistance of nonprofit aid organizations like the Red Cross. As a result, postwar Japan played host to legions of American secretaries, housewives, nurses, policy experts, and children, as well as soldiers. While the numbers of foreign personnel dwindled somewhat following the return of Japan's autonomy in 1952, sizable U.S. military bases, whose presence in Japan was negotiated in the Treaty of San Francisco, ensured a significant population of temporary American residents in Japan for years to come. Most of these Americans, especially officers' dependents and civilian employees, would come to enjoy a lifestyle not unlike the privileged position of nineteenth-century European imperialists stationed in colonial outposts. During the occupation, American personnel and their families were billeted in segregated neighborhoods, where they commandeered some of the finest homes left standing in Tokyo, often with a staff of six or seven local servants on hand. While most of the Japanese population was struggling to survive on inadequate food rations supplemented by overpriced black market purchases, Americans could choose from a variety of household supplies and carry home all the meat and sugar they wanted from the military post exchange.[1]

In keeping with such an elevated social position, some soldiers and occupation employees adopted a role not uncommon for many Orientalists, that of the white observer who "goes native." As part of a peacetime force, many Americans had ample opportunity to experience their local surroundings and become at least superficially acquainted with Japanese lifestyles and culture. Homemakers and children especially were in a unique position to interact with native household servants and local playmates eager to make friends. According to a book by *Stars and Stripes* cartoonist Bill Hume, *When We Get Back Home from Japan*, servicemen became accustomed to bowing, wearing *geta* (wooden sandals), sitting and sleeping on the floor, eating raw fish with chopsticks, and removing their shoes before entering a house. GIs in the book also use words like *sayonara*, *doozo* (please), *dai jobu* (okay), and *moshi moshi* (a telephone greeting). In his commentary on the cartoons, fellow *Stars and Stripes* contributor John Annarino explained, "The servicemen in Japan have a word for it. They call it 'Asiatic.' It means that they've been in Nippon for too long. Their American customs have thrown in the social towel, and Japanese customs have been tagged the winner."[2] Annarino and Hume joked that they and their fellow occupation personnel had completely immersed themselves in Japanese culture, attaining the ability to migrate seamlessly between the United States and Japan.

Attaining full understanding of the habits and customs of another nation over the course of one military tour of duty would of course be highly unlikely (let alone the fact that almost no servicemen learned the language fluently). Instead, according to historian Donna Alvah, many Americans stationed overseas following World War II viewed themselves as "unofficial ambassadors." Believing that their patriotic duty was to promote understanding between the United States and other nations, Americans felt a willing obligation to share their values and ideas with their foreign neighbors and employees. Later, those stationed in Japan would bring home newfound knowledge and newly purchased souvenirs to teach their friends and families in the states about foreign nations and their customs.[3]

Some of these self-appointed diplomats adopted Japanese hobbies, often taking classes sponsored by the military to promote cultural exchange. They then carried these leisure pursuits back to new American audiences, two of the most popular being ikebana flower arranging and bonsai miniature tree cultivation. Over the following decade, both spread throughout the United States, eventually becoming status symbols of fashion and taste among upper-middle-class Americans. Many hobbyists and consumers came to embrace these horticultural art forms. Promoters of each practice cited the shibui aesthetic, claiming these plants had a distinguished modern look whose cultivation required an appreciation of nature and level of discipline that were both uniquely Asian. However, neither ikebana nor bonsai practitioners held strictly to these ideals. In some cases, avant-garde ikebana arrangements threatened to break out of their particular Japanese mode and embrace more universal contemporary aesthetics. Meanwhile, some "lower middlebrow" American consumers began to take an interest in bonsai for the "wrong" reasons. Instead of admiring its modernist style and letting its demanding practice serve as an Oriental foil to postwar convenience, they appreciated its strange miniaturized appearance and cultivated bonsai using quick and easy American methods. Turning on its head the concept of what elements were supposed to be familiar and what aspects foreign, these particular bonsai owners created their own balance of the exotic and the comfortable in consuming Japanese culture.

Ikebana: An Art for the Modern Well-Heeled American Woman

Ikebana flower arranging dates back at least as far as the fifteenth century, and its practice has continuously evolved in the years since.[4] One rule that has remained unchanged is that any arrangement must contain plant materials of three varying lengths that represent heaven, man, and earth. Three main Ikebana styles were well established in Japan by the mid-twentieth century.

FIG. 3. Ikenobo arrangement by Yoshiko Nakamura on display at Seattle Center as part of the 2008 Cherry Blossom Festival, April 19, 2008. Photo by Joe Mabel. Wikimedia Commons.

FIG. 4. Example of Saga Goryū moribana kōseitai (hidarigatte) style. Wikimedia Commons.

The oldest is *seika*, which follows strict rules of placement and displays plant material in a shallow dish, holding it in place with a spiked metal plate called a needlepoint holder. Over the years new styles emerged, adapting and evolving these rules, including *nageire*, whose main requirement is that arrangements must be displayed in a tall vase. A third style, *moribana*, became the most popular in the United States. Emerging in the nineteenth century as part of the wider Meiji-era project to westernize and democratize Japan, moribana aimed to become a more accessible style, not adhering strictly to any set of rules, save that arrangements be displayed in a shallow container. These three styles are further divided into numerous schools, each with a master who developed his own particular guidelines for arranging.

During World War II, Japanese nationalists had promoted ikebana as a symbol of their special character; most ikebana masters were dispatched to Japan's colonies as propaganda agents to instruct and indoctrinate Japan's new Southeast Asian imperial subjects. However, during the occupation, few Americans seem to have been aware of the art form's wartime co-optation. When U.S. military vehicles arrived outside the home of renowned master Sofu Teshigahara, he feared they were there to arrest him as a collaborator. Instead, Gen. Douglas MacArthur's wife, Jean, had dispatched the officers after seeing Teshigahara's arrangements on display. She wanted to commission an exhibition of his works at the Ernie Pyle Theater in the American section of Tokyo, which later proved to be very popular among military personnel and their dependents.[5]

A significant number of American women were not content to merely admire these arrangements on display. In their desire as unofficial ambassadors to improve international relations, they sought to understand more deeply the fundamentals of Japanese culture and practice ikebana themselves. Many army posts that offered adult education classes soon received frequent requests for ikebana lessons. By 1955, according to a *Chicago Tribune* correspondent, "Japanese flower arrangement has by far the greatest attraction" of any hobby in the city. "Classes meet all over Tokyo in private homes, clubs, recreation centers, and even in temples." *Tokyo Monthly* magazine reported two years later that approximately half of all women living in security forces housing had taken at least one course on ikebana. It also pointed out that the wives of diplomats and businessmen living in Japan had taken up the practice, some of them becoming trained experts in the field. In 1955, *Time* estimated that six thousand military wives had taken classes in ikebana, with more than four hundred receiving certificates licensing them to teach the art themselves.[6]

Once their tours of duty were complete, many of these women set to work on the other end of their cultural bridge, by providing lessons to their friends back in the United States. Many organized demonstrations in their communities, in department stores, garden clubs, YWCA centers, and churches.[7] In 1960 *Flower Grower*, a mid-twentieth-century magazine aimed at the home gardener, declared, "Any evaluation of the course of flower arrangement today must take account of one overwhelming trend—interest in Japanese styles. . . . [They] are predominant." Three years later, the *Chicago Tribune* listed ikebana as one of the three most popular flower-arranging styles in the country.[8]

By far the biggest driving force behind white American women's interest in ikebana was the organization Ikebana International (II). At first consisting mainly of the wives of officers and diplomats stationed in Japan, by 1962 its membership had expanded over five continents. The club was founded by Ellen Gordon Allen, a woman whom colleagues described as possessing admirable organizational skill and seemingly boundless energy. She moved to Tokyo in 1950 with her husband, an army general in the occupation. A friend in Washington DC had advised her to study Japanese flower arranging, and she found herself immediately drawn to the art. Her appreciation grew after her husband left Japan to fight in the Korean War, and she discovered that practicing the hobby helped to soothe her when she worried about his safety. She threw herself into the pursuit so completely that she simultaneously studied both seika arranging and the Ohara school of moribana, at a time when few Japanese practitioners engaged with more than one school in a lifetime.

Following her husband's two-year tour in Asia, Allen embarked on a new vocation teaching the art of ikebana. After her return to the United States, she founded several local clubs, taught classes, and published a short book entitled *Japanese Flower Arrangement in a Nutshell*. She also returned periodically to Japan, where she made her first efforts to start an organization to promote ikebana to foreign nationals living in Tokyo. She approached several instructors, including Houn Ohara, who would later advise the organization, and made remarkable headway for someone who did not speak the language. But her husband's reassignment to Italy put a temporary halt to her plans. Upon his retirement in 1954, Allen returned to Japan to continue her ikebana study. In August 1956, a Japanese friend asked her to deliver a speech on ikebana at a local army officers' club. While there, according to II lore, she surveyed the wives sitting in the room, gauged a positive reaction, and spontaneously decided to invite them all to found a new ikebana club. A week later, twenty-one women gathered at Allen's hotel for Ikebana International's first meeting.[9]

The organization's original membership drew mostly from a close-knit group of white American military wives living in the Washington Heights security forces housing area in Tokyo.[10] Within several months, they began to branch out, forming local chapters in the United States. The first was in Washington, Allen's hometown. Others quickly followed, and in the next year, chapters appeared in St. Louis, Nashville, Los Angeles, and New York. The group also established a foothold in a number of smaller towns like Cleburne, Texas, Panama City, Florida, and Lake Charles, Louisiana. Most of these chapters were near military bases, where officers' wives returned after their tours in Japan. Allie Uyehara, one of the organization's founding members, hailed from Chinook, Montana, a town so small it did not have its own flower shop, but the chapter she started there preceded the establishment of clubs in Atlanta, Boston, Seattle, and San Francisco. By 1959 there were so many local groups wanting to join the larger organization that II developed a complex system for approving new chapters, involving three separate stages of application and review by headquarters. Once established, each chapter maintained close ties to Tokyo, sending regular dues and correspondence and receiving their monthly newsletter and magazine. By the mid-1960s, II was a highly structured and sophisticated multinational organization with seventy-one chapters in the United States, Japan, Italy (where Allen maintained connections), England, Hong Kong, Australia, and Argentina.[11]

According to accounts offered in *Ikebana International Magazine*, interest in ikebana spread quickly across the United States. In 1958 Japanese ikebana instructor Seiko Ogawa visited Chinook as part of a national tour and described her experience: "After the exhibit so many people came to thank me and to shake my hand. There were many elderly ladies in the audience and many of them had tears in their eyes—they said it was the first time

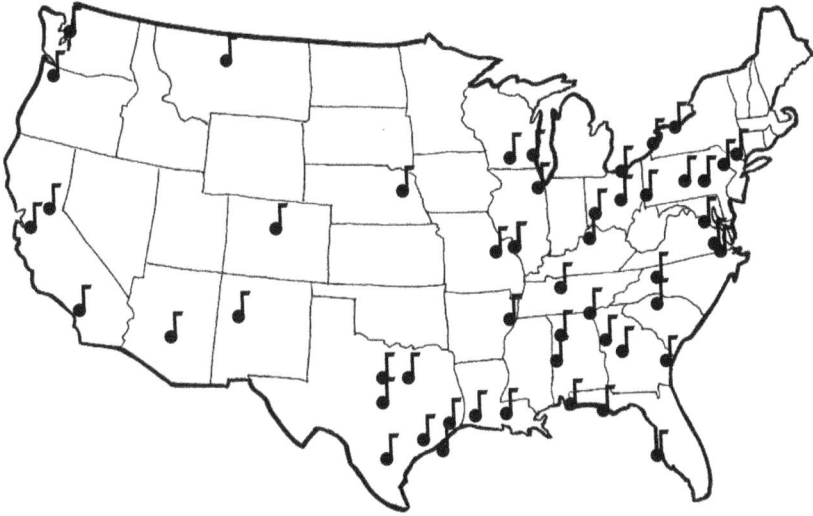

FIG. 5. Map of Ikebana International chapters in the United States in 1962. Image from *Ikebana International Magazine*.

in their lives they had seen Japanese ikebana and had enjoyed it so much." While not every small town chapter's experience was quite so lachrymose, many followed a similar pattern. One woman or group of women who had studied ikebana in Japan would demonstrate the art for her friends, and they in turn would practice their newfound hobby with other like-minded women.[12] In large cities, II attracted more members by actively promoting the practice and appreciation of ikebana with demonstrations, exhibits, public lectures, television appearances, flower shows, and house and garden tours. The organization's headquarters also sponsored multicity lecture tours for Ogawa, Ohara, and Australian ikebana master Norman Sparnon.[13] In 1959 the group's reputation received a further boost when *Better Homes & Gardens* magazine sent a reporter to II's Tokyo headquarters to produce a three-page article on the organization, accompanied by color photographs.[14]

In promoting ikebana, many II members felt they were serving a higher purpose than simply informing American women about an intriguing new hobby; they viewed their efforts as a way to encourage unity and cultural understanding not only between the United States and Japan, but throughout the world. The notion originated at the very first meeting of II, when Allen concluded her inaugural speech: "I see no reason why Ikebana International cannot become a veritable garland of flowers surrounding the world with beauty and binding us together in real and lasting friendship—a magnificent contribution from Japan to the world at large!" This proclamation betrays a certain degree of American chauvinism, in Allen's casual assumption that a cadre of white American women were the most appropriate spokespeople for a Japanese art form. But most members appeared oblivious to this incongruity in embracing her more noble One Worldist optimism. When Stella Coe, founder of the London chapter, coined the pithy slogan "Friendship through Flowers," it quickly caught on among the entire organization's ranks. Some expressed similar sentiments when they wrote letters to headquarters in Tokyo. "I am proud of the beautiful job you did for international relationships," remarked Miss Helene Hashmill of Washington, North Carolina. To which Mrs. Thomas N. Tanimoto of Monterey, California, added, "I feel that II can bind all nationalities in peace through one object, flowers." Their efforts were recognized by the U.S. ambassador to Japan, Douglas MacArthur II, when he wrote a note of congratulations to the organization in 1960, asserting, "It might be said that flowers, like music, speak a universal language." Similarly, in 1965 the Foreign Cultural Division of the Japanese Foreign Ministry awarded Ellen Gordon Allen the Order of the Precious Crown, fifth class for the group's work in helping to spread Japanese culture around the globe.[15]

Overall, the membership of Ikebana International was largely homogeneous, consisting almost entirely of upper-middle-class white women. It appears that men had a tendency to feel unwelcome in the organization, viewing it as a predominately female space. A *New Yorker* reporter visiting an ikebana class discovered a husband patiently waiting for his wife at a distance outside the door. One male II applicant felt the need to ask headquarters, "Will you accept an American man into your membership?" Allie Uyehara recalled that such gender disparity was often due to contemporary assumptions about men and women's respective places in society. "Mostly women joined Ikebana International at the outset, as in those days women had the time to become involved in such things, whereas men were the breadwinners and did not participate." In addition to supposedly lacking leisure time, it was considered emasculating for American men to take an interest in flowers. In the introduction to his 1960 book on ikebana, Sparnon (a white Australian) complained of "the notion more or less prevalent in Western nations that the appreciation of floral beauty, or of nature itself, is necessarily a womanly weakness to which the male must never succumb." Meanwhile, it appears such gendered assumptions were not as ingrained in Japan, where in fact the majority of ikebana masters were men, some of whom served as advisors to Ikebana International. But their presence did little to convince many white American men that ikebana could indeed be manly.[16] As citizens of a defeated nation whose culture as a whole supposedly valued quietude, subtle beauty, and other stereotypically ladylike attributes, Japanese men were themselves presumed feminine due to their race.

Along with gender segregation, there was also a looser, but nonetheless noticeable, sense of class exclusivity within the organization's ranks. The price of tools and materials typically kept ikebana out of reach for working-class women. According to Uyehara, "It is expensive to take lessons [and] purchase the equipment, plus fresh flowers, so it is the well-to-do that join." This proved to be the case when New York's Museum of Natural History offered classes in 1960. The course was limited to fifteen students and cost $20 (approximately $160 in 2017 currency) to enroll for four weeks. The aforementioned reporter attending the class discovered that the woman working next to her owned a country home near the Stockbridge Bowl and a membership in the Berkshire Garden Center, both prestigious New England addresses.[17] It was clear ikebana would emerge as an "upper middlebrow" pursuit.

Since most of the women involved in II were military officers' wives, or at least affluent homemakers, they also tended to be overwhelmingly white, as did the organization's leadership. However, some Asian women did become members. The first to do so were Japanese women who worked in clerical positions at headquarters, employed because of their English skills. Coverage of local chapter activities in *Ikebana International Magazine* suggests that most stateside members of Japanese ancestry were war brides; all women in the publication were identified by their husband's names, including some visibly Asian women labeled with Western-sounding names. Many of these newlywed wives found themselves cut off from other Japanese people, as they settled with their white husbands in small towns scattered throughout the country. Feeling isolated, perhaps they saw ikebana as a link to their homeland, as well as an opportunity to participate in a new social network in an unfamiliar locale. Others members appear to have been Japanese American, signing letters to the editor as women with English first names and Japanese surnames.[18] The Los Angeles–based Japanese American news-paper *Rafu Shimpo* further offers reports of Nisei women participating in ikebana exhibits aimed at white audiences throughout the 1950s.[19]

One notable example of a prominent Japanese American II member was Mary Takahashi, who not only founded the Chicago chapter but also ran an ikebana school, went on lecture tours, made an appearance on local televi-sion, and organized an exhibit of a complete Japanese garden at the Carson Pirie Scott department store. She even spread her reputation nationwide, designing a set of ikebana-themed placemats as a giveaway for Johnson's Wax (now the S. C. Johnson Company) in 1959. *Ikebana International Mag-azine* suggested with admiration that "no small part of the breezes that give Chicago its nickname are activated by the wonderfully energetic Miss Takahashi." However, there was more to Takahashi than simply being an enthusiastic woman enamored of flower arranging. Born in California as the daughter of a bonsai expert, she took an early interest in brush painting as well as ikebana, but trained as an optometrist. Interred with the rest of the West Coast Nisei during the war, in 1943 she applied and was approved to relocate from camp as a "loyal citizen." Like most who left the camps early, she moved to Chicago and found a job helping fit war industry workers with safety goggles. When the war was over, her more artistic side won out when she became a wallpaper designer and later opened her own interior design studio, establishing a successful market for her services among a wide clientele. Yet she never abandoned the Japanese American community that emerged in Chicago following the war. In 1948 one of her first exhibits of traditional Japanese design was held at a community center for resettled Nisei. However, unlike many of her fellow former prisoners, who held tightly to their assimilation as a preemptive shield against prejudice, she made a career of promoting traditional Japanese arts to the white American public in an attempt to improve international and interracial relations.[20]

While neither newspaper coverage nor *Ikebana International Magazine* reveals exactly what Takahashi said to her audiences in her lectures, it is probably safe to assume that regardless of her racial heritage, she professed the same opinions as other American enthusiasts and presented ikebana as emblematic of traditional Japanese culture. Ikebana's promoters praised its subtlety and minimalism, both characteristics that American art experts regularly attributed to Asian aesthetics. They contrasted ikebana with the fullness and brightly colored flowers of traditional Western arrangements, since it used far less plant material in one vase, with far fewer petals and leaves. Sanae Yamazaki, a war bride who became a cartoonist for *Stars and Stripes*, made fun of this typical American impression of ikebana. In one comic, a young boy tags along to his mother's class and comments on the instructor's pruning techniques, declaring: "I think she's wasting an awful lot."[21] But unlike the naïve boy who simply found its appearance strange, most ikebana promoters saw great aesthetic value in ikebana's spareness. In another of many "how-to" books, Nina Clark Powell listed the ingredients of the art as "subtleties of thought . . . suggestions of ideas . . . symbolism" and "an appreciation of clean line." Rachel Carr, an American ikebana master and guidebook author who had lived in both China and Japan, explained in *Flower Grower*, "The reason for this appeal to western taste is precisely the quality of simplicity and restrained beauty so typical of Oriental art. . . . Behind a Japanese arrangement lies the answer to its graceful beauty and effortless charm—simplicity."[22] With its supposedly Eastern subtlety, ikebana offered an intriguing alternative to more established American styles and, by extension, reinforced the image of a nonthreatening traditional Japan from which contemporary Americans could profitably learn.

Another benefit of ikebana's inherent Japanese qualities, enthusiasts claimed, was its spiritual rewards; assumed to stem from a timeless Orient, the quiet antimodern practice of ikebana could provide respite in the loud and stressful twentieth century. Some authors drew direct ties to Shintoism or Buddhism, both of which appeared ancient and exotic to most white Americans in the early 1950s. In *Japanese Flower Arrangement in a Nutshell*, Allen called ikebana "an antidote to worry" and reminded readers that "Japanese flower arrangement was not practiced solely for the satisfaction of arranging flowers beautifully according to the rules, but because the art became imbued with a deep philosophical and religious significance." These spiritual qualities, Allen and others claimed, could offer solace to Americans leading hectic lives. In her guidebook, Lida Webb put forth the assumption, common to many westerners at the time, that Japanese people possessed an inborn appreciation of nature. "In the stress of this scientific industrial age, we need opportunity to turn now and again to the peace and tranquility to be found in nature. Through the ages nature has been a source of refreshment to man's spirit."[23] In using natural plant materials to create works of tasteful beauty as Japanese had done since time immemorial, ikebana could serve as a foil to a contemporary world that had become overly stressful.

The mainstream press took up this same line of reasoning, further asserting Japan's exoticism, but also the inherent peaceful and nonthreatening aspects of its culture. The *New York Times* explained how the philosophy behind ikebana is based on a yin/yang dichotomy, and *Flower Grower* warned that "Americans' lack of knowledge of Oriental symbolism and meditation" might hinder their ikebana study.[24] But it was American ikebana master Rachel Carr who probably did the most to link ikebana practice to an inherent Japanese sense of the spiritual and artistic. Contributing multiple articles to both the *Times* and *Flower Grower*, she posited repeatedly that ikebana was "akin to [Japanese] philosophy and their way of life." She referred to Japan as "a nation of artists," at another point referencing "the Japanese genius which, through a love of naturalism, developed an art of sublime beauty with unlimited opportunity for expression. . . . They have allied expressive art with nature to a greater degree than any other people.

In fact, the celebrated [haiku] poet Basho once said: 'Follow nature and turn constantly to nature.'"[25] In all of these examples, characteristics of spirituality, meditative repose, harmony, and a general love of nature contrast sharply with previous media images of Japanese violence and deviousness. The promotion of ikebana thus helped, however unintentionally, to reinforce the postwar image of a wise yet compliant ally.

In addition to serving the ends of international relations, ikebana could appeal to American women on a personal level as well. In using few flowers to create austere and reserved designs, ikebana arrangements avoided the alleged gaudiness of typical American arrangements, and thereby became a marker of sophisticated, affluent tastes. Ikebana also adhered to a highbrow set of values in providing a form of character-building leisure. Unlike more passive and supposedly banal pursuits, like the still-novel activity of TV viewing, the demanding practice of ikebana could cultivate patience and self-discipline. Allen tried to assure readers that the art was "extremely easy and simple to learn." Yet on the same page, she mentioned "obstacles confronting any beginner" and advised students to "be patient, persevere and work hard." A 1955 cartoon by Anne Cleveland, an illustrator living in Japan as the wife of a British businessman, depicts some of the obstacles a woman could face if she tried to casually take up the hobby. After admiring an arrangement, her character Mrs. West tries her own hand, only to find herself pulling out a hacksaw, attempting to strangle a branch, and eventually creating a jerry-rigged arrangement that includes tangles of string and a nailed up two-by-four. But rather than interpreting ikebana's demanding aspects as stumbling blocks, some hobbyists promoted them as valuable challenges, often linking them to the art form's Oriental origins. Helen Van Pelt Wilson of *Flower Grower* claimed it built character and skill and that "there is no better discipline than that offered by a study of the traditional Japanese styles." Carr further explained in a *New York Times* article that ikebana study in Japan was a lifelong pursuit. Most experts began their training in childhood, and once they received a master's degree from their chosen school, they still required years of practice before they were allowed to create distinctive or original arrangements.[26]

But while ikebana often seemed essentially Eastern in its subtle aesthetics, spiritual appreciation of nature, and adherence to strict discipline, there were some occasions when modernist arrangements appeared to transcend particularly Japanese aesthetics and perhaps contradict ikebana's reputation as timeless and traditional. Some American experts did indeed recognize that the art was constantly updating, often displaying evidence of inter-action with American styles. Most of the Japanese ikebana masters who advised II, like Ohara and Tomoyuki Minomura, tended to favor the most recent styles, which they promoted to their American pupils.[27] Teshigahara, who offered classes to Ikebana International's members, had a reputation in Japan as a supporter of the avant-garde art scene. The Sogetsu school's great hall played host to displays of cutting edge art and theater through-out the postwar era. Sofu's son, who would eventually inherit the school, was the neorealist director Hiroshi Teshigahara, most famous for his 1964 film *The Woman in the Dunes*. As the son of a prominent ikebana master himself, in his youth Sofu provoked his father's ire by declaring he wanted to create his own style of arranging that would allow for more individu-alistic expression. In 1953 he showed a *New York Times* correspondent how Western techniques had influenced his arrangements. "Americans put many flowers in one vase," the journalist paraphrased. "Japanese use few flowers. Mr. Teshigahara has combined the two tendencies. Americans use garden flowers. The Japanese like twigs. Again Mr. Teshigahara has borrowed a bit from each. He believes the combination of American mass and Japanese line will make for the best style." Teshigahara later told II members that he created his own school of ikebana because "the centuries-old style of flower arranging, stiff and formal as it had to be, was getting outmoded" and could not keep pace with the encroaching Western influence on Japanese living.[28] The result was a school that followed fewer rules, incorporated more flowers and plant material found outside of Japan, and kept pace with the times as a dynamic art form.

In some cases, both Teshigahara and Ohara modernized their works to the point that they bore little resemblance to the typical American notion of a flower arrangement. One example was a highly abstract nine-foot-tall,

FIG. 6. Example of jiyuka freestyle arrangement. Wikimedia Commons, Sorin Mazilu.

six-foot-wide arrangement Ohara created in 1959 for a Houston bank meant to capture his impression of the Texas Gulf Coast as seen from the air.[29] These works were in keeping with a new form of moribana that emerged around 1950, known as freestyle. It required only that materials be arranged in a triangular asymmetrical form; any type of material could be used in any type of container. This style emerged partly out of necessity in postwar Japan, where fresh flowers were difficult to find, but urban rubble offered abundant free material.[30] By the mid-twentieth century, some ikebana masters were creating designs that used no live plants at all but consisted of objects like driftwood, chunks of mortar, and discarded metal, creating pieces that looked more like abstract sculptures reflecting disaster and decay than joyous and colorful flower arrangements.

In a 1963 issue of *Flower Grower*, Rachel Carr reported on a show at an Osaka department store that included such pieces. She saw arrangements that incorporated scrap metal, wood, iron wheels, concrete, engine mufflers, rope, and cork. She explained, "New forces of expression in the modern movement have invaded the traditional arts.... Now the realm of ikebana encompasses free expression approaching the abstract and extending to avant-garde sculptures, mobiles and reliefs that may, or may not, include flowers."[31] In 1964 another freestyle arrangement graced the entrance of the Manufacturers Hanover Bank in Manhattan. It consisted of a ten-foot magnolia tree decorated with pine and juniper branches, metallic painted leaves, plastic flowers, and a peacock feather.[32]

While such arrangements signaled a departure from the more traditional methods that she practiced and advocated, Carr was nonetheless an admirer of the new designs. "Pure form and color seem to obey their own laws, resulting in masterful control of rhythm, balance, and harmony. The scope of creative vision is endless." Helen van Pelt Wilson also praised the new expressive nature of freestyle ikebana. She contrasted the quiet simplicity of traditional schools with newer arrangements that "mirror[ed] the harassed modern spirit, its desperation, revolt and fury, the brutality of the times reflected in truncated limbs and inverted designs."[33] In these cases, arrangers appear more like modern artists trying to speak to an audience from any nation, and instead of capturing some essence of a timeless past, they address and reflect the challenges of twentieth-century life. In these instances, ikebana broke free from the typical shibui mode for understanding Japanese culture by offering art that was both universal and contemporary.

But instead of significantly disrupting white Americans' understanding of ikebana as traditional, serene, and uniquely Eastern, these arrangements were more commonly dismissed by spectators as too bizarre for their taste. Yamazaki again humorously interpreted this American tendency. In another cartoon, a husband stands above his wife's arrangement, which consists mainly of artfully arranged twigs and stumps, and asks, "I know it's modern, but where are the flowers?" His smug expression coupled with her obvious annoyance reveal that his query was less a genuine question than a dig at her new hobby. One observer of the display at Manufacturers Hanover Bank told the *New York Times*: "All you need is an old worn-out cedar tree and lots of attachments. Give me a Christmas tree any day." In 1964 Robert C. Cherry, president of the Florists' Telegraph Delivery Association (commonly known as FTD), wrote an editorial in the *New York Times* in which he complained of the lack of flowers in ikebana arrangements. He doubted the appropriateness of "Japanese traditions" that "place high premium on distortion and often suppress flowers in favor of abstract design," and derisively referred to it as "the straw and scrap metal school." Of course, Cherry's words might be taken with a grain of salt, coming as they did from a man whose business was selling flowers.[34]

Perhaps allaying his fear, most American enthusiasts, Carr included, tended to prefer more traditional arrangements that were at least based in live plant material. Few of the arrangements featured in the pages of *Ikebana International Magazine* were done in abstract freestyle. Far more common were moribana designs that incorporated flowers and branches in the kind of subtle arrangements that white Americans had come to recognize as typical ikebana by the end of the 1950s. With its promises of serenity and tastefulness, ikebana developed a large following among potentially harried, upwardly mobile middle-class women. However, it failed to reach as wide an audience as some other popularized Japanese art forms, as its challenging nature suggested it was not a hobby for everyone. Not only were men largely discouraged by assumed gender roles, but becoming skilled at ikebana also required a woman to possess a high level of persistence and spare time that most working-class women lacked. As a result, ikebana remained an exclusive and refined art, reserved for those women with the time and the talent to master it. Within this circle, American practitioners created painstaking arrangements that adhered to their understanding of Japanese culture as sophisticated, spiritual, and subtly tasteful, which could rarely be described as anything but shibui.

Bonsai: An Exotic Hobby for the Busy Suburbanite

The same cannot necessarily be said for bonsai, another botanical Japanese art that became popular in the postwar United States and attracted a wider following than ikebana. Properly pronounced "bone sigh" (as guidebooks of the time liked to remind readers), it is also a centuries-old practice whose earliest known record is dated 1310.[35] While techniques for cultivating bonsai have changed over time and been updated with advances in horticultural techniques, the end result has remained the same: trees grown in miniature size to mimic the picturesque twisting and knotting of their full-grown counterparts. One popular manual described the bonsai specimen as "a forest tree seen through the wrong end of a telescope."[36] Bonsai are kept small through techniques including the use of shallow pots and special fertilizers and the strategic pruning of roots, branches, and buds. Sometimes plants are purposely twisted into artful shapes using wire wrapping and other training methods. Once they attain the desired form, specimens must be meticulously cared for on a daily basis, to maintain the fine line between proper dwarfing and starving the plant. In order to keep their size, they can only receive a small amount of water at a time. If a tree misses this regular watering for only a day or two, it could easily dry out and die. Some remarkable bonsai are kept alive under such conditions for decades. In October 1962 a thief managed to steal one of these long-lived bonsai from the Brooklyn Botanic Garden valued at $2,000 (approximately $15,600 today).[37] But most specimens were far more modest, kept on the patios and in the living rooms of suburban American homes.

American interest in bonsai began, like ikebana, among U.S. military forces stationed in Japan. Before World War II, few white Americans even knew of bonsai's existence, and they were understandably fascinated when they encountered the plants for the first time. Kyuzo Murata, later dubbed the "Father of Modern Bonsai in Japan," was surprised one afternoon during the occupation when two American servicemen arrived at his nursery in a jeep. At the time, his business was on the verge of bankruptcy, since postwar economic conditions left few Japanese with the means to afford such luxuries as bonsai. But naval lieutenant Leo R. Ball and war correspondent John R. Mercier had heard about his famed bonsai garden and were interested in purchasing some trees. Realizing he had a potential customer base in occupation personnel, Murata decided to keep his business open, and it eventually regained financial stability. Not long after the occupation ended, another bonsai expert, Yuji Yoshimura, was invited by the U.S. embassy in Tokyo to stage a demonstration of bonsai pruning for an American

FIG. 7. Example of bonsai. Kyoto botanic garden, 2008. Photo by the author.

audience. The event generated so much interest that Yoshimura agreed to offer classes to American military families, assisted by his German colleague and translator Alfred Koehn. The course quickly caught on in popularity, attracting roughly three hundred students in its first several years, leading one II member to describe it as "a must for foreigners in the Tokyo area."[38]

After most bonsai purchasers returned to the United States with their plants, however, many discovered that their trees wilted or became sick. For bonsai owners in the New York area, the most logical place to seek help was the Brooklyn Botanic Garden (BBG), which had an established interest in Japanese horticulture. Since 1914 the Garden has been the home of a three-and-a-half-acre Japanese garden, and in 1925, retiring nursery-man Ernest F. Coe of New Haven, Connecticut, donated his collection of thirty-two bonsai trees to the BBG. Military personnel began arriving at the garden in the late 1940s with their dying plants looking for answers on how to cure them. Unfortunately, Coe's collection had not proved popular among New York audiences in the 1920s, and no one had bothered to learn how to maintain the trees. BBG director George Avery, who knew almost nothing of bonsai himself, was thus at a loss, but requests for advice from servicemen kept coming. Eventually he decided to seek help from other botanic experts to assemble a handbook on the care of bonsai. His reply from most American specialists tended to take the same condescending and dismissive tone; as Elizabeth Scholtz, director emeritus of the BBG, phrased it: "Bonsai is for the birds—and the Japanese." Avery next turned to Kanichiro Yashiroda, a botanical garden director in Japan with whom he regularly corresponded. Yashiroda agreed not only to offer his own advice, but also to recruit other Japanese experts to contribute articles to the handbook, including Yoshimura. Once assembled, the slim glossy volume was translated into English and published in 1953. Over the following ten years, it proved to be the BBG's most popular publication.[39] The BBG also began to hold periodic exhibits of bonsai grown by local amateurs and organized the first bonsai classes in the United States to be offered outside of the Japanese American community.[40]

The Brooklyn Botanic Garden's first bonsai instructor was curator Frank Okamura. A landscape gardener who had moved to California from Hiroshima at age thirteen, he was interred at Manzanar during the war and then relocated to New York, where he was hired at the BBG in 1947 to maintain the Japanese garden. Many former GIs visiting the park who encountered him assumed that any gardener of Japanese ancestry must know about bonsai and began hounding him for advice. After repeated requests, he took it upon himself to add bonsai cultivation to his repertoire. While he may have been drawn to the art begrudgingly at first, over time he embraced the role of bonsai master and was eventually recognized by the Japanese government for his contributions to cross-cultural understanding when he received the Order of the Sacred Treasure, sixth rank in 1981.[41]

Other distinguished bonsai growers would soon follow as BBG instructors. The next summer Yashiroda left the public garden in his home village of Kawaga-ken to come to New York and teach classes. Earlier in life, he had studied horticulture at the Royal Botanical Gardens at Kew in London, where he learned English, and was thus a natural choice as an instructor.[42] In 1958 the Garden recruited Yoshimura to offer his popular Tokyo classes in the United States. Following the initial success of his course, he had published an English-language book on bonsai cultivation for Americans, translated by one of his most skilled pupils, Giovanna Halford. After his first round of classes in Brooklyn, he took another position at Longwood Gardens in Pennsylvania, offering instruction to Philadelphia-area bonsai hobbyists. Later that year, he founded a bonsai company in upstate New York and returned to teaching classes at the BBG. In 1963 he helped to found the Bonsai Society of Greater New York and embarked on a lecture tour that included stops in Cleveland, San Francisco, and Southern California.[43] Throughout his career, he accomplished more than any other single bonsai promoter to bring his craft to a wide American audience.

As Yoshimura's career suggests, interest in bonsai spread far beyond Brooklyn. Bonsai grower George F. Hull provided a sense of its reach in his 1964 book *Bonsai for Americans*. "If a map of the fifty states were used to chart the interest made evident by bonsai organizations and by public reaction seen in attendance to exhibits, the large bright dots would be found on the West Coast, with concentration in San Francisco and Los Angeles areas … with a strong mark at Denver, Colorado, a scattering of dots in the mid-continent cities, and a number on the East Coast, with a special mark at New York City." He then mentioned several geographically scattered bonsai enthusiasts he knew living in rural areas in Georgia, Virginia, Kansas, and Tennessee. Scholtz, then BBG educational director, remembers that people would fly in to take classes from cities like Washington, Boston, and Chicago. In 1962 the nationwide organization Bonsai Clubs of America was founded to coordinate and oversee the activities of local societies. Most clubs hosted exhibits and demonstrations to promote bonsai to the larger public. Typical of such events was the Midwest Bonsai Show, held in 1960 near Chicago in Dundee, Illinois, which featured a large display of bonsai specimens, an amateur plant competition, and a lecture by Japanese expert Kaneji Domoto.[44]

Evidence suggests that the "bright dots" on the West Coast were due to the presence of Japanese American communities. Dr. Daniel Torrance of

Ruxton, Maryland, who attended Yoshimura's class at the BBG, had originally discovered bonsai trees before the war in a Seattle-area specialty nursery run by a Japanese American. In 1964 *Sunset* magazine listed a dozen bonsai clubs and societies in the San Francisco Bay Area, but not all of these clubs were founded for the purpose of educating white Americans. The list included a special section of "Clubs for Japanese Speaking Students," suggesting that some catered more exclusively to an Issei membership who practiced the hobby among themselves in their native language. Yet some Nisei bonsai experts did indeed decide to encourage new white practitioners. Examples include Bob Goka of Frank's Nursery in Los Angeles and Kenneth Sugimoto, president of California's Peninsula Bonsai Society, both of whom offered suggestions in popular home and garden magazines.[45]

Among white bonsai converts, there was far less exclusivity in terms of gender as compared with ikebana. In Japan, bonsai was most popular among middle-aged businessmen and was spread to the United States in part by male soldiers. Since the art dealt with gender-neutral trees as opposed to supposedly feminine flowers, and also seemed to fit into the category of landscaping more than gardening, it was more widely accepted as a masculine activity. II member Gertrude H. Stewart noted that her husband, who would never join her in practicing ikebana, did in fact accompany her to Yoshimura's bonsai classes in Tokyo. When a *New Yorker* reporter attended one of Okamura's lectures, he counted an audience composed of thirty women and half a dozen men. Scholtz remembers the number of male participants as being even higher, estimating the gender ratio for most BBG classes at about fifty-fifty.[46]

But even if bonsai was considered more manly than ikebana, it still reflected a restrained, as opposed to a vigorous, masculinity. Many bonsai experts promoted their art in the same ways as ikebana enthusiasts, emphasizing its refined and spiritual qualities, assumed to be inherent to serene Japanese traditions. The government-sponsored Japanese Travel Bureau published a guidebook on bonsai for westerners in 1950. Wanting to recuperate their international reputation following the war, they joined Americans in promoting an image of their national arts as subdued and nature-loving. Author Norio Kobayashi posited, "Here, as in other branches of Japanese art, sobriety is the keynote. . . . Appreciation of the beautiful as expressed by the Japanese is characterized by a love of subdued effects." Like the sparseness of an ikebana arrangement, bonsai offered minimalist beauty, which Kobayashi stated "can best be explained as the reverse of garish and gaudy." Frank Okamura would also emphasize bonsai's spiritual qualities as he came not just to accept but to embrace his role as an expert on the culture of his birthplace. In 1957, while talking with a *New York Times* reporter who compared him to "a figure in an eighteenth-century Japanese print," Okamura explained, "Every tree has its own art . . . every bonsai, like any good artistic creation, has truth, goodness and beauty." Despite the fact that, according to Yashiroda, fewer than 10 percent of Japanese people actually cultivated their own bonsai, Okamura would discuss the art as if it were imbued with an underlying Japanese spirituality. He insisted that "there must be harmony in bonsai," and lectured his students on its five characteristics: humanity, justice, courtesy, wisdom, and fidelity. He added that cultivating bonsai "would be beneficial to many of us today, caught up as we are in the rapid tempo of time." Like ikebana, bonsai could offer practitioners an antidote to the stress of modern life. Renowned Japanese actor and miniature bonsai (*mame*) grower Zeko Nakamura noted in the BBG's handbook: "It seems to me that this pursuit is good for hasty men in big cities in this hurried age; I feel such impatient men learn to be deliberate as they become interested in growing mame bonsai."[47] The discipline required to grow and care for bonsai, both its Japanese and American advocates argued, harkened back to a simpler, more self-sufficient premodern era, and therefore helped build character as well as provide relief from the modern world.

But it soon became apparent that not all bonsai enthusiasts necessarily appreciated the art for such high-minded reasons. For instance, one army colonel reportedly told his instructor in Tokyo that he took up bonsai with no higher motives than "simply to waste time." Some Americans also may have purchased bonsai in order to appear fashionable. Given its associations with highbrow values of discipline and subtlety, bonsai came to signify elegant, sophisticated taste to American consumers. In 1959 the Pomona Tile Company tried to lend its product cachet by placing a bonsai tree alongside a fashionably dressed woman in one of their advertisements.[48] More generally, Yoshimura complained that many American students failed to understand bonsai's true nature and treated them like houseplants. Such criticism might imply that white Americans were culturally unequipped to fully appreciate a Japanese hobby. Yoshimura insisted bonsai needed to be kept outdoors, instead of in the living room, to receive sufficient sunlight and air. However, BBG leadership disagreed with this particular proscription, realizing that apartment-dwelling New Yorkers would never take up the hobby unless some adaptations were made to its original Japanese form. They developed techniques and began to offer classes for growing "indoor bonsai," creating a hybrid form that melded Japanese aesthetics with American needs.[49]

They would not be the last to do so. The biggest disagreement between bonsai masters and amateur practitioners occurred over the subject of proper maintenance, specifically the level of dedication and difficulty required. Early guides like Kobayashi's called bonsai "an art that demands not only scientific observation but also care born of motherly affection." He emphasized that bonsai plants required diligent attention, as "The price of neglecting to water your bonsai in midsummer even for a day will have to be paid with a withered plant. You might as well plough the field and forget the seed as commit such negligence." In his guidebook, Yashiroda criticized some of the elitist Japanese he had encountered who frowned upon Americans' attempts to raise bonsai, but nevertheless cautioned that whoever tried to practice the hobby without proper instruction "will be bothered and will find himself incessantly busy, trying to maintain them in perfect condition." Okamura concurred with his colleagues, yet reminded his pupils that such demanding practice added to bonsai's spiritual qualities: "People think these things require patience [but] when you are creating art, there is no question of time."[50]

Yet unlike ikebana practitioners, who tended to be wealthy women devoting hours of leisure time to their art, some bonsai owners were less affluent suburbanites for whom time was something that always seemed in short supply. Various gardening magazines of the era offered pointers and techniques for creating faster, easier bonsai, often on the premise that Americans lacked either the time or the racially inherent discipline of Japanese growers. In one article entitled "We Tell the 'Secret' of Bonsai," *Popular Gardening* magazine assuaged its Caucasian readers' fears, claiming, "No special Oriental patience is required [to grow bonsai] and no more gardening skill than that possessed by many home gardeners." In 1963, *Sunset* felt "many westerners who appreciate the subtle beauty of bonsai lack the patience to grow them by traditional methods," and therefore suggested "air layering," a process of growing new trees from the roots of older ones that proved much faster than cultivating a plant from a seed. Other time-saving suggestions included special root pruning techniques, buying saplings from local nurseries that already resembled dwarfed trees, and artistically pruning an outdoor bush in the shape of a bonsai.[51] Eventually, it almost seems as if some of these publications began a race to see who could create the fastest bonsai. In 1959 *Flower Grower* told its readers they could "Grow Miniature Trees in Less than One Year" by shopping for already stunted specimens, and in 1963 George Hull was still promising *New York Times* readers plants in "a season or two." But later that same year, *American Home* magazine claimed, "You can . . . make an enchanting facsimile of a bonsai in a day." If that wasn't fast enough, *Flower Grower* declared that "good specimens can be grown in a few hours." But the quickest time of all appeared in a November *House & Garden* article that told readers: "You can make a true and lovely bonsai from a nursery-grown plant in half an hour."[52]

While some of these articles' claims may have appeared implausible, they did advocate legitimate shortcuts, often by utilizing recently developed horticultural techniques. The same cannot be said for an advertisement that appeared in the *New York Times* Sunday magazine section in February 1958. A company called Miniature Forests offered a mail-order bonsai growing kit that retailed for $3.98 (about $33.00 today) and promised customers "automatic results." "You Work Only 5 Minutes! You Don't Even Dirty Your Hands! And You See Your First Baby Trees—In Just 4 Short Weeks . . . Or Your Full Money Back!" The rather dubious process for growing these miracle bonsai relied on an unspecified "new scientific invention" and involved growing seeds in pots made from "an amazing new natural material" that combined just the right amount of plant food, fungicide, and moisture, allowing purchasers to avoid "long, tortuous hours of careful work." The kit succeeded in making bonsai cultivation resemble any other convenience-based product familiar to Americans of the time. In 1953 Yashiroda had predicted, "I get the impression that American bonsai growers or instructors are intending to have mass production of bonsai, disregarding the wise words of Henry Hicks: 'Plants are . . . not standardized merchandise that anybody can buy and sell.'"[53] Had he later discovered Miniature Forests Inc., he surely would have found them the worst offender in this regard.

The advertisement further undermined the message of most bonsai promoters in a more pernicious way as well. Instead of promoting its product's subdued elegance or natural harmony, it revived older stereotypes of Japan by playing up the exotic novelty of bonsai's diminutive size:

> Yes! Imagine your friends walking into your home, and seeing on your living room table—in breathtaking miniature—an actual forest tree! One of the largest and most beautiful living creatures in the world—transformed—as if by magic—*into an exquisite living miniature no higher than an ordinary book!* Imagine the look of astonishment on your friend's face as he bends down and begins to examine this living miracle.[54]

In the late nineteenth century, authors like Lafcadio Hearn created an image of Japan as a nation filled with small, delicate people who adhered to mysterious, almost magical, religious beliefs. In this instance, with its seemingly supernatural smallness, bonsai could well be a relic from such a fairy-tale land. Miniature Forests was not the only one to appreciate bonsai for its seemingly fantastic qualities. Most BBG visitors who expressed their impressions of the garden's bonsai exhibit found a specimen's age to be its most remarkable characteristic, amazed that trees so old could be kept so small. Some bonsai hobbyists played up what they viewed as their trees' charming sense of foreignness by adding tiny houses and people to their bonsai to create dainty Oriental scenes. While this interpretation of a

Japanese art as essentially cute might still have made for a more flattering stereotype than the maniacal kamikaze pilot, many Japanese people bristled at the suggestion that they were petite and dainty. Yashiroda, for one, called the practice of creating miniature bonsai scenes "repugnant."[55] Nor would such a characterization help further American political interests, as a nation that seemed so diminished as to be miniaturized would not serve as a sufficient bulwark against communism.

While most bonsai masters who popularized their art in the United States were unified in the message that it promoted a typically Japanese sense of subtle beauty and served as a foil to industrialized modernity, they had no guarantee that such a message was always received. Unlike ikebana, bonsai enthusiasts varied in terms of gender and class, with no dominant nationwide organization keeping them in line. As a result, while few botanic garden visitors and nursery patrons left records as to why they appreciated bonsai, coverage in the popular press suggests that many held different interpretations of the miniature trees than the experts. Some may have feared that as white people living in the hectic modern suburbs, they would never be able to take the time to truly comprehend and practice bonsai in its authentic form. Attracted to the plants for their exotic or fashionable qualities, they preferred less demanding Americanized versions that looked elegant but accommodated the modern world instead of resisting it.

The practices of bonsai and ikebana arrived in the United States through similar military channels and were initially promoted for the same reasons. They embodied a set of characteristics including subtlety, restraint, and discipline that Americans understood as inherently Japanese traits, yet neither seemed alienating in their foreignness. The simple lines of their aesthetic design adhered to the same minimalist principles as modernist art from the West. Ikebana and bonsai both seemed to encourage the values of self-discipline and love of nature, allowing them to serve as exactly the kind of answer to tacky industrial postwar America that many affluent people of the time were searching for. Thus, as they were appreciated by experts and affluent consumers, ikebana and bonsai appeared familiar in their modern-style form, but served a function as a counterweight to easy convenience by requiring "Oriental" amounts of painstaking labor.

There were moments, however, when both of these arts nearly defied that pattern. The designs of Sofu Teshigahara and other avant-garde ikebana masters used almost no blooming plant material and bore no resemblance to traditional flower arrangements from any nation. Instead they created a transcendent abstract style that spoke to contemporary concerns instead of offering sage lessons from the past. However, Americans often dismissed such creations as fundamentally weird, and freestyle ikebana never caught on among the affluent homemakers of Ikebana International. Adapted versions of bonsai, in contrast, appear to have become the preferred technique among consumers by the 1960s, allowing the art to gain even more popularity in the United States than in its native land. Instead of requiring hours of character-building hard work, in keeping with a supposedly ancient ethos, these adapted trees insinuated themselves seamlessly into middle-class suburban life. Yet this is hardly to say that updated bonsai lost its association with Japan, since its distinct and curious appearance drew most middle-brow consumers to purchase plants in the first place. Here, bonsai became familiar in function—serving as a houseplant or conversation piece—yet remained foreign in form. But in all cases, Americans from different class backgrounds ended up reinforcing Japan's "junior partner" status by making its culture appear recognizable yet exotic, friendly but enticingly different.

CHAPTER 4

HOW TO BE AMERICAN
WITH SHIBUI THINGS

Japanese Aesthetics in the American Home

In 1959 and 1960 both *Better Homes & Gardens* and *House Beautiful* magazines featured photo spreads of the Hillsborough, California, home of Frank D. Stout. Stout was not a particularly prominent man, only an affluent homeowner with intriguing design tastes. In this case, the celebrity was the house itself. As visitors approached its entrance, a pebble-paved court led them under exposed roof beams to hand-carved wooden front doors. Once inside, they found *tatami* mats on the floor, exposed wood ceilings, sliding *shoji* screens, brush paintings on the walls, kabuki lamps sitting on lacquer end tables, and in the center of the living room, a large *fusuma* cabinet. The rest of the house was decorated with Japanese objects, including hanging scrolls, paper lanterns, and bathroom towels embroidered with imperial-looking crests. *Better Homes & Gardens* claimed that this Asian theme "soften[ed] the rather severe lines of this modern California house." *House Beautiful* concurred, observing that the use of Japanese aesthetics gave the house "an over-all simplicity and coherence" and a "kind of meditative calm and repose." But while his house may have attempted to imitate a traditional Japanese home from many angles, both articles reveal that Stout still enjoyed many of the conveniences of U.S. postwar prosperity. Stout's tatami were made of machine-woven fabrics instead of traditional straw, his kabuki lanterns were wired with electric bulbs, and the fusuma opened to reveal a wet bar and hi-fidelity stereo system.[1]

Few Americans went as far as Stout in trying to imitate Japanese design in their own homes, but his house serves as the epitome of a larger postwar trend wherein homeowners introduced Japanese elements into the design and decoration of their suburban houses and gardens. Architectural historian Myungkee Min identifies three ways in which Americans have historically adapted Japanese design: by exact imitation, by incorporating individual elements, and by borrowing underlying principles.[2] During the 1950s they engaged in all three, sometimes at the same time. Architects and landscape designers revived an interest in Japanese design when they noticed similarities between its fundamental concepts and Western modernist aesthetics. These professionals, as well as the middle to upper class homeowners who could afford to hire them, tried to adopt some of these principles into their designs, without necessarily imitating the exact appearance of Japanese homes. In contrast, suburbanites living in newly developed tract housing lacked such an ability, and instead incorporated Japanese style into their homes through their interior decorating. In doing so, they often put actual Japanese objects to new practical purposes or grafted Japanese motifs onto Western furniture. In this case it was not aesthetic philosophy that inspired Japanese touches as much as their elegant or exotic appearance. While professional designers familiarized the new postwar image of a friendlier Japan by lending Eastern-inspired functionality to Western structures, consumers gave Japanese forms new American functions.

The Japanese Influence on Architecture and Landscaping

American interest in Japanese home design was nothing new in the 1950s. Architecture and interior decoration made up a large part of the turn-of-the-century wave of japonisme, as artists, designers and wealthy homeowners studied and tried to duplicate Japanese aesthetic concepts. Japanese design first came to the American public's attention in 1876, when the Centennial Exhibition in Philadelphia featured a Japanese "dwelling," tea house, garden, and "bazaar." The 1893 Columbian Exposition in Chicago similarly included a large Japanese pavilion composed of three structures known collectively as the *hoo-do* or Phoenix Villa. Other examples appeared at various exhibitions around the country in cities including San Francisco, Buffalo, and St. Louis. Each of these displays, often sponsored by the Japanese government, portrayed the Japanese as a hardworking, refined, and industrious people, who were highly skilled in creating everyday objects of beauty. Yet festival visitors often simultaneously viewed the Japanese condescendingly, as diminutive in their meticulous attention to detail and primitive in their techniques. While amazed at the skill behind Japanese handicrafts, Americans also prized them for being premodern and serving as contrast to the encroaching industrialization in their own society.[3]

The first American book to enumerate the principles behind Japanese design appeared in 1886. East Asian specialist Edward Morse's *Japanese Homes and Their Surroundings* proved highly influential throughout the American architectural profession. It inspired the young architect Frank Lloyd Wright, who took a lifelong interest in Japanese woodblock prints and went on to create buildings that echoed the horizontal layout and lack of external ornament typically found in Japanese houses.[4] Some of Wright's contemporaries followed suit, including Charles Sumner and Henry Mather Greene, the latter constructing a number of distinctive Japanese-inspired homes throughout Southern California in the early twentieth century.

Despite the fact that late nineteenth-century Japan was undergoing a massive project of westernization that included the importation of new types of architecture, or the fact that Japanese of different social classes in different localities lived in various types of houses, American designers treated one particular historical style as the archetypical "Japanese Home."[5] The *sho-in* style (pronounced "show een") was developed in the fourteenth century and persisted as a common model for residential design among the elite samurai and scholar classes through the nineteenth century. Sho-in's hallmarks included the use of exposed support beams, sliding interior walls and floor-to-ceiling windows, tatami floor mats, a tokonoma display alcove, and a general lack of furniture or ornament. In the twentieth century, its

FIG. 8. A typical sho-in style interior with walls removed. Note exposed beams, sliding shōji doors, and standardized tatami mats. Wikimedia Commons.

popularity began to decline, as most urban Japanese citizens continued to adopt Western styles of living, including houses and furnishings.[6]

Turn-of-the-century and midcentury observers alike noted several key characteristics of Japanese homes that they found particularly instructive. The first and most fundamental was a lack of unnecessary ornament. Morse declared, "The Japanese dwelling is in every bone and fibre of its structure honest and our dwellings are not honest." Wright, who generally advocated simplicity over cluttered late Victorian interiors, similarly praised the Japanese house for its "elimination of the insignificant." Commentators also praised sho-in's openness and flexibility. Sliding or removable walls could be pushed aside to either expand a room or open the house to the outside and allow spaces to be used for multiple purposes. A third element was modularity, exemplified by the use of standardized and interchangeable tatami. Every mat in every sho-in house in Japan had the same measurements of approximately three feet by six feet. Homeowners arranged them in various patterns to create rooms of differing sizes to suit the requirements of day-to-day living, and the number of mats per room became a standard measure of interior space throughout the nation.[7] In a 1956 article in *Holiday* magazine, industrial designer George Nelson contrasted the cramped, cluttered feeling of many American homes, particularly in urban areas, with the openness of post and beam construction found in traditional Japanese houses. However, he did break away from some turn-of-the-century enthusiasts, dismissing "Gilbert and Sullivan" images of a diminutive Japan to declare, "The Japanese house no longer looks like a toy." Instead, the most salient aspects of Japanese culture Nelson found were its appreciation of simplicity and attunement with nature, evident in sho-in style's choice of building materials, including its polished framing structure, which needed no further adornment than the beauty of the wood itself.[8]

Other postwar designers admired the Japanese house's efficiency and modularity, highlighting an American stereotype of Japanese people as meticulously organized and standardized in order to increase productivity and achieve results. This assumption appeared threatening during the war, especially when describing the military training of recruits or mobilizing the public.[9] In the late twentieth century, the natural Japanese talent for efficiency served as a convenient explanation for why the nation's high-end electronics and compact cars were outselling American products. But in the 1950s, with a pacified Japan and its weak economy, such efficiency rarely seemed sinister. Instead, architects considered it a valuable asset that enabled cost-effective housing designs. Nelson went on to argue that this particular skill was another piece of traditional wisdom Americans could learn from Japan. Eliminating unnecessary decoration in American houses reduced costs, and the use of standardized modular elements could further lower the price of materials.[10] A trait that a decade prior had been seen as a mark of Japan's inherent ruthless, militaristic nature was neutralized in peacetime as proof of its people's talent in design.

This sense of efficiency in particular led many 1950s design experts to draw comparisons between Japanese architecture and modernist styles that had emerged since the turn of the century. The 1920s and 1930s witnessed the rise of the "International School," which eschewed unnecessary ornament and emphasized functionality. Characterized by the work of European architects Le Corbusier and Mies van der Rohe and the German Bauhaus school of design, it often featured exteriors composed of efficient grid-patterned window walls with modularly apportioned space on the inside. American architects took note of the fact that, despite their centuries-old influences, traditional Japanese houses shared these characteristics with newer designs. In 1963 architectural historian Clay Lancaster analyzed the epitome of modern building, the skyscraper, to find that its features "are related to Far Eastern architecture rather than traditional Western architecture." He drew attention to most skyscrapers' lack of weight-bearing walls and the presence of flexible interior partitions found in sho-in houses.[11] Yet while American commentators closely studied many principles used by long-dead sho-in builders, they rarely called on the expertise of present-day Japanese architects to further their understanding of contemporary design. According to their viewpoint, traditional Japanese architecture was interesting and unique, while contemporary designs were simply copying the West and therefore had little to offer. In fact, when most American design specialists did take note of modernist buildings in Japan, it was to lament their presence as a sign of industrialization encroaching on the traditional charm of the Japanese landscape.

Many Americans were first exposed to sho-in style by touring a model house constructed at New York's Museum of Modern Art in the summer of 1954. The exhibit's organizer was John D. Rockefeller III, then serving as president of New York's Japan Society and continuing his efforts to promote understanding between the two nations. Taking a cue from earlier world's fairs and knowing that the Museum of Modern Art had already sponsored two displays of model homes in its garden, he took his plans for a sho-in home to curator Arthur Drexler (fittingly also a friend of George Nelson), who readily agreed that the next house in the series should be Japanese. Rockefeller and Drexler traveled to Japan, where they formed the Special Rockefeller Architectural Committee and recruited the financial support of numerous corporate donors who wished to further the image of their nation as artistically skilled. The committee's members concluded that a sho-in house would be the best choice to favorably represent Japanese culture, noting its historical status as the preferred style of the respectable upper-class samurai. The Committee then selected Junzo Yoshimura of the Tokyo Art College as chief architect. The house was constructed in Nagoya and later disassembled into 736 carefully labeled crates for shipment to New York in the spring.[12]

The exhibit opened on June 20 to more than 1,200 visitors. Each paid 60 cents admission, then removed their shoes and toured the house in complimentary slippers, so as not to damage the rice straw tatami.[13] In the pamphlet museum visitors received upon entering the home, Drexler described the similarities between modern architecture and Japanese design, praising both for their ingenious efficiency and functionality. He drew attention to the house's simplicity and respect for nature, as evidenced by the fact that both decorative elements and furniture were integrated into its structure and that retractable walls could be pushed back to integrate home and garden.[14] Drexler elaborated on these concepts in his book *The Architecture of Japan*, available at the museum gift shop, which featured photographs he had taken while visiting Japan with Rockefeller that highlighted details of famous Japanese buildings in traditional styles. The model house was so popular that the museum reopened the exhibit the next summer. At the end of its second season, MoMA agreed to dismantle and ship the house to Philadelphia to be reassembled in Fairmount Park, where it remains today. By the time it left New York, the exhibit had attracted more than 50,000 visitors and garnered nationwide press coverage.[15]

Reviews of the exhibit reiterated ideas Drexler presented in his pamphlet. Lewis Mumford, architectural critic for the *New Yorker*, discussed the similarities between the house and the designs of Wright and Mies, noting in particular the modernist modularity of tatami. But he placed more emphasis on the differences between Japanese and Western architecture, listing several lessons he felt Americans should learn from the former. The first emphasized subtlety and "associa[tion of] purification and cleanliness with beauty." Decorative elements could be derived from "changes in the color and texture of the surfaces" of the wood used in constructing the house, instead of added ornament. The second lesson related to minimalism, lack of furnishings, and "how much beauty can be achieved merely by quiet repose, by selection and elimination, by stripping every human requirement down to its essentials." The last pertained to the Japanese love of nature which insisted that "no building is aesthetically finished until" the visitor can look from "the interior outward and back again," as open construction integrated the natural world into the house.[16] None of this argument seemed surprising coming from Mumford, a man who had long criticized American industrialization and unbridled consumption. For him, the humanity, nature-centeredness, and serenity unique to the traditional Japanese home seemed to offer the perfect counterweight to his own society's faults.

One exhibit patron, who according to the *New York Herald Tribune* "sounded as if she lived in a brownstone house," agreed with Mumford, wondering aloud why the city of New York didn't just tear up its older, less-efficient houses and replace them with new sho-in structures. Her "male companion" replied that "if Americans copied this type of architecture, they'd make it garish."[17] Luckily for him, in adapting Japanese design, most professionals concentrated on underlying concepts and philosophy rather than direct imitation. *Life* magazine first observed in 1951 that "elements of Japanese home design . . . are having their impact on the West's modern architecture." The article mentioned new features of the American home like all-purpose rooms, indoor-outdoor living rooms, and exposed wood surfaces that were "like the functional simplicity of their whole design, old ideas in Japan, newly fashionable in the U.S." Almost ten years later, a *New York Times* reporter commented that Americans were still subtly incorporating Japanese features into their homes, including "airy, graceful building contours, the occasional use of stilts," and "exotic rooflines." A contributor to *House Beautiful* magazine similarly noted, "Our preoccupation with the exotic aspects of Japanese architecture is beginning to fade and . . . some more general appreciation of the lessons of Japanese architecture, as they may apply to our way of living, is replacing it." Many Americans wished to borrow from Japan the principles of simplicity, efficiency, and openness, but not necessarily its tile roofs or stone lanterns.[18]

The first houses to follow such a pattern appeared on the West Coast. The overwhelming majority of Japanese Americans lived in this region, and their aesthetic influence had such deep roots by the mid-twentieth century that Japanese aesthetics no longer appeared so exotic to white homeowners that they would shy away from copying them. Furthermore, the climates of central Japan and the Pacific Northwest are similar in average temperature and rainfall, making this type of house appropriate to both locales. By 1960 homes adhering to the principles of Japanese design had become a common sight in Washington, Oregon, and Northern California. When the American Institute of Architects announced the winners of their biennial Western Home Awards in 1959, they highlighted the latest local trends in design, some of which were also features of the MOMA house. These included the elimination of "unneeded posts and walls" to provide openness, and integration with surrounding gardens. Indeed, most homes featured in *Sunset* magazine (the competition's cosponsor) throughout the late 1950s followed Japanese design patterns. They lacked attic or basement, relied on heavy post and beam construction, and featured windows integrated into the house as walls.[19]

Before long, sho-in design influence could be found in other houses around the country. Many homebuilders were motivated by practical concerns, reasoning that they could borrow from Japanese builders' centuries of accumulated wisdom to provide cost-effective building and maintenance solutions. The Frazel family of Wayne, Illinois, chose to build their interiors of Japanese-style natural wood in order to avoid continuous repainting or repapering, claiming that "by use of natural textures, upkeep and maintenance are practically eliminated." In 1958 Norman F. Carver of Kalamazoo, Michigan, took inspiration from his visit to Japan on a Fulbright Fellowship. He found the traditions of using open post and beam construction and incorporating furniture into the structure of the room helped him save money on both labor and materials. One Baltimore designer discovered that open construction provided more natural lighting, cutting down on electric bills, and a family with a summer home on the nearby Magothy River noted that tatami held up better than carpeting under sandy bare feet.

Another summer house, designed by Chicago area architect Robert Tyler Lee, included sliding screens inside the windows, to "provide wonderful light control and guarantee complete privacy when it is desired." Shutting the panels in the off-season also hid the contents of the house to discourage potential thieves.[20] Designers of suburban tract housing joined the trend as well.[21] Cherry Hill, an upscale Chicago area development, offered a "shibui" model that included a "shoji room." Irv Miller, vice president of the development company, claimed the house "gives you a feeling of serene tranquil calmness, with its lovely Japanese settings," because "in the fast-paced world in which we now live, it is hard for a person to relax."[22] In this case, an already low-cost house promised its inhabitants the distinct form of serenity Americans were coming to associate with Japan.

Such elements of efficiency, simple beauty, and calm repose, assumed to be inherent to Japanese culture, could be achieved through interior decoration as well as the structure of the house itself. In the late nineteenth century, as part of the same movement that admired Japanese architecture, wealthy Americans hung lanterns from their parlor ceilings, decorated their walls with brush paintings, fans, and print wallpaper showing Asiatic scenes, and entertained their friends with china tea sets. Advice magazines of the time praised "the Japanese taste," claiming that its underlying philosophy reflected important moral values. Paintings depicting supposedly typical Japanese subjects like flowers and birds were meant to enhance their owners' appreciation of nature. The attention to balance, harmony, and simplicity of Japanese objets d'art conveyed a lack of ostentation and a degree of honesty. The display of such items in the home came to signify not only worldliness and refinement but also good character.[23]

In the 1950s, women's magazines were once again in the vanguard of promoting Japanese styles. In the late summer of 1960, *House Beautiful* devoted back-to-back issues to the subject of Japanese design. The August issue discussed Japanese aesthetics in their original context, echoing many architects' praise for their functionality. The magazine offered a typical postwar depiction of Japan, highlighting the culture's respect for nature and simplicity, but placed even more emphasis on its supposedly feminine qualities like grace and modesty. The magazine's lead article posited that the Japanese people had a long-standing inherent appreciation of beauty, claiming that they "have not distinguished between the beautiful and practical." Even mundane elements of Japanese houses and household objects, its editors argued, may have appeared simple at first glance, but actually contained subtle and complex beauty. The Japanese home was meant to reflect "an attitude to beauty which had made of it something to consume and experience every hour of every day." As in Western modernist designs, form followed function, but remained pleasing to the eye. Another article repeated this theme of subtle elegance and introduced the concept of *shibui* as "the hidden treasure waiting for discovery, the giant's unused power, the modesty that lets the thing speak for itself, and the creation of wealth by discarding the unnecessary and the trivial." It added, "If we could learn something of the balance between freedom and discipline that gives Japanese art and design its serenity, the quality of *shibui*, we might find a clue to lead us toward a recapture of the tranquility and harmony that our machines have stolen."[24] While a house's structure and architecture might conform to contemporary Western tastes, the Eastern antimodern attributes of its interior design offered relief from the harried twentieth century.

This theme was reiterated in the September issue, which focused on American uses of Japanese design. In doing so, it defined a new style of home decoration: "the shibui syndrome." (In this case, the term *syndrome* referred not to a disease or neurosis but its less common definition of a pattern or motif.) In articles entitled "How to Be Shibui with American Things" and "New Home Furnishings with the Shibui Concept of Beauty," the magazine, taking a cue from professional designers, suggested ways to embrace Japanese design concepts using American objects. The editors explained, "We feel the current interest [in the Japanese look] is prompted ... by a search for meaning and richness, after the arid sterility of the Modern movement." The American objects they labeled "shibui" were fashioned from natural fabrics and wood, as opposed to the precision-made chrome and glass of some modern furniture. Their handmade quality "connotes rather a lack of artifice, a spontaneity," reflecting the individual character of the craftsman.

Their humble design lent them an atypical and thus more complex kind of beauty. "One of the characteristics of a thing that is *shibui* is that at first glance it looks plain and simple but on subsequent examinations it reveals more and still more."[25] Supposedly grounded in an Oriental past before mass production was possible, handmade shibui objects reflected human warmth and found beauty in their humility. The role of Japanese objects in the American home had come to echo the broader relationship between the two nations: Japan offered useful help to Americans, but only through its role as a static, nonthreatening, premodern country.

Meanwhile, beyond the home's exterior, professional interest in Japanese gardens revived as well. Just as Japanese houses were spare in their use of ornament, Japanese gardens avoided using large amounts of colorful flowers or dense foliage in favor of manicured bushes and trees. But while plant life was often highly cultivated, it was paradoxically trimmed in such a way as to appear completely natural; asymmetrical and unregimented, trees and shrubs complemented preexisting features like large rocks and uneven topography. Many gardens also featured either naturally occurring or man-made water features and meandering stone paths that encouraged visitors to linger and admire its landscaping from various angles. David Engel, probably the best-known white American proponent of Japanese gardens in the postwar era, published an illustrated guide to Japanese gardens that praised their "naturalness, strength, simplicity, humor, and human warmth. Their elements are arranged to convey the feeling of the partnership of nature and art. In effect, the symbolism is that of man and nature in a pact of friendship, sealing it, as it were, with a hearty handshake." He claimed that the Japanese garden succeeded in directing nature without necessarily taming or subduing it. In contrast, Western gardens were more domineering in forcing plant life into an overly contrived arrangement. Osamu Mori, head of the architecture department at the National Cultural Properties Research Institute in Nara, agreed. In his first book written for an American audience, he explained that the fundamental philosophy behind Japanese gardens "comes from the inherent view of nature of the Japanese people themselves—to see nature at its roots and take only the

FIG. 9. Garden at Kyoto Imperial Palace. Wikimedia Commons by moja, 2004.

most intrinsic out of it. In thus abstracting nature, there have been a set of tacit rules and agreements" to ensure that it was not overly confined or restricted.[26]

Prior to the publication of his book, Engel had in fact designed a garden included in the MoMA Japanese house exhibit, which reinforced principles similar to the house, such as minimalism and an appreciation for nature.[27] Throughout the 1950s, several major cities also revived Japanese gardens that had been closed during the war. San Francisco had maintained its Japanese tea garden in Golden Gate Park since the Midwinter Exposition of 1894. After the city temporarily tried to hide its association with the enemy by renaming it the "Oriental" tea garden, it reverted to its original appellation in 1952 and was once again a popular destination for family outings. The Brooklyn Botanic Garden featured a Japanese style garden that was originally constructed in 1914. In 1938 a wooden Shinto shrine on the premises burned down, possibly the work of an anti-Japanese arsonist. This structure too was restored and reopened in 1960. In Seattle in 1957 at the University of Washington Arboretum, planning and construction resumed for a three-acre public Japanese garden that was originally proposed in 1937 and had been put on hold once war was declared.[28] Each of these cases provides a direct example of the connection Americans drew between the nation of Japan itself and the importation of its culture. Municipal leaders' willingness to reject or embrace Japanese aesthetics proved to be firmly tied to diplomatic relations between the two nations at a given time and could vary just as dramatically, with Japanese gardens being treated alternately as a threatening or friendly alien presence within their own city limits.

A large part of Americans' admiration for Japanese gardens in the 1950s was based on the assumption that the Japanese possessed a unique understanding and respect for the natural world. In *House Beautiful*'s September shibui issue, Engel posited that Japanese gardens were inherently attuned with nature, and he presented them as peaceful places to escape the overly mechanized aspects of American life. Both Engel's article and another by landscaper June Meehan contrasted Japanese gardens with those that followed European traditions or with contemporary American front yards. Meehan claimed that in the West "man is supreme (and busy) and nature has to revolve around him" while "the traditional gardens of Japan are dedicated to nature." Engel added, "While we tend to mow lawns, edge garden plots, and remove rocks, aiming at an artificial, man-made-looking smoothness and order . . . the Japanese garden . . . is unmown, unedged, and carefully disordered." The two argued that the American garden had become too neat, too planned, too divorced from the natural world and perhaps overly standardized in keeping with an industrial age. Meanwhile, Japanese designs served as a counterweight to such tendencies by creating a kind of controlled chaos of plant life.[29]

However, when Americans borrowed from Japanese gardens, both Engel and Osamu Mori warned against direct imitation, encouraging gardeners to instead apply underlying principles and be personally creative with plant materials native to their local climate. Mori complained about the haphazard use of exotic touches like "glaring red bridges, grotesque dwarfed pine-trees, out of place stone lanterns, and *torii* gates." He concluded his book with the admonition: "The fact should always be remembered that any 'imitation-for-imitation's sake will never do in the creation of true Japanese gardens in Western countries. Simply discard all that cannot be copied in foreign countries and try to grasp the 'spirit' rather than the 'physical appearance' of Japanese gardens. This way and only in this way, Japanese gardens will be a true success in Western countries." Like houses that incorporated eastern concepts but kept their Western appearance, gardens too could apply foreign ideas to familiar contexts.[30]

Here as well, the trend began on the West Coast. In 1955 *Sunset* profiled the garden of Mr. and Mrs. Harry Belshore of Carmel, California, who had asked designers to create a Japanese garden around an old pine tree in their yard. A 1962 article showcased a spacious garden in Sausalito with winding stone paths and another in San Francisco that exhibited nature in a "handkerchief size" plot.[31] By 1959, *Flower Grower* observed, "The Japanese influence in American gardens" was "gradually moving eastward."[32] Indeed, in the late 1950s and early 1960s flower shows in New York, Chicago, and Philadelphia featured model Japanese gardens. In 1961 *Chicago Tribune* columnist Mary Merryfield commented on the large number of artists in the Lincoln Park neighborhood who had planted Japanese gardens outside their homes, as the trend of using Japanese techniques to improve upon American gardens spread across the country.[33]

Perhaps the most notorious example of Americans copying Japanese garden design was the BBG's replica of the Ryoanji temple rock garden in the summer of 1963. The exhibit did not actually follow the patterns of the most common styles of Japanese gardens, but instead imitated the particular style of the Zen rock garden. Appearing even more foreign and exotic to Western eyes—the garden's director told members it "would be like comparing abstract paintings with traditional art"—it did not include any plant material at all, but was instead composed exclusively of carefully placed stones. The exhibit consisted of fifteen granite rocks arranged in an asymmetrical clustered pattern, within a tennis court–sized enclosed yard, surrounded by white gravel raked to resemble the wave patterns of

FIG. 10. The original Ryoanji garden in Kyoto. Wikimedia Commons by Stephane D'Alu, 2004.

a river flowing around the rocks in a technique known as *karesansui*. Visitors were asked to pay twenty-five cents admission and don paper slippers before stepping out on an elaborately constructed viewing platform. In the summer it opened, 24,236 guests visited the exhibit.[34]

The idea for the replica of the rock garden began when George S. Avery, the BBG's director, visited Ryoanji temple with his wife in 1960 while on a bonsai-hunting trip to Japan. With motives similar to Rockefeller and Drexler, he decided to re-create the garden in New York to help expand Americans' cultural horizons and improve their understanding of Japanese traditions. He hired Takuma P. Tono, a Japanese landscape architect who had taught at Columbia University, as a consultant on the project to oversee plans and construction. Avery and Tono also convinced their mutual friend Alden Dow, architect and Dow Chemical heir, to help sponsor the project. Dow had recently toured Japan himself, at a time when American tourism was steadily increasing, and was excited at the prospect of helping to promote Japanese arts in the United States. Further assistance came from the members of the

BBG, who were asked to scour their neighborhoods for the perfect rocks fitting the color and dimensions of the boulders in the original Ryoanji.[35]

Not only were a number of local rocks included in the exhibit, but the gravel used was also of American origin. Organizers traveled all over Japan to find the most authentic-looking stones to match the original, but eventually discovered it at a poultry grit supplier in North Carolina, suggesting that geology doesn't always neatly adhere to cultural divides. Boundaries were blurred yet again as the gravel was meticulously raked on a daily basis by an African American groundskeeper whom the staff jokingly referred to as their official "monk." But to better reinforce a sense of geographical and racial specificity, the museum exclusively hired young Japanese women to serve as interpreters, despite the fact that some of these employees had little proficiency in English. Most were art students studying in Manhattan for the summer, who engaged in westernized lifestyles outside of work, but were asked to wear kimono to lend the exhibit an air of timeless authenticity.[36]

Yet at the same time, the exhibit's brochure compared the garden to modernist art like an abstract painting or symphony, claiming that "because simplicity is the key to the design, this type of garden makes a strong appeal to contemporary taste," adding that although the garden was "created by unknown artists and nearly 500 years old, it is as modern as tomorrow." In a similar vein, Avery told the *New York Times* that "Japanese garden concepts, which started independently from ours, bring a fresh viewpoint to American gardening."[37] As with ikebana and bonsai, the modernist aesthetics were familiar, but the concepts behind them were refreshingly foreign. Such views were echoed by many landscape designers of the time, although few of them went so far as to copy austere Zen rock gardens.

Nor did many of these gardeners arise from the Japanese American community, a fact which bears a certain irony. Both before and after the war, so many Japanese immigrants worked as landscapers and gardeners that it soon became a stereotype.[38] But few white commentators gave credit to Japanese American garden designers by name in print. Certainly some professionals took advantage of the phenomenon and were able to attract new clients once their ethnicity transformed from a liability into an asset.

But just as easily, many may have chafed at white homeowners' sudden interest in Japanese design, after hearing for decades that they should try harder to assimilate. Moreover, many Nisei were trying to move beyond the stereotypes of the past, and they viewed the practice of gardening as a step backward in terms of gaining acceptance among whites. Diarist Charles Kikuchi, an outspokenly pro-assimilationist Nisei, spotted a garden one Issei internee had cultivated at the Tanforan Assembly Center. He admitted it was "laid out beautifully," but criticized its creator for clinging too tightly to "old Japan," exactly the kinds of ethnic traditions from which he wished to distance himself once the war was over.[39]

The one Japanese American who did receive attention for designing a rock garden was in fact a sculptor whose "garden" could probably more correctly be called a fountain. In 1964 Isamu Noguchi created an arrangement of stones at the Chase Manhattan Bank building that many critics at the time compared to Ryoanji. Several years prior, he had attempted to create a public sculpture adhering precisely to Japanese rock garden design principles at UNESCO headquarters in Paris. After vigorous disagreements with his Japanese consultant, Touemon Sano, he ended up unsatisfied with the project and decided he could never again "embrace orthodoxy" in his work.[40] Arguments arose from the fact that while Sano wanted to closely follow traditional methods, Noguchi was a sculptor who created transcendent art that refused to conform to any cultural norm. The son of a Japanese poet and an American translator who spent his life between Japan and the United States, he never felt entirely at home in either nation, nor did he ever seem comfortable with his identity as a Nisei. Living in New York when relocation began, he voluntarily committed himself to the Poston, Arizona, camp to organize art classes among the internee population, but left the camp several months later feeling out of place there as well. While at times he would praise Japanese culture along lines similar to other American designers, his work reflects not only the influence of Japan and the United States but numerous other cultures he absorbed over the years, including French modernist, Indian, Indonesian, and Native American. In this regard, he remained true to his body of work when approaching the

Chase Manhattan design, which instead of just bringing the East to the West, was meant to reflect his own experience incorporating various influences. While he did use rocks imported from Japan placed in a formation that resembled many Zen gardens, he also set them in a tile floor and flooded the sculpture during the summer months, more in keeping with European public fountains. Refusing to solely reflect what Americans had come to understand as a timeless Japanese tradition, he created his own design to capture a more universal aesthetic.[41] While Noguchi's work had the potential to make Americans question their deep-seated sense of an East/West divide, as well as the notion that Japanese Americans were inherently "Japanese," observers at the time were instead quick to emphasize the fountain's resemblance to Ryoanji above all its other attributes. Such an outcome was by then a familiar experience for Noguchi, as throughout his career U.S. critics had strained to find essentially Oriental qualities in his work.

Or perhaps, less perniciously, at a time when Japanese gardens were enjoying the height of their popularity, they were simply lodged in the forefront of many critics' and journalists' minds. By then, most had settled into an understanding of how Japanese design could be useful and applicable to Americans while still remaining distinctively foreign. Design professionals applied values of efficiency and economy, and incorporated antimodern attributes reflecting spiritual, nature-loving qualities to provide respite from modern machine age life. Architects designed buildings with flexibility of space and lack of unnecessary ornament, interior designers created elegant living spaces with deceptively humble handmade objects, and landscapers planted beautiful gardens that tamed nature without dominating it. In doing so, they all gave credit to traditional sensibilities that Japanese people had supposedly possessed since time immemorial. Most American designers ignored any twentieth-century developments in architecture or gardening in Japan—or really any since the 1600s—and treated Japanese design as if it was then what it had always been: the sho-in house and the Zen rock garden. As such, they relegated these styles a particular place in the design canon; remaining perpetually static, Japanese aesthetics served to provide lessons to the present straight from the past.

Japanese Aesthetics and the American Homemaker

Of course, design professionals only made up a small portion of the American population, and middle-class consumers often formed their own opinions regarding the merits of Japanese design. In fact, there was noticeable resistance from the public toward MoMA's Japanese house exhibit. Part of visitors' reluctance to embrace Japanese styles likely lay in the format of the exhibit itself. Protected and roped off as an essentially noninteractive museum piece, the house was removed from the public and placed on display as a work of art to be admired, not a dwelling to be lived in. Even if it did look modern, the house appeared to the public more as a fascinating aesthetic curiosity than a home that people might actually use on a daily basis. Journalists from all over the country visited the house, and some did indeed pass on portions of the museum's official message to their readers, especially regarding the house's modernist look and its lack of clutter. But many seemed to take a far greater interest in its exotic aspects, like the rule that visitors had to remove their shoes before entering. One columnist from Hartford, Connecticut, directly contradicted the museum's pamphlet, declaring, "It seemed to me that the spirit of this Japanese house was as different from contemporary, Western domestic architecture as chalk from cheese," and reminded readers that modernist architecture is rooted in Germany. Other visitors doubted the pamphlet's claims that Japanese design could be applied in their own homes. One complained that the house had no place to put a TV. Another remarked he could never live without modern plumbing and kitchen appliances. A third seemed to prefer cluttered spaces to clean and empty ones, reportedly asking a museum employee "'Where is the television set, the radio, record player and records? The shelves of books? The piles of magazines and newspapers that flood in on every mail? Where is the desk, the piano, children's toys, hobby junk, tropical fish, model planes, butterfly collection, oil paints, dolls' clothes, tennis rackets, fishing poles, and golf clubs?'" While their tone was facetiously critical of postwar abundance, few visitors seemed willing to give up the convenience of appliances or the creature comforts of a contemporary lifestyle in favor of what they perceived as a more austere and traditional form of living.[42]

Neither were visitors entirely enthusiastic about the BBG's Ryonaji rock garden. Some did indeed draw parallels between its simple, subtle beauty and Western art. One female guest described it as a Japanese *Mona Lisa*, and *Newsweek* added that attendees at the formal opening ceremony "debated the mysteries of the garden like art students puzzling over the Gioconda smile." However, few subsequent visitors seemed eager to embrace the austere foreignness of a Japanese rock garden. A Brooklyn housewife reportedly wondered, "If it's a garden, where are all the flowers? . . . and what are all those stones doing here?" Elizabeth Scholtz, serving as the BBG's director of adult education at the time, remembered that while some guests would sit and meditate for long periods of time, more would remark: "It's just a lot of sand," or "Why did I have to pay extra to see this stupid thing?" She added that by the closing of the exhibit most days, carelessly discarded paper slippers littered the garden.[43]

While professionals made valiant efforts to promote Japanese design on their terms, it appears more often than not that their message was only partly received by the general public. To the museum patrons who raised their eyebrows at the house or garden, Japanese aesthetics were still too foreign to import wholesale, all similarities to modernism notwithstanding. This is not to say that American consumers rejected Japanese design outright; they sought to adapt it and valued it for their own reasons. For the homemakers in the vanguard of this trend, it was the foreignness of Japanese objects that was most appealing, so long as it remained in small doses. Displaying any foreign artifact in the home suggests that the owner possesses a certain level of cosmopolitanism and worldliness, and the particular popularity of Japanese design among the nation's elites in the 1950s only strengthened shibui objects' affiliation with upper-class taste. Instead of having their inherent "Japaneseness" resist the faults of American consumption, they served as status symbols in U.S. society. For many Americans, home decoration had long been, and continues to be, one of the prime markers of social class distinction. In her book on the cultural and political significance of home furnishing, historian Leora Auslander offers an illustrative example of this process at work. In the postwar era, her maternal grandmother wished to identify with the working-class Jewish community where she had grown up. In her home she displayed "aesthetic norms that would probably be described by a sociologist as working class," which included Formica tables, La-Z-Boy chairs, and wood veneer bookshelves. Her other grandmother, a more secular Jewish woman, wanted to distance herself from her working-class past. She chose to furnish her home with pieces that conformed to middle-class values of taste, including "simplicity, elegance, quality, purity of line." Her living room included a glass and metal coffee table, Danish modern furniture, and modular shelving units.[44]

Her choices conform to the observations of social critic Vance Packard in his 1959 best-seller, *The Status Seekers*. In outlining recognized markers of class standing in 1950s America, he asserted that working-class women liked to decorate with bright colors and a lot of frills, while wealthier women preferred more austere, less-ornamented furnishings, or in his blunter terms "the primly severe" over "the frankly garish."[45] Similar advice was dispensed in McGraw-Hill's home economics textbook *The Home and Its Furnishings*, which warned its pupils against using busy ornamentation. When selecting objects for their living room, the book instructed readers to "look at the decoration, if there is any. Is it a structural part of the decoration that seems to fit the object and be part of it? If the decoration has been stuck on, like the Victorian wool roses on a fly swatter, not harmonizing with either the shape or function of the object, turn your back on it firmly."[46] *House Beautiful* promoted Japanese objects in precisely this vein. "*Shibui* must never be attention-demanding. It must have depths of interest that are so unobtrusive you will almost miss them."[47] It must always be subtle and understated, never flashy, busy, or gaudy; if the use of loud patterns denoted a lower-class home, the shibui syndrome decidedly signified affluence.

House Beautiful indeed served as a source to instruct American women of any class about what was currently fashionable among the elite. It was one of many American women's magazines to collectively reach their peak circulation in the 1950s. With prevailing gender assumptions of the era suggesting a woman's place was in the home, these large glossy periodicals offered her advice and instruction on almost every aspect of everyday domestic living including cooking, relationships, childcare, and housekeeping.[48] *House Beautiful* was specifically directed toward upper-middle-class women; the suggestions it gave were meant to reflect an exclusive taste that projected a certain level of elegance and refinement. However, as contemporary observers noted, women of lower income levels often aspired to appear as if they too possessed money and sophistication. To help create this impression, they read such magazines and took their advice, but adjusted it slightly to fall within their budget. In 1950 novelist and cultural critic Mary McCarthy noted in the *Reporter* that women of all backgrounds were avidly reading the up-market *Vogue*. "Southern women, Western women with moderate incomes pored over it to pick up 'hints', carried it with them to the family dressmaker, copied, approximated, with a sense, almost, of pilferage.... (What would *Vogue* say if it knew?)"[49] As women beyond the intended audience purchased these magazines, they discovered the styles they featured and were able to follow the tastes of wealthier homeowners.

For many of these women, designing a new home according to Japanese principles or hiring a landscaper to plant a Japanese garden in their backyard was simply beyond their financial means. But they could still give their home an air of Japanese aesthetics through interior decoration, as *House Beautiful* had suggested. It appears few women followed the magazine's dictates to the letter by seeking out American items with inherently shibui qualities. Instead, they took the more direct route of buying items that immediately and obviously looked "Japanese." In the early 1950s, examples of such products included paper lanterns, painted screens, ceramic tea sets, and lacquer trays. In many cases, these Japanese items were not simply on display but served practical household purposes. In a collection of her cartoons depicting Americans living in Japan, Sanae Yamazaki included a section entitled "This Will Make a Nice ...," in which white women appropriate ceramic pitchers as vases and chopsticks as hairpins.[50] The practice was continued by American homemakers who used lacquer ware as waterproof coasters or screens as room dividers.

Also popular was Western style furnishings with Japanese-looking motifs grafted onto them. For example, a 1959 dining set called "Kyoto" alluded to Japan with a plastic tabletop patterned to mimic teak graining and brass chair legs and backs sculpted to resemble bamboo.[51] *New York Times* interior design expert Betty Pepis had criticized this trend on the grounds that traditional Japanese homes did not include most Western forms of furniture, and therefore a chair with Japanese accents could hardly be authentic.[52] Nevertheless, such furnishings remained popular among white middle-class Americans who had found an affordable way to incorporate sophisticated-looking Japanese touches into their homes.

They were aided in this pursuit by a number of business entrepreneurs, both American and Japanese, who capitalized on the trend. A Japanese import store in Manhattan named Shibui that opened soon after the MOMA house built off the exhibit's success. Another shop, Charles E. Gracie and Sons, had been operating as a small two-story import store in Manhattan for more than thirty-five years, but was able to move to a nine-story showroom once business increased significantly by the late 1950s. Their products ranged from inexpensive bamboo chopsticks, to mid-priced grass wallpaper, to luxurious silk wall coverings.[53] In 1960 they even offered a full-size prefabricated teahouse. Designed by a Japanese artist and constructed mostly out of cedar, the structure cost $8,000, and buyers were asked to wait six months for delivery. According to a *New York Times* reporter, the teahouse reproduced distinctly Japanese architecture that "today symbolizes for many Americans utter serenity in a shelter," but made it available in the type of prepackaged form that was becoming increasingly familiar to postwar American consumers.[54]

Japanese trade representatives also seemed eager to profit from the trend. In 1954 the government's Ministry of International Trade and Industry established the External Trade Recovery Organization (JETRO) to explore foreign markets and promote Japanese goods overseas.[55] That same year, the National Home Fashion League, Inc. recognized their efforts by bestowing its annual award for "outstanding promotion of home furnishings in this country by a foreign power" to the nation of Japan. In 1958 the Japan Trade Center, JETRO's public relations branch, offered an exhibit of new styles of Japan-inspired furniture in their Fifth Avenue headquarters. The goods on display consisted mostly of American-style items containing elements suggestive of Japan, for instance "curved arms and back of a chair" were "reminiscent of a pagoda roof." Additionally, the exhibitors suggested ways in which Americans could adapt traditional Japanese items to suit their own needs, such as "a hibachi (charcoal cooking urn) makes an unusual outdoor grille or can be converted into a planter or umbrella stand. Japanese rice bowls make original finger bowls or soup bowls. And rice containers can be used as catchalls for almost anything." They even suggested using a large cupboard to "house a hi-fi set."[56]

The most prominent entrepreneur to promote imported Japanese goods to American consumers was Michio Kushi. After earning a degree in political science at Columbia University in the late 1940s, Kushi opened several small specialty shops throughout New York City, but later set his sights on something larger and more profitable. His plan was to create a full-sized department store that would promise a virtual visit to Japan, and in 1958 he persuaded one of Japan's biggest department store chains, Takashimaya, to open a branch in Manhattan. Kushi promised that the store would "offer some consolation for frustrated citizens who can't make the trip [to Japan]." Once opened, it employed the advertising slogan "How to reach Japan by subway." As the store's chief architect, Kushi hired Junzo Yoshimura, the designer of the MOMA house, to create a two-story façade meant to evoke traditional Japanese design. Like the BBG, he exclusively employed young Japanese women to wait on customers while wearing kimono. While the merchandise varied largely in price to accommodate a wide customer base, Kushi was adamant that his store did not sell cheap souvenirs. It did carry some modern items like the Japanese-made watches and transistor radios that were becoming increasingly popular among American consumers. But the store's overall focus was clearly on selling items reminiscent of traditional Japan in keeping with the shibui decorating trend. Products included simple items like bamboo coasters and chopsticks as well as expensive decorated screens, pearls, and kimono, with *zabuton* pillows, paper lamps, dolls, and stationery in between.[57]

One particular item carried by Takashimaya, as well as many other American stores by 1960, was the shoji screen, which provides an illustrative case study of how American homemakers consumed Japanese inspired décor. In the Japanese home, *shoji* refers to the sliding partitions that separate interior rooms, or the interior from the exterior of a house. They are usually made of wood and rice paper and decorated with a grid pattern in a particular five blocks high to three wide ratio. In America, the term *shoji* came to refer to stand-alone folding screens, which may or may not have featured the distinctive grid pattern, typically imitating the appearance, but only occasionally the original purpose, of Japanese shoji.

The shoji screen was one of the first Japan-influenced items to interest American consumers, and its popularity continued to grow throughout the 1950s. In 1960 a comical retrospective of interior design in the *New York Times Magazine* declared 1953 the year that shoji "inva[ded] from the East," and featured a cartoon of perplexed visitors lost in a cramped apartment overrun with folding screens. A 1956 ad for *Esquire* listed the many cutting-edge trends the magazine had discovered in recent years, including the use of shoji screens as room dividers. The next year, a New York shutter store noticed a decline in its sales of Western-style window treatments in favor of shoji. By 1959 the term may have become overused, as Chicago department store Carson Pirie Scott labeled a set of wood and fiber screens with no grid pattern as "shoji," apparently assuming that the word applied to any eastern-looking folding screen.[58] By that point, most major department stores, including Bloomingdale's, Gimbel's, and Macy's, carried shoji-style screens, most retailing at a price between $30 and $40 for a three-panel screen. This would equal a price range of about $250 to $330 in the 2010s, making shoji a significant purchase, but one that most financially comfortable middle-class customers could afford.[59]

In 1960 an Atlanta newspaper declared that shoji "screens . . . although mentally linked with the land of the cherry blossoms, are standard equipment in the U.S."[60] Indeed, it appears most homemakers purchased the screens because, while they evoked traditional Japan in their appearance, they were quite functional in American living spaces. Despite her distaste

"Shoji" Our Japanese
screen expresses Oriental charms

3-panel screen
each panel 16" x 68" $32

FIG. 11. Shoji in the United States, a free-standing folding screen with a similar grid pattern. Bloomingdale's advertisement in the *New York Times*, September 1958.

for inauthentic Japan-inspired furniture, Betty Pepis suggested that her readers use shoji to conceal awkwardly placed windows in their apartments. The *Chicago Tribune* also mentioned some possible uses in the American home, including separating a living room from a dining room, or baby's sleeping area from its parents; serving as "unusual window treatments," and hiding "bad architectural features" or clutter in the corner of the room.[61] However, none of these articles noted that the shoji screen's form had been significantly altered in the process of importation, with only the veneer of its original appearance remaining.

Besides being transformed from sliding walls into stand-alone screens, American shoji were adapted in other significant ways. They were often manufactured out of more durable materials than their traditional wood and rice paper construction. Gracie & Sons specially treated their models to withstand the steam heat used in many New York apartments, and the *Tribune* mentioned that many American shoji were made with plastic instead of paper. In some cases these designs discarded shibui restraint in favor of more colorful taste, pressing plants and butterflies within the plastic. Other models were made to be more cost-efficient. In 1959 Mandel Brothers of Chicago offered a wrought iron frame shoji for only $9.99, one-third the price of most screens. A year later, the *New York Times Magazine* featured instructions for do-it-yourself shoji, claiming it could be "built by any handyman." The article suggested using pretreated wood that would not warp or shrink and translucent white fiberglass, because rice paper "would not be practical on a portable screen since the paper could be very easily torn or punctured." By the end of the decade, there were in fact few sho-in elements left to American shoji, save its distinctive grid pattern.[62]

To some homemakers, the grid was what mattered most for its ability to outwardly signify Japanese style. Commercial furniture makers incorporated the shoji pattern onto the fronts of chests and wardrobes, the backs of chairs, and as "a veneer pattern on table tops." One Chicago homemaker decided to place painted strips of wood across her living room windows to create the illusion of shoji. Mrs. H. Licht, also of Chicago, applied black

126 | HOW TO BE AMERICAN WITH SHIBUI THINGS

tape to the white doors of her bedroom closet to imitate a shoji pattern. Professional architects had initially praised shoji for its function: providing well-lighted and flexible interior space. High-end tastemakers like magazine editors later appreciated its form for its understated attractiveness. For these consumers, attractiveness took precedence. Prohibited financially from installing actual shoji in their home, they could at least suggest an affluent sense of style by copying its most prominent superficial elements.[63]

Another piece of Japan-inspired furniture whose popularity was admittedly smaller in scale was the *hibachi* grill. In Japan, a hibachi is a charcoal brazier used inside the home for cooking and keeping warm in the winter. Traditionally they were compact and concealed, often by necessity as houses made of wood and paper and filled with grass mats could be highly inflammable. In the 1950s, when Japanese homeowners were purchasing electric stoves and installing central heating in increasing numbers, Americans adopted the device, and hibachi-centered cocktail parties became a fashionable trend. The concept was first introduced in 1953 by high-end magazines *House Beautiful* and *Vogue*. Both publications touted the hibachi party on the grounds that the novelty of cooking in the living room would keep the festivities lively. *Vogue* claimed it worked "better than drink or a dancing poodle, partly because of audience participation." No guest could stand around bored or at a loss for words as they participated in the exotic experience of grilling their own hors d'oeuvres. (Hibachi predated the American fondue craze by over a decade.) *House Beautiful* also pointed out that a hibachi made party preparation easier and called hibachi-grilled appetizers "delightfully 'irresponsible,'" as the hostess simply set out ingredients and let guests do most of the work themselves. But while the main appeal of the party lay in its fascinating foreignness, the hibachi table itself was adapted to suit American needs as a piece of furniture. *House Beautiful* included a photograph showing how, after the party was over, the grill could be removed and the hole in the center of the table then used as an attractive planter. *Vogue* also pointed out that "some people have removed the old braziers and put in electric grills, which is *not* on a par with putting a clock in the stomach of the Venus de Milo, but simply means that those not raised in the charcoal tradition can be sure of temperatures and results." Not to mention the fact that it would be far less smoky in an American living room with no chimney or removable walls. Hibachi hostesses could thus appear fashionable and fun by creating the appearance of intriguingly primitive Oriental cooking, while being aided by modern technology.[64]

This particular fad further illustrates the trickle-down nature of some of these Japan-inspired trends. After 1955, the *New York Times* hardly mentioned living room hibachi anymore, suggesting that well-to-do New Yorkers had lost interest. Yet coverage of hibachi cookery increased in the more humble Midwest. In the late 1950s and early 1960s, the *Chicago Tribune* reported on celebrities and other personalities who enjoyed hibachi cooking and featured a number of recipes. In 1960 cooking columnist Mary Meade suggested that her readers use their hibachi to grill food like shrimp with mushrooms, lean beef or lamb, and fish balls. After the column appeared, friends criticized her for omitting the fact that cocktail franks, a food commonly associated with lower-income diets, were "perfect for hibachi cookery." Meade responded: "I didn't mention cocktail franks . . . simply because they are what everyone cooks on hibachi," and proceeded to lay out her recipe for "Cocktail Franks Oriental." By this point, hibachi parties were hardly an exclusive elite affair, as they spread out among hostesses of varying social backgrounds and tastes.[65]

The example of the hibachi illustrates the overall pattern of how Japanese aesthetics and objects spread throughout the American postwar suburbs. Lower-middle-class American women would learn from design experts and tastemakers in high-end magazines that the shibui style was currently fashionable among the nation's elite consumers and decide they could make their own home appear more elegant and sophisticated by purchasing Japan-influenced objects or pieces of furniture. In many cases, when Japanese objects failed to suit their needs exactly, homemakers or manufacturers adapted them in ways that did, often making them more affordable in the process. Rather than utilizing functional aesthetic principles, they were more likely to graft superficial Japanese elements onto familiar furniture or appropriate new American functions to Japanese items. With their exotic appearance, such décor could immediately project a homemaker's cosmopolitan appreciation for fashionable foreignness, regardless of how authentic it might have been.

In prioritizing exotic appearance and social status over shibui principles in decorating their homes, upwardly aspiring suburban homemakers were willing to adapt Japanese objects to better fit their everyday lives. But should they be criticized for tampering with tradition by electrifying their hibachis or building fiberglass shoji? On the one hand, such acts could appear disrespectful, taking items that functioned perfectly well in Japan and assuming they could always be improved by superior American ingenuity. On the other hand, such transformations tend to be par for the course in any cultural exchange. Japanese people had in fact been doing the same thing to Western furniture for decades, incorporating objects like chairs and tables into their homes, but sitting down at them to eat Japanese cuisine with chopsticks as they had always done. Neither side held to strict authenticity in the use of each other's household objects, nor could they be expected to, as they made them relevant in new contexts and part of their daily lives.

Design professionals, in contrast, treated Japanese homes as museum pieces (at times literally). They did make Japanese design principles seem more familiar to American homeowners by unobtrusively integrating them into otherwise Western home designs. However, in singling out particular historical styles, like sho-in and karesansui, and defining them as quintessential "Japanese design," they created the impression that all Japanese architects and homeowners followed those principles throughout time and into the present. In fact, Japanese architects were promoting a kind of mirror image process in the 1950s, amalgamating Western materials and furniture with more traditional designs.[66] But rarely did American design professionals acknowledge the presence of contemporary building styles in Japan, and if they did, it was often to condemn it as a symptom of encroaching west-ernization. Nor did they typically consult Japanese or Japanese Americans for suggestions on contemporary designs, unless it was as experts on his-torical styles. While American designers' opinion of Japanese aesthetics was undoubtedly complimentary, helping to boost Japan's reputation as a worthy ally, they nevertheless played a part in making Japan appear perpet-ually foreign in its timeless tradition, by hiding from Americans' view the skyscrapers and Western furnishings that reflected the modern, dynamic place recovering Japan actually was.

CHAPTER 5

SATORI IN AMERICA

Intellectuals and Artists Discover Zen Buddhism

On Saturday, April 18, 1959, Sarah Lawrence College in Bronxville, New York, held a one-day conference entitled "Zen Buddhism in American Culture." Speakers from the fields of religious studies, art, music, literature, and psychiatry had assembled to offer their views in a series of student-moderated panels. Representatives from the First Zen Institute in New York were on hand to answer questions and demonstrate meditation techniques, and Takashimaya department store had supplied a home furnishings display that enhanced the event's Japanese atmosphere.[1] The morning's keynote address—an introduction and overview of the Zen religion by University of Delaware philosophy professor Bernard Phillips—ran long, postponing lunch by more than an hour. Following lunch, the now somewhat disgruntled participants divided into panels centered on the themes of religion, the arts, and psychology, all fields where Americans were making extensive use of Zen concepts and practices. The arts panel included modernist composer John Cage, Beat poet Gregory Corso, Pace College art department chair Peter Fingesten, and psychotherapist Vera Brensen. Once discussion began, several minor disagreements arose between Brensen and the artists over questions of art and communication, later giving way to a more heated debate over how well acquainted Zen practitioners should be with Western philosophy before exploring Eastern religious beliefs. At one point Professor Phillips stood up in the audience and forcefully declared that Corso needed psychological help. A student covering the conference for the school newspaper described the scene: "Mrs. Brensen is just trying to find out what's going on. The audience has stopped trying. It's just enjoying itself." Meanwhile, the situation at the religion panel was similarly dissolving into a "three-cornered tug-of-war" over whether or not Zen should be "all-embracing," which left the reporter puzzling, "All-embracing what?" An event meant to foster sedate academic discussion of a religion based in serenity had instead deteriorated into chaotic debates that undergraduate attendees found farcical. The student reporter eventually concluded, "Seeing Zen discussed by so many experts, one realizes there is no one thing called Zen."[2]

This last observation seems particularly apt to describe the phenomenon that the U.S. press came to dub the "Zen boom" of 1957–60, which swept up prominent artists, intellectuals, and religious scholars, as well as more modest Americans. The increasing interest in Zen was no doubt tied to the rising popularity of other Japanese traditions, since most American Japan enthusiasts interpreted Zen philosophy as the foundation of all Japanese culture.[3] Appearing ignorant of the facts that Shinto was an equally popular religion in Japan, that many Japanese practiced other denominations of Buddhism, or that the exact version of Zen as they understood it was actually formulated less than a century before, Americans came to believe that *rinzai* Zen underlay all forms of Japanese art and ceremony. With its emphasis on meditation and quietude, this peaceful, feminized, nonviolent approach to the world appeared to be the font of serenity and minimalism from which all other shibui traditions had sprung.

For some prominent painters, musicians, writers, psychologists, and religious leaders, Zen philosophy could expand beyond its supposedly timeless origins predating all Japanese culture and function as a set of ideas to address problems faced by many Americans in the mid-twentieth century. Artists used it as a lens through which to examine and critique twentieth-century U.S. society, or they were inspired by its methods to create new forms of expression. Psychologists found its techniques of meditation and introspection could help patients combat particular forms of stress unique to postwar suburbia. Religious scholars began to pay more attention to Zen as part of a wider move toward ecumenism, that is, finding value in religions besides one's own particular sect. Some Catholics even began to promote Zen study to infuse new energy into their religious practice and appeal more to younger adherents. But while all of these "highbrows" who took an interest in Zen did so with a serious dedication that sought to understand the religion, as the anecdote above suggests, various self-appointed Zen experts were often prone to infighting over the finer points of Zen belief, including whether it was primarily a religion or a philosophy. Yet one characteristic they often shared in common, whatever particular type they subscribed to, is that they interpreted Zen as emerging unchanged from a timeless Oriental past. Like other examples of Japanese culture, Zen Buddhism ultimately derived its power from a seeming ability to offer an ancient, exotic alternative to the contemporary American worldview.

Americans' Concept of Zen and the Experts Who Promoted It

Zen is a sect of the Buddhist religion that originated in China at least one thousand years ago. Zen does not include the notion of a personified God, and according to its cosmology, no single being exists to exercise control over the universe or to provide humans with an established set of moral laws required to avoid eternal damnation. Instead, as twentieth-century Americans came to understand it, the Zen world is subject to a succession of random occurrences that are neither good nor bad. Births, deaths, war, peace, disease, and good fortune all happen because that is simply the way of things, and Zen thought excludes any kind of judgment that would categorize these events as either positive or negative. In denying the universe an underlying structure, this outlook also eschews intellectual theorization and logical thought, on the grounds that they impose an overly structured false sense of order. Instead, Zen favors more simple, direct, and spontaneous ways of thinking, which adherents referred to as a clear "mirror" mind.[4] However, none of this is to imply that Zen envisions the world as amoral chaos.

Adherents believe that every living being and the actions they perform are fundamentally connected to all others, not just in the sense that actions have consequences, but as part of a deeper spiritual unity, often called "Buddha" (referring not to the religion's founder but to a sense of pervading essence). They can achieve peace by relinquishing their sense of an individualized self and realizing their position within this cosmic unity. As in most Buddhist denominations, the process involves renouncing distracting attachment to material possessions and practicing meditation, that is, sitting still and silent for long periods of time and clearing the head of ego-centered thoughts, to become attuned to the nature of existence as a unified whole.

Like Japanese architecture, Zen Buddhism made its initial impressions on the American public well before the 1950s. In the 1870s, following Japan's Meiji Restoration and during the new government's subsequent attempts to create a more unified state, Buddhism was subjected to a short-lived but intense repression as a "foreign" religion due to its Indian and Chinese origins. Perceiving their faith was under attack, Zen followers strategically courted allies in the West. Since many late nineteenth-century Japanese were consciously borrowing from Europe and the United States in an effort to become more modern, endorsements from westerners carried significant weight. Zen advocates packaged their religion for export abroad in a strategic way, emphasizing characteristics of the sect that either suggested universalism or seemed to be in keeping with modernist philosophy.[5] Prominent intellectuals in Europe and Anglo-America had recently begun to question then-dominant modes of positivist thinking, which assumed the natural world and human behavior functioned according to a set of discernable and constant laws. Finding that chance, contingency, and general disorder played a larger role in the world than their predecessors were often willing to admit, they turned their intellectual gaze toward the uncertain and the irrational.[6] Observing this trend, Japanese Zen promoters emphasized the fact that their religion relied little on strict rules and allowed room for chance and disorder. They also emphasized Zen's seeming compatibility with scientific rationality—as compared with Christianity—an appreciation for simplicity and the mundane and an underlying sense of universal interconnection. Therefore, when Americans "rediscovered" Zen fifty years later, what they actually uncovered was one particular version of the religion that had essentially been prewesternized.[7]

Most of the men who first promoted Zen to westerners subscribed to the rinzai Zen sect, primarily distinguished from the other major Japanese denomination, *soto*, by its use of koans. A koan can be a question, such as the now famous riddle "What is the sound of one hand clapping?" Or it can be an anecdote involving the enigmatic actions of a past Zen master that the novice is asked to explain. An example of this second type often quoted in 1950s Zen literature involves a monk who asks his master, "What is Zen?" to which the master responds, "Three measures of flax." For many students, discovering a satisfactory response to a koan could take years of rigorous meditation practice, or *zazen*. Some eventually experienced *satori*, the moment of realization at which the illogical nature of Zen suddenly made intuitive sense. In the meantime, they were expected to meet with their *roshi* on a regular basis and discuss their koan in meetings known as *sanzen*.[8] Traditionally, roshi very rarely had kind words for their pupils during these sessions, and rinzai masters in Japan had a reputation for doling out numerous verbal and physical reprimands.

The man most responsible for initially promoting modernist rinzai Zen in the United States was the Japanese scholar Shaku Soyen. He reached his first significant American audience at the World Parliament of Religions, held in conjunction with 1893 Columbian Exposition in Chicago. Arranged by scholars from the emerging field of comparative religions, this meeting brought together representatives of many faiths to offer lectures and discussions explaining their beliefs.[9] Over time interest grew in Soyen's version of Zen, as influential American intellectuals came to draw parallels between Zen and their own country's philosophical currents. In 1897 journalist Lafcadio Hearn published *Gleanings in Buddha Fields*, one of several travelogues of his experiences in Japan. The book expressed his admiration for Zen belief, finding it more "capable of being reconciled with the widest expansions of nineteenth-century thought" than Christianity. Specifically, he posited that Zen's critique of the ego-centered worldview reinforced recent theories on human sense perception and that Zen's lack of a specific moral code could help promote tolerance in a seemingly shrinking world.[10] Around the same time, Paul Carus, a German American religious scholar and editor of the religious studies journal *The Monist,* produced a series of books on Asian religion through his Open Court Publishing Company, including *The Gospel of Buddha* in 1904. His publications in general sought to uncover what he termed "the religion of science," a web of rational truths underlying the world's varied religions, and found Zen an excellent fit for his project, as it appeared to contain many universalist concepts.[11]

After the Columbian Exposition had ended, Soyen's student Yeita Sasaki, known to fellow Zen adherents as Sokei-an, stayed behind to continue the mission of spreading Zen in the United States. In 1931 he founded the Buddhist Society of America in New York, later to be renamed the First Zen Institute. The institution offered meditation sessions, sanzen with Sokei-an, and a small library of Zen literature. It also published a semiregular newsletter entitled *Cat's Yawn* (after Sokei-an's constant feline companion, Chaka), which offered translations of older Zen texts, as well as essays by institute staff. While its membership remained small and was subject to scrutiny by law enforcement during World War II, the society operated through the postwar period as a Zen outpost in midtown Manhattan. In 1944, threatened by both heart disease and a fear of internment, Sokei-an married one of his more formidable students, Ruth Fuller, who would take the helm of the institute following his death less than one year later.[12] (While speculation persists as to whether their nuptials were mainly for legal reasons, friends and family maintained that the two were genuinely in love.)

After the war, organizations like the First Zen institute enjoyed higher membership than ever before and continued to promote the same form of Zen as they had at the turn of the century. In the aftermath of the most destructive conflict in history, atrocities like the Holocaust and the use of atomic bombs seemed to call into doubt everything Americans thought they had known about human nature, morals, and reason. Modernist thought's uncertain, disordered worldview began to move beyond academic intellectual circles and into the mainstream. Even the realm of the natural sciences, which might have been the last bastion of solid objectivity, saw the rise of Einstein's theory of relativity and Heisenberg's uncertainty principle, which placed limits on humans' ability to know and quantify the physical world.[13] British Zen scholar Alan Watts wrote that since the war, "We find ourselves adrift without landmarks in a universe which more and more resembles the Buddhist principle of the 'Great Void.' The various wisdoms of the West, religious, philosophical, and scientific, do not offer much guidance in the art of living in such a universe, and we find the prospects of making our way in so trackless an ocean of relativity rather frightening. For we are used to absolutes, to firm principles and laws to which we can cling for spiritual and psychological security."[14] Since Zen had been grappling for centuries with the question of how to lead an enlightened life in a random universe, Watts argued, it would hold important lessons for survival in the postwar intellectual and moral climate. The Zen idea that the universe is fundamentally unstructured seemed more appropriate in this environment than the concept of a God who was fully in control yet allowed such tragedies to occur. The trauma of war similarly encouraged most intellectuals to abandon the idea that humanity was constantly progressing toward a more perfect state, a notion that Zen, with its acceptance of the universe on its own terms, had rejected long before.

To learn more about this philosophy, Americans had a handful of experts to whom they could turn, who presented and interpreted Zen ideas in accessible English. Ruth Fuller Sasaki, D. T. Suzuki, and Alan Watts most notably offered direct advice on the theory and practice of Zen, as well as how Americans could apply these ideas to their lives. After Sokei-an's passing at the end of the war, his wife Ruth took over the helm of the society, and it became clear rather quickly that she held dissimilar ideas from her late husband in terms of popularizing Zen. It was not that she was against gaining as many dedicated adherents as possible, but she was opposed to the concept of adapting what she perceived as an ancient religion to fit more modern tastes. A product of elite Chicago society, she first took an interest in Buddhism around 1920, as a harried new mother searching for a sense of peace. In 1932 she made the decision to begin Zen training under Nanshinken roshi in Japan, aided by a translator. She thus bypassed Soyen's Western adapted Zen and was not disposed to find any modernist parallels in Zen thought. Throughout her career, she would insist that it was first and foremost a religion that required rigorous and exacting practice. Unlike Sokei-an, who offered lectures at the First Zen Institute explaining Zen to American visitors in accessible terms, Ruth preferred to translate centuries-old historical works and let them speak for themselves. On the rare occasions when she did write for a general audience, her pamphlets took the form of practical guides to serious study, as opposed to her late husband's explanations of Zen philosophy for the uninitiated. For example, her "Rinzai Zen Study for Foreigners in Japan," published in 1960, essentially discouraged the faint of heart from practicing Zen by outlining its demanding meditation sessions and self-denying lifestyle.[15] She complained to *Time* that many people who visited the Institute in the late 1950s were "faddists, or just curious, and Zen is not for them.... Zen is not a cult. The problem with Western people is that they want to believe in something and at the same time they want something easy. Zen is a lifetime work of self-discipline and study." Nevertheless, casual visitors kept appearing, leading her to require in 1962 that new institute members pass a written entrance exam in order to keep dilettantes and "beatniks" at bay.[16]

But while her approach to Zen was exclusive, under her leadership the institute expanded significantly, opening a second branch in Kyoto in 1956. Taking over the Ryosen-an subtemple at Daitoku-ji, it provided a venue for westerners to study Zen in Japan. Visitors would engage in the same traditional meditation practice of koan contemplation as many Japanese monks, but with some concessions, such as indoor plumbing, electricity, sanzen in English, and American cuisine. For administrative purposes, Fuller Sasaki was ordained as a Zen "priest" officially serving as "abbot" of the temple. In 1957 and 1958, the center added a new library and meditation hall, or *zendo*. The number of students increased as well, from several of Fuller Sasaki's personal acquaintances to fifteen to twenty long-term visitors. In 1960 the institute constructed a temporary dormitory facility called Zuiun-ken to accommodate these students. The majority of them

FIG. 12. Ryosen-an, 2008. Photo by the author.

came from backgrounds that could be described as highbrow; many were university professors from the United States or Japan, perhaps attracted to Zen because of the emphasis that rinzai places on rigorous individual study, much like academia. In addition, the institute played host to pianist Walter Nowick, artist Donatienne Lebovich, Dutch novelist Janwillem van de Wetering, and a banker couple from Egypt. Its most famous guest was the poet Gary Snyder, who arrived while still a graduate student in Asian languages at the University of California at Berkeley.[17] After returning to the United States in the 1960s, he went on to found the Ring of Bone Zendo in Northern California and work as an environmental activist, but he is best known as the inspiration for Jack Kerouac's fictional character Japhy Ryder in the novel *The Dharma Bums*.

Back in New York, the original branch maintained a healthy core of loyal adherents under the direction of institute secretary Mary Farkas. Members ranged in age and background from young single white Anglo-Saxon

Protestants to middle-aged Jewish and German Americans and included a Russian immigrant in her late sixties. Stephen Tichachek, a carpenter by trade, had worked as a set designer with Farkas's husband. A longtime sufferer of Parkinson's disease, he was losing his ability to perform his job and was in search of new meaning in his life. He was so grateful to the institute for aiding him spiritually that one of his last acts before the disease took his life in 1961 was to repaint and plaster the zendo.[18]

Records also suggest that there was a near 50/50 gender ratio among institute members; if there was any discrepancy, there were slightly more women present at meetings. Despite its reputation as virile and masculine in Japan, in the United States Zen was more gender neutral. In Japan, Zen monks far outnumbered nuns, and some masters at Daitoku-ji were reportedly scandalized to hear that a woman was appointed head of Ryosen-an.[19] In the United States, by contrast, female leadership seemed fairly common. In addition to the efforts of Fuller Sasaki and Farkas, author and lecturer Nancy Wilson Ross published widely on the subject. Instead of emphasizing rigorous discipline and manly self-denial, most American interpretations of Zen focused instead on its sense of serenity and inner peace, desirable attributes for both men and women. The presence of so many female leaders within the movement may also stem from American women's long-standing active participation in various religious denominations.

Spiritual seekers of both genders were interested in learning important lessons from Zen, but many lacked the dedication or resources to regularly attend meditation sessions like the members of the First Zen Institute. For them, other avenues opened through the prolific writings of D. T. Suzuki and Alan Watts. Unlike Fuller Sasaki, neither man sought to preserve Zen in a completely authentic state, instead offering adapted versions that allowed Americans to borrow ideas without necessarily adhering to practice. But even in its more Americanized forms, Zen's appeal continued to draw from the fact that it was rooted in a mysterious and wise Eastern past.

In 1957 Suzuki delivered a well-attended series of lectures at Columbia University that first inspired magazine editors to start paying attention to the growing popularity of Zen. But his first opportunity to promote Zen in the United States came much earlier when he accompanied Soyen to the World Parliament of Religions as his translator. Afterward, Carus hired him to help with translations for Open Court. Over time, Suzuki became an enthusiastic and prolific writer in his own right, eventually publishing more than thirty books in English.[20] His early works were mostly translations and explications of older Zen writings, but through interactions with American and British Zen enthusiasts, he developed his own social science–based approach to the religion. The result was an expository style that incorporated sayings and anecdotes from centuries-old Japanese texts, but often read like Western philosophy, echoing the modernist style of Zen that Soyen had promoted several decades earlier.[21]

In January 1957 *Vogue* mentioned lectures he was delivering at Columbia University in its "People Are Talking About" section, an act credited with launching the boom as well as Suzuki's reputation. A feature-length profile in the *New Yorker* in August 1957 and a half-hour interview on the NBC television network two years later, along with his prolific publishing, helped make him a nationally recognized figure.[22] Suzuki's colleagues and admirers often credited his clear writing style as well as his personal charisma for his ability to explain Zen's complex belief system in a way ordinary Americans could understand. Psychologist Erich Fromm characterized Suzuki as vibrant but humble, claiming, "His love for life, his freedom from selfish desires, his inner joy, his strength . . . tended to make one stronger, more alive, more concentrated. Yet without ever evoking that kind of awe which the great personality so often does." In the *New Yorker*, Winthrop Sargeant claimed that Suzuki wrote in "a language whose clarity might be the envy of many metaphysicians." Catholic monk and author Thomas Merton added, "I can venture to say that in Dr. Suzuki, Buddhism finally became for me completely comprehensible, whereas before it had been a very mysterious and confusing jumble of words, images, doctrines . . . and so forth."[23]

Yet, while many observers touted his warm and relatable personality, his portrayal in the American media was just as likely to resemble cultural scholar Jane Naomi Iwamura's archetype of the exoticized, inscrutable "Oriental Monk," even though Suzuki spent most of his career as a lay scholar.

Such a figure served as an effective symbol for a friendly, nonthreatening Japan; weakened by age, he welcomed all comers who sought his timeless wisdom. One of the typical monk's primary characteristics was his esoteric spirituality, which appeared puzzling to westerners. Indeed, in contrast to readers like Merton, some reviewers described Suzuki's books as enigmatic. Daniel Bronstein of the *Saturday Review* felt it necessary to "warn the reader that unless he is a patient man he may find himself developing an inferiority complex as he reads Dr. Suzuki's exposition of Zen," due to its many "ciphers." Other articles depicted Suzuki visually as an Oriental monk. Photographed wearing traditional kimono, despite the fact that he typically dressed in slacks and sports jackets, his shaved head and uncombed bushy eyebrows added to the overall effect of his exotic appearance. Such images, combined with descriptions of his "quiet, cheerful" demeanor and the "absent-minded rubbings of his forehead," like those provided by Sargeant, helped cast Suzuki in the role of a kindly, wizened Oriental sage.[24] While he addressed westerners in language some could comprehend, he did so through a persona that appeared thoroughly steeped in Asian tradition.

Alan Watts, by contrast, came across as a white Western spiritual seeker exploring the lessons of Asian religion, just like much of his audience. In keeping with such a role, he published books that felt even more straightforward to American readers than Suzuki's. Born in Kent, England, and ordained as an Anglican priest, he was later attracted to Zen because it offered an alternative to certain aspects of Christianity that Watts found too doctrinaire. For example, he claimed that the commandment "Love the Lord thy God" was in fact impossible, since no human being could forcibly will themselves to love. Zen, in contrast, felt such directed effort could only prove futile in a world where things happen as they will, and was thus more forgiving of its adherents.[25] As Watts learned more about the religion, often from British scholars familiar with modernist westernized Zen, he became more enamored of its concepts of universal unity and nonduality. Eventually he reached the conclusion that Zen inspired human beings to exercise compassion more effectively than Christian commandments did, by endowing practitioners with a sense of sympathy and discouraging them from passing judgment. By the time Zen began to grow in popularity, Watts had completely rejected Christianity and its emphasis on a distant otherworldly afterlife. Zen, he believed, offered a means to salvation in this world: a life based on personal serenity, understanding, and well-being.[26]

Watts made a successful career out of popularizing this interpretation of Zen. He published his first book, *The Spirit of Zen*, in 1935 at the age of twenty-one. Although he would later call the book "unscholarly" and "misleading," he reissued it twice with new prefaces in 1954 and 1958. He tried to improve upon his efforts in a lengthier 1957 work entitled *The Way of Zen*, intended for the more "advanced student," which was followed by a collection of essays on Zen and spirituality entitled *This Is IT* aimed at a much wider audience. In 1951 he helped found the short-lived American Academy of Asian Studies in San Francisco, where he and like-minded colleagues taught graduate courses on diverse subjects including Hinduism, Islam, Sanskrit, yoga, and *sumi-e* brush painting. Throughout the 1950s, he broadcast a radio series on KPFA in Berkeley, achieved increasing popularity as a seminar speaker, and appeared in his own television miniseries in 1959–60, *Eastern Wisdom and Modern Life*. Although he became a longhaired and bearded "New Age" guru in the late 1960s, which is how most people remember him, in the 1950s he was still relatively "square," clean shaven, with a crewcut and sport jacket.[27]

Watts and Suzuki's attempts to make Zen more accessible for a wider audience at times led to significant disagreements between the two men and the First Zen Institute. Sokei-an had complained about Suzuki fashioning his own brand of Zen according to Western stereotypes. "The tea ceremony is what Americans think Japan is," he wrote in his memoirs, "and when Dr. Suzuki takes seventy-five dollars for a lecture, he must give them that and not Zen." Fuller Sasaki wrote to one of Suzuki's Japanese colleagues that he was telling people "the use of meditation" was "out of date" and "unsuited to the West," and she worried that his idea of replacing sanzen with casual conversations would corrupt rinzai traditions. She also left numerous argumentative remarks in the margins of her copies of both Suzuki's and Watts's books, including a declarative "nonsense!" appearing multiple times throughout the pages of *This Is IT*.[28] Despite his marriage to Ruth's daughter Eleanor, in his autobiography Watts characterized Ruth as an elitist, arguing that the texts she created were intended for an exclusive circle of scholars whom he derisively referred to as "the in-group of academic Orientalists who, as librarians, philological nitpickers, and scholarly drudges dissolve all creative interest into acidulated pedantry." For his part, Suzuki lashed out at Watts, claiming that at least some practice should be required of a self-proclaimed Zen expert. In a Japanese scholarly journal, he described Watts as a "fake," speculating, "He is still young, so if he trained for ten years he would get better. . . . Still, it's probably useless from the start to hope for him to do that."[29]

But while all three argued over the finer points of Zen practice, like the amount of study and meditation required to attain true enlightenment, they nevertheless agreed on the basic premises that Zen provided a novel spiritual outlook for Americans who felt something lacking in their Christian or Jewish beliefs and that it did so grounded in ancient Asian traditions. As such, the opinions of all three clashed fundamentally with most Buddhist practitioners of Japanese descent. In Japan, the popularity of Zen Buddhism was at an ebb at the same time it was cresting in the United States. Fuller Sasaki observed that "modern Japanese are existentialists, Marxists—anything but Buddhists." Zen scholar Gary Snyder found himself labeled a political conservative by his Kyotoite friends, since many Japanese considered Zen the outdated "religion of the samurai." The image of Zen priests praying with kamikaze pilots before sending them into battle had further associated the sect with the type of wartime militarism that many Japanese were eager to put behind them.[30] By the late 1950s, enthusiasm about Zen was in fact stronger among Americans than it was among the Japanese people who allegedly lived in its spirit every day.

Nor did this particular version of Zen agree with how many Japanese Americans practiced Buddhism. Few were rinzai Zen adherents; those who followed Zen tended to belong to the soto sect. But even greater numbers adhered to *jodo shinshu* Buddhism, believing that upon their deaths, they would be welcomed by the Buddha into the heavenly "Pure Land," not through their own efforts in study and meditation but through the grace of the Buddha spirit. Seeking acceptance in racially prejudiced U.S. society in the early twentieth century, Japanese American Buddhists had begun a process of de-exoticizing their religion. Many gathered for services on Sunday mornings, following a Christian model, in houses of worship they called "churches," where they sang adaptations of hymns like "Onward Buddhist Soldiers." Living in San Francisco in 1952, Alan Watts offered his opinion of this practice in a local Buddhist newsletter. He first wrote, "It is very understandable that Americans of Japanese origin want to adapt themselves to American life, and to fit in with the social patterns which they find in this country." However, as someone promoting the Zen sect as a font of Eastern wisdom that offered benefits to contemporary white Americans precisely because of its foreignness, he felt, "This copying of Christian church-organization is most unfortunate." Similar debates played out in other venues between Japanese Americans and white American Buddhists, with white converts fighting to preserve Zen in a supposedly pristine authentic form, and Japanese Americans continuing to adapt and assimilate. As a consequence, few participants in the Zen Boom looked to the Japanese American community for guidance, and they, in turn, did little to promote Zen on a national scale.[31] The version of Buddhism popularized in the United States, despite also having been adapted to suit the taste of white westerners, had to be disguised as the wisdom of an ancient Oriental past.

Artists and Intellectuals Find Zen a Useful Tool for Their Work

Throughout the 1950s, a variety of artists and other professionals decided to borrow ideas from this version of Zen Buddhism and apply them to their own work. Composer Jackson MacLow attested that his fellow artists and musicians could always be found in large numbers at Suzuki's Columbia lectures.[32] While many discovered Zen through their own individual paths, most formed interpretations similar to Suzuki's, making links between their modernist ways of thinking and Zen belief. In doing so they often used Zen's supposedly ancient Eastern concepts of unity, antimaterialism, and an appreciation of simplicity to critique the popular culture of their own time.

Some of the most prominent artists known for their Zen inspiration either taught at or graduated from the Cornish School, a prestigious private college in Seattle specializing in the visual and performing arts. By the mid-1950s it had gained a reputation for its faculty and students' affinity for Asian aesthetics. In 1957 the U.S. Information Agency selected paintings from the school for an international goodwill tour to promote American art to "the elite of Europe and Asia." According to a *Time* reporter, USIA made this decision because "the general Orientalism and mysticism of the Northwest painters were thought likely to be received sympathetically in the Far East." Although response to the mostly abstract artwork among visitors was admittedly "indifferent," the agency still considered the tour a success in terms of promoting goodwill abroad; they had been able to at least suggest to an Asian audience that open-minded and benevolent Americans had come to appreciate their philosophies and values.[33]

Several of these Cornish School artists came to embrace Buddhism following what they described as revelatory experiences. Painter and instructor Mark Tobey traveled to China and Japan in 1934 to study calligraphy and spent four months in a Kyoto monastery studying Zen. Knowing he was an artist, the abbot instructed him to meditate on a *sumi* ink painting of a large circle, which he did to no avail, a failure he attributed to his Caucasian background. "Day after day I would look at it," he would later write. "Perhaps I didn't see its aesthetic and missed the fine points of the brush which to a trained Oriental eye would reveal much." But eventually he did develop an appreciation for such a minimalist style of art and later wrote that Zen paintings reflected a sense of "Simplicity, Directness, and Profundity" lacking in Western art, expressing complex concepts and emotions with the use of only a few well-placed lines.[34] Morris Graves, a younger Cornish School painting instructor who became Tobey's mentee, first visited Japan at age seventeen as an ordinary navy seaman. Even then, he was impressed by the country's traditional arts: "I was interested . . . in the gardens of Japan. You could get out into the countryside from Tokyo—it was only half an hour by train. In Japan I at once had the feeling that this was the right way to do everything. It was the acceptance of nature—not the resistance to it.

I had no sense that I was to be a painter, but I breathed a different air."[35] Gaining firsthand exposure to Japanese traditions, both painters found that these ancient cultural forms offered a different approach to art and a new worldview from what they had previously studied in the United States.

Graves later formed a specific appreciation for Zen at the age of twenty-five. Following the sudden death of his father, he sought solace in religion at a local Buddhist temple. For Graves, Zen's greatest appeal lay in its emphasis on intuition over intellect. He once argued, "I think it is possible for one section of your mind, the rational, to intrude upon yourself and hamper deeper insight." Zen provided a vehicle for him to get in touch with his emotions and work through the grieving process in a way that Christianity did not.[36]

Graves's friend and Cornish School music student John Cage similarly came to Zen out of personal hardship. According to several accounts, he first turned to Zen around 1950 in the midst of the stressful process of divorcing his wife. Other accounts reveal that Graves had earlier laid the groundwork for Cage's interest after persuading him to attend a lecture on Zen given by Nancy Wilson Ross at the Cornish School in 1939.[37] By the time he reached the height of his fame, Cage openly professed Zen beliefs, but decided to put them into practice following his own methods. He once told an interviewer, "Rather than taking the path that is prescribed in the formal practice of Zen Buddhism itself, namely, sitting cross-legged and breathing and such things, I decided that my proper discipline was that one to which I was already committed, namely, the making of music. And that I would do it with a means that was as strict as sitting cross-legged."[38] Like Graves, Cage too found Zen's sense of spontaneity and contingency to be its most salient attribute, in contrast to the dull regimented routine of conformist American life. He invented a method of composition known as "chance operations," in which he tossed a coin, or threw sticks as in the Chinese *I Ching* fortune-telling method, to decide the next note, sequence, or action a piece would take.[39] He also attempted to capture the sense of quietude and serenity experienced during meditation with his most infamous piece, *4'33"*, a piano composition that consisted of nothing more than four minutes and thirty-three seconds of silence. It was arranged in three "movements"—which the performer signified by raising and lowering the keyboard cover—of random duration Cage determined using his *I Ching* sticks. Its debut performance took place on August 29, 1952, at Maverick Concert Hall in Woodstock, New York, with pianist David Tudor at the keyboard. During the first movement, the only sound to be heard in the hall was the wind blowing outside. At some point during the second, it began to rain, producing a somewhat musical pattering on the roof overhead. In the course of the third movement, the sounds increased as audience members began talking and walking out. Alan Watts would later seem to concur with their assessment, referring to Cage's piece as "therapy . . . not yet art," and accused Cage of using Zen aesthetics to shock his audience just to gain attention without really teaching them anything.[40] But Tudor for one found *4'33"* to be the spiritual experience Cage had intended, later telling *Harper's Magazine*, "[It's] one of the most intense listening experiences you can ever have. . . . You're hearing everything there is. . . . It is cathartic—four minutes and thirty-three seconds of meditation, in effect."[41]

While Cage challenged the noise, busy-ness, and conformist social structure of 1950s middle-class America through musical performances reflecting Zen-based quietude and spontaneity, Mark Tobey and Morris Graves registered similar critiques through their paintings. In his "Hollyhocks" series (1953), Tobey tried to capture a sense of spontaneity by allowing dots of paint to run down the canvas in a random fashion. He also drew inspiration in his sumi ink paintings (most completed in 1957), where he applied the paint in random blotches, zigzags, and splatters, borrowing from Zen's underlying philosophy as well as Zen artists' most common medium. Graves employed similar techniques in works like *Restless Ink* (1943), which features swirls of sumi ink, or *Machine Age Noise* (1957), in which he doused a broom in sumi and splattered it against the canvas. Other paintings emphasized Zen's appreciation of nature and sense of antimaterialism, which both painters used to critique their society. Tobey titled one painting *The Void Devouring the Gadget Era* (1942). Featuring a mess of chaotic shapes disappearing into a quieter field of color, its title made clear it portrayed the defeat of materialism in the face of Zen's all-encompassing oneness, which scholars like Suzuki often referred to as "the void." Graves's painting *Bird with Possessions* (1943) depicts a malevolent looking crow furtively guarding several small seeds, like an overly materialistic American who goes against Zen teaching by cherishing his personal goods above all else. His later *Spring with Machine Age Noise #3* (1957) critiqued the encroachment of midcentury industrialization on the natural world that Zen valued by featuring dissonant lines of red and black paint splotches polluting an otherwise peaceful marsh scene.[42]

For these paintings as well, Watts had harsh words, claiming Tobey's work was nothing more than a "haphazard drooling of paint or uncontrolled wandering of brush."[43] But at the same time, established and influential critics and museum curators expressed admiration for all three artists. In 1956 the Whitney Museum staged a retrospective of Graves's work, and two years later Tobey won the top award for painting at Venice Biennale, as well as an American Art Award. That same year, New York's Town Hall honored Cage with a retrospective that included his chance operation pieces.[44] In giving these Cornish School artists such stamps of approval, the leaders of the American art world ensured that wide audiences would experience their work and along with it their modernist interpretation of Zen, whose intriguing worldview would challenge many Americans' acquisitive, conformist, and hurried approach to life.

Outside of the Cornish School, the artist with the biggest reputation as a Zen enthusiast was author J. D. Salinger. According to *Time* magazine, Salinger also turned to Zen to relieve depression. Psychologically damaged by his experiences on the European front of World War II, he found some spiritual comfort after bohemian friends in Greenwich Village introduced him to Zen philosophy. A decade later Salinger had notoriously retreated to a life of seclusion in rural New Hampshire, but he still interacted with his neighbors, including the renowned Judge Learned Hand, who noted his great affinity for Japanese traditions. "In fact," Hand told *Newsweek*, "whenever Japan is mentioned, his face seems to light up. He seems to adore everything about Japan."[45]

His penchant for Zen as one specific Japanese tradition is apparent throughout his body of work. He chose a koan as the epigraph for his *Nine Stories* (1953)—"We know the sound of two hands clapping. But what is the sound of one hand clapping?"—and the collection concludes with "Teddy," a short story about a precocious boy who meditates, loves Japanese poetry, and believes he was a Buddhist monk in a past life. Salinger's last two books, *Franny and Zooey* and *Raise High the Roof Beam, Carpenters, and Seymour: An Introduction,* both center on the Glasses, an upper-middle-class New York family with seven children, all of whom had starred on a radio quiz show for prodigies. The eldest two sons, Seymour and Buddy, share Salinger's interest in East Asian religion and poetry. In the "Zooey" section of *Franny and Zooey,* originally published as a short story in the *New Yorker* in 1957, Buddy explains their approach in helping raise the two youngest siblings: "Seymour had already begun to believe . . . that education by any name would smell as sweet, and maybe much sweeter, if it didn't begin with a quest for knowledge at all but with a quest, as Zen would put it, for no-knowledge. Dr. Suzuki says somewhere that to be in a state of pure consciousness—satori—is to be with God before he said, Let there be light."[46] "Seymour: An Introduction" (first published as a short story in 1959), a tribute composed by Buddy to his older brother, is similarly peppered with musings on haiku poetry and Buddhist belief. Many literary critics of the time mentioned Salinger's affinity for Zen in their reviews. Some treated it as a superficial characteristic of his writing, dismissing his penchant for Eastern mysticism as a form of rebellion or an attempt to appeal to disaffected youth while the Beats were also studying Zen. But others found that a Zen-inspired longing for truth underlay his writing at a fundamental level. In the *Western Review,* Ihab Hassan interpreted Salinger's interest in Zen less as a mystical quest and more as a practical strategy for confronting mid-twentieth-century urban life, writing sympathetically that "Zen itself, in Salinger's work, makes up an odd way of criticizing contemporary failures."[47] As with the Cornish School artists, Zen endowed Salinger's characters with a spiritually trenchant worldview, separate from the one shared by the shallow, materialistic Manhattanites that populated his social milieu: the type of people his most famous character, Holden Caulfield (*Catcher in the Rye*, 1951), would disparagingly refer to as "phonies."

In addition to artists from various media, Zen concepts also inspired some well-known psychologists of the era, which seems fitting given that most Americans taking an interest in Zen did so to aid their spiritual well-being and by extension their mental health. During the 1950s, psychoanalysis was at its peak in the United States, its popularity bolstered by the immigration of prominent European Jewish psychologists fleeing the Nazis, as well as the success that psychoanalytic techniques appeared to be having on shell-shocked war veterans. Partly to aid the health of soldiers recovering from trauma, in 1946 President Truman signed the National Mental Health Act, which significantly expanded federal funding for psychiatric education and research. Many psychologists believed that most serious mental illnesses could be successfully combatted if detected early, while the patient was still leading a relatively "normal" life. Therefore community clinics funded by the NMHA were established throughout the country to help average Americans cope with everyday stress and neuroses before they developed into more serious conditions. Throughout the 1950s, weekly newsmagazines ran articles profiling prominent psychoanalysts and highlighting successfully treated cases. They also reported on movie stars and other celebrities in therapy and helped spread the image of a typical patient as a young, urbane, and intelligent person. The stigma associated with mental health treatment eroded, and it soon became common, even fashionable, for those who could afford a therapist to consult one regularly. In affluent urban circles, it was eventually considered a status symbol to be analyzed by a prominent psychologist.[48]

Against such a backdrop, where middle-class Americans were almost expected to make personal efforts to improve their well-being, it would only seem to make good marketing sense for Zen promoters to emphasize their religion's impact on mental health. Suzuki and Watts had both felt for a long time that Zen had much to offer the field of psychology and vice versa. Suzuki was friends with several psychologists and reportedly once told a colleague that "psychoanalysis could in part take the place of Zen" by substituting therapeutic breakthroughs for satori. Watts often employed terms borrowed from psychology like "self-consciousness" and "double bind" in his writing, and some of his essays at times sound like they might belong in the genre of self-help literature. Meanwhile, Fuller Sasaki characteristically objected to such adulteration of the Zen religion. In one pamphlet she wrote, "A lively interest taken in Zen by psychiatry has given rise in some quarters to the view that Zen is a kind of psychotherapy. Here again a warning is necessary . . . do not expect [your roshi] to have insight into your private neurosis or be able to cure it for you through koan study." Nevertheless, the fact that she felt compelled to issue such a warning speaks to the growing number of Americans turning to Zen to aid their mental health. Furthermore, the library at the First Zen Institute in Kyoto maintained a collection of books on psychology, suggesting at least a few of her colleagues weren't quite as strict on this point.[49]

In 1960 the field of psychiatry officially recognized Zen as a "related field" in *The American Handbook of Psychiatry*.[50] But the practice among mental health professionals of using Oriental beliefs to uncover alternative forms of therapy dates well before that. In the 1910s and 1920s, Carl Jung incorporated Buddhist concepts into his theories, most notably that of a collective unconscious. In 1952, noted German psychologist Karen Horney began researching Zen and traveled to Japan with Suzuki, determined to create a Zen-based form of therapy. However, she died several months thereafter, leaving others to continue her work.[51] One was a colleague, Japanese psychologist Akihisa Kondoo, who posited that Freud and Zen held a mutual appreciation for "a state of wholeness." In a special 1958 issue of the *Chicago Review* devoted to the subject of Zen, Kondoo discussed the enormous psychological benefits of the practice of meditation, or "sitting" as he called it. At first, he reported, many patients felt restless when being forced to remain alone and quiet, mulling over their problems. But in time they worked through their anxiety and experienced a sense of personal wholeness, which led them to become "charged with more psychic energy and vitality" as well as mentally refreshed.[52]

It was expatriate German psychologist Erich Fromm, however, who did the most to present Zen as an alternative form of mental therapy. He first learned about Zen from Karen Horney and later attended Suzuki's lectures at Columbia. Having fled the Nazis in the 1930s, he remained engaged in liberal political causes throughout his career and did much to promote his ideas to a middlebrow lay audience. His theories often stemmed from his belief that all human beings possess an inherent need to receive compassion from others, leading him to emphasize concepts of unity and oneness in his interpretation of Zen.[53] In 1957, while living in Cuernavaca, Mexico, he organized a conference for American psychologists interested in Zen, with Suzuki as its keynote speaker.

Following the event, he published three conference lectures as a book called *Zen Buddhism and Psychoanalysis*. An essay by psychologist Richard De Martino attempted to bring Zen up to date by explaining how the process of koan study led to satori in psychoanalytic terms. In contrast, the other two lectures by Suzuki and Fromm assumed a better defined East/West contrast, in arguing that Japanese wisdom could offer answers to American problems. Fromm used case studies to prove that Zen served as an effective antimodern counterweight to the mental stresses of life in industrialized society. He observed a *mal du siècle* in his patients, which entailed "the deadening of life, the automatization of man, his alienation from himself, from his fellow man, and from nature. . . . Where the roots of Western culture [once] considered the aim of life the *perfection of man*, modern man is concerned with the *perfection of things*," leaving him "in a state of schizoid inability to experience affect, hence he is anxious, depressed, and desperate."[54] Fromm went on to demonstrate how societal emphasis on conspicuous consumption had led his average American patient to place too much value on acquisition and ambition. His recommended cure was Zen meditation. The product of a premodern time that valued serenity over material things, it held the key to putting patients back in touch with their inner feelings, in effect making them well again.

Finally, a seemingly unlikely group of Zen interpreters emerged from the Catholic Church. They claimed Zen, or at least its philosophy, could in fact coexist harmoniously with their own religion. Admittedly, some Christian leaders were apprehensive about a competing religion's rise in popularity, especially among young parishioners. Prior to the boom, many religious experts and Catholic journalists had dismissed Buddhism as too exotic and foreign to be beneficially applicable or even relevant to American life, and most refused to change that stance following Suzuki's rise to fame.[55] In 1959 artist Peter Fingesten, the same Zen detractor who several months later would argue with Cage at Sarah Lawrence, published an article criticizing Zen in the magazine *Christian Century*. He admitted there were some similarities between Zen and Christianity. "Zen Buddhists make a tremendous effort to understand life from the point of view of eternity and at the same time to preserve their childlike directness in relation to it. This attitude too is a cornerstone of Christianity." However, his goal in writing the article was not to promote Zen but to convince Christians tempted to stray from the church that their own religion already offered many of the spiritual solutions they sought. He cautioned readers that Zen was too alienating with its foreign concepts, and subscribed to "the irrational and unproved premise that life, nature and God are 'void,'" arguing that it promoted nihilism and a dangerous disengagement from the real world. In some ways Zen might have looked familiar, according to Fingesten, but ultimately it threatened American spirituality by opposing traditional Western faith and values.[56]

However, there was a small but vocal group of Christians who felt Zen's foreign aspects would do more to refresh their religion than undermine it. Seeking connections with, and trying to learn from, other faiths was in fact part of a larger trend among many postwar American churches toward ecumenism. At times used politically to close ranks against "godless" communism, the ecumenical approach to religion nevertheless created and instilled unity across different Christian denominations, who later reached out to Jews and non-Western religions as well.[57] The Catholic Church became explicit about its willingness to find value in all religions at the convention of the Second Vatican Council, now commonly referred to as "Vatican II," held in 1962. The council issued a declaration urging Catholics to "acknowledge, preserve and encourage the spiritual and moral truths found among non-Christians, also their social life and culture."[58] Church members were thus able to learn and borrow from Asian religions like Zen with full approval of the Catholic hierarchy.

One famous Catholic who put such ideas into practice was Thomas Merton, a Trappist monk originally from France who spent most of his religious career in Kentucky's Gethsemani monastery. Best known for his peace activism, he filled his days by writing prolifically about his personal beliefs and ongoing spiritual journey, and his autobiography, *Seven Storey Mountain*, published in 1948, sold more than 100,000 copies within a year.[59] He would later succinctly express his personal sense of ecumenism in his diary. "Latin America, Asia, Zen, Islam etc., all these things come together in my life. It would be madness for me to attempt to create a monastic life for myself by excluding all these. I would be less a monk. Others may have their way of doing it but I have mine."[60] In 1959 he began a correspondence with D. T. Suzuki about a book he was writing on "The Desert Fathers," a group of early church mystics who lived in Egypt and practiced seclusion. His letters were enthusiastic, noting an affinity between the monks' adherence to a lifestyle based on simplicity and clear-mindedness and similar practices in Zen monasteries. Suzuki would disagree with Merton in terms of specifics, finding more points of difference, but the two colleagues concluded that on a fundamental level, Zen and Catholic mysticism agreed in terms of attaining spiritual insight by losing oneself in a sense of universal connectedness. According to this interpretation, Zen would not so much challenge or undermine Catholicism as encourage Catholics to appreciate their religion with newfound perspective. Merton elaborated more publicly on such ideas in the Catholic magazine *America*, arguing that "Zen has provided us with a deadly weapon against pious illusions" by "exploding all forms of self-importance." By encouraging egoless humility, Zen philosophy could make Americans better Catholics, or as he more colloquially phrased it, "we can filter a little Zen into our lives without losing our souls or becoming beatniks."[61] Just as Zen could aid an artist's spontaneous impulses, or help a neurotic patient better cope with the stresses of life, so too could it rejuvenate a Catholic's relationship with their faith.

While Merton was attracted to Zen's seeming universalism, most of the artists and psychologists who embraced Zen placed more value in its distinct Japanese-ness, treating it as timeless Oriental wisdom with the potential to counteract the materialism and busy abundance of modern American life. Most of these promoters and enthusiasts seemed unaware (or in Suzuki's case, purposefully forgetful) of the fact that this form of Zen was in fact a westernized version of the religion that was less than a century old, behaving instead as if they had discovered ancient teachings wholly crafted in a foreign environment. But they also understood that this supposedly timeless philosophy held certain aspects that could be usefully borrowed and applied to their own historical moment in the United States. In fact, its ancient and exotic veneer is what made Zen appear to offer such a novel outsider perspective in the first place, specifically one that could serve to combat the selfishness, conformity, materialism, and general spiritual shallowness of the postwar era.

Furthermore, this particular version of Zen served to reinforce Americans' postwar image of Japan as serene, docile, and essentially feminized. In the *Chicago Review*'s special Zen issue, Gary Snyder actually did paint a masculine and vigorous image of Zen study, describing monks' highly rigorous routine, enduring long periods of meditation and self-denial of food and sleep.[62] Yet such details were rarely echoed elsewhere by other Zen experts. Most discussions of Zen by authors, painters, and scholars depicted it as an outlook on life that encouraged self-knowledge and spontaneity, but above all a sense of even-keeled, relaxed quietude. In emphasizing simplicity, antimaterialism, and a general sense of personal peace with the universe, this version of the Zen worldview could not only provide inspiration and spiritual solace but it could also support the foundational image of a humble, serene, and peace-loving Japan.

CHAPTER 6

ZEN GOES "BOOM"

The Popularity of Zen Buddhism, Both Beat and Square

Interest in Zen may have started among a small group at the First Zen Institute, then spread among artists, psychologists, and religious scholars, but to truly constitute a "boom," its popularity grew much wider with remarkable speed. In 1957 *Vogue* announced in its "Everybody Is Talking About" section a series of lectures delivered by Japanese scholar D. T. Suzuki on the subject of Zen. Soon thereafter, *Time* proclaimed, "Today a 'Buddhist boomlet' is under way in the U.S. Increasing numbers of intellectuals—both faddists and serious students—are becoming interested in a form of Japanese Buddhism called Zen."[1] Other mass circulation magazines like *Mademoiselle* and *Harper's Weekly* took note of the trend. These articles then created a kind of snowball effect; the more they proclaimed the phenomenon's existence, the more readers perceived that "everyone" was studying Zen and decided to do so themselves. At no point before or since did the religion inspire as much interest in the United States as it did in the short period between 1957 and 1960. It would be impossible to determine the exact number of suburbanites who took a passing interest in Zen, but contemporary sources suggest it was indeed substantial. In a 1958 *Mademoiselle* article, novelist and Zen promoter Nancy Wilson Ross described a young woman who attended a fashionable New York cocktail party where "everyone" was talking about Zen. Ruth Fuller Sasaki, the first American to be ordained as a Zen priest, similarly noted that Zen had become "the magic password at smart cocktail parties.... Radio and television comedians consider it natural for spoofing. Zen jokes appear in the daily papers, and a recent magazine contains an excellent satire on it."[2]

With such widespread popularity, it is not surprising that, as the earlier mentioned conference at Sarah Lawrence suggests, the varieties of American Zen study were numerous. In 1958 Alan Watts attempted to at least categorize these various strains into three broad types in a widely read *Chicago Review* article entitled "Beat Zen, Square Zen, and Zen." He described "Beat Zen" as the countercultural, often rebellious form of Zen practiced mostly by young poets and artists like Jack Kerouac and Allen Ginsberg who subscribed to the Beat movement. "Square Zen" was the label Watts gave to the form practiced mostly by intellectuals that placed a premium on following rules and required years of study under a master or *roshi*. But "real" Zen, he argued, followed the spirit more than the letter of this ancient Japanese religion and helped to ease people's spiritual ills regardless of nation or time period.[3] Most middlebrow Americans would come to adopt this final interpretation of Zen, treating it as an intriguing foreign philosophy that offered an alternative to the traditional Western worldview and could be applied to their everyday lives almost like a self-help ideology.

Middlebrow Americans and the Zen Boom

In 1961 poet Felicia Lamport published a humorous collection called *Scrap Irony*, containing a section entitled, "The Fifties Recollected in Tranquility," where she poked fun of such decade-defining trends as McCarthyism, the sheath dress, and the *Twenty-One* quiz show scandal. She included the following verse on the Boom:

BUDDHISM NOW AND ZEN

Conceptual dichotomy
Had primed me for lobotomy
Until I met a Buddhist fan

And man!
He really got to me

Shoot the dharma
To me mharma![4]

By decade's end, not only had *conceptual dichotomy* and *dharma* entered common parlance, but the term *Zen* itself began to appear in unexpected places.
In 1958 a *New York Times* article about the return of rambunctious children
from summer camp advised parents to "'live loose' for a week or so . . . and
to float, as followers of Zen Buddhism are said to do, 'like ping-pong balls
on the stream of life.'"[5] Actor Burgess Meredith (who would later achieve
fame as the Penguin on TV's *Batman* and crusty trainer Mickey Goldmill
in the movie *Rocky*) went on a somewhat spurious "Zen-macrobiotic diet
kick." He dined frequently at the upscale Musubi Restaurant in Manhattan,
specializing in "yin-yang cuisine." Others who were interested in this new
regimen could attend the Zen Macrobiotic camp sponsored by the diet's
founder, George Ohsawa.[6] Zen, it seemed, was everywhere.

The rising popularity of other Japanese arts and fashions throughout
the 1950s laid the groundwork for this widespread fascination with Zen in
the postwar period. Watts hypothesized that Zen's appeal was "connected,
no doubt, with the prevalent enthusiasm for Japanese culture which is one
of the constructive results of the late war."[7] By mid-decade it appeared to
be common knowledge among American Japan enthusiasts that the simplified aesthetics of ikebana, bonsai, and rock gardening were inspired by
a Zen belief in humility and serenity. The likely source of this notion was
D. T. Suzuki's best-selling *Zen and Japanese Culture*, originally published in
Japan in the 1930s and translated into English in the 1950s. Ironically, the
book had initially been written to promote a spirit of wartime nationalism
and exceptionalism among the Japanese population.[8] The author argued
that the nation's strength lay in the unique spirit of Zen inherent in all
Japanese people and expressed through their culture in both peaceful
craftsmanship and violent swordplay. Regardless of its original intent,
Americans latched on to this claim and seemed to skim over the chapters

on kendo sword fighting in favor of Suzuki's discussion of Zen quietude and restraint, which supposedly undergirded the minimalist aesthetics of all Japanese traditions. The book also encouraged readers to perceive Zen as the exclusive domain of the Japanese people, despite the fact that the religion was practiced in other parts of the world as well. In publishing a book for Zen beginners in the late 1950s, Chinese master Chen-Chi Chang felt obliged to use Japanese terms and names, since Americans would be more familiar with them than Chinese pronunciations.[9] Even today, when the word *Zen* is used regularly in commercial marketing as a recognizably "Asian" term, very few Americans are familiar with the word *ch'an*, its Chinese equivalent.[10]

Yet it is questionable how much Zen traditions actually mattered to people living in Japan in the late 1950s. In reality, Zen had about as much direct influence on bonsai and architecture as kabuki did on Kurosawa: each arose independently as products of their own times and circumstances.[11] Nor did Zen consistently conform to the staid minimalism or discipline associated with the term *shibui*. The kinkaku pavilion at the Rokuonji temple in Kyoto, for instance, is a highly ornamented structure painted in bright, beaming gold, hardly in keeping with the austerity of sho-in house.[12] A group of monks at Kobe's Shofukuji temple caused an international scandal in February 1959 when *Time* reported that they spent their time playing mah-jongg, drinking with bar hostesses, and "happily gaping at pictures of virtually naked women."[13] Outside most Americans' basic conception of Zen, in Japan both the religion and its adherents could be flashy and loud, more in keeping with what shibui Japanese culture was supposed to fight against than with its presumed essence.

In addition to the popularity of Japanese culture more generally, the Zen boom was furthered by a concurrent phenomenon in the book publishing world: the rise of the paperback reprint. Introduced in 1939, the practice of offering inexpensive editions of best-selling books grew dramatically in popularity and profitability over the following twenty years, with a peak corresponding almost exactly with the Zen boom. In 1958 over 375 million copies of paperback books were sold nationwide, a 25 percent gain over the previous year.[14] Zen served as a staple subject for paperbacks. Books like *Zen in the Art of Archery* and *Spirit of Zen* as well as translated sutras and Suzuki's numerous works became popular titles. In 1959 a drugstore in New York's Greenwich Village frequented by members of the Beat movement demolished its soda fountain to make room for a paperback rack. "Any book with the word *Zen* on it sells fast here," the proprietor reported, rattling off titles. "We've sold 'The Way of Zen,' 'Zen Buddhism,' 'Buddhism Zen,' 'The Way of Zen,' 'Zen and Japanese Culture,' 'Zen Flesh, Zen Bones.'"[15]

Evidence suggests that not only Village Beats but also "square" suburbanites purchased such titles in attempts to learn about Zen relatively easily and inexpensively, without fully devoting themselves to its practice. Religious scholar Thomas Tweed has sought to break down the dichotomy between religious "adherents" and "nonadherents," referring to those who merely dabble in Zen as "nightstand Buddhists." The name stems from the fact that many fair-weather Buddhist practitioners "place a how-to book on Buddhist meditation on the nightstand . . . read it before they fall to sleep, and then rise up the next morning to practice, however imperfectly or ambivalently, what they have learned the night before." Such Americans "have some sympathy for a religion but do not embrace it exclusively or fully. When asked, they would *not* identify themselves as Buddhists. They would say they are Methodist, or Jewish, or unaffiliated. If we could talk to them long enough—or better yet visit their homes and observe their daily routine—we would notice signs of interest in Buddhism."[16] Chen-Chi Chang observed a similar phenomenon in 1959. "Most Westerners, after reading a few books on the subject, treat it as a pastime or topic of conversation. . . . A few even practice meditation with high hopes of Enlightenment, or at least having some interesting experiences." Similarly, in his introduction to a collection of Suzuki's essays, William Barrett predicted, "For the readers of this book, the question will hardly arise of becoming a Buddhist, but that does not lessen the importance of Zen for them."[17]

Some of these Nightstand Buddhists at times would attempt more serious study along the lines of the First Zen Institute, but many quit once they found meditation too demanding or simply too strange for their tastes. In the late 1950s, it became common at the institute to see first-time attendees chatting perplexedly outside the zendo during services trying not to distract those engaged in meditation. One member reported witnessing "people walking out during the chanting just doubled up with laughter."[18] The Ryosen-an branch as well saw its share of halfhearted adherents. Philip Yampolsky, who worked as the subtemple's librarian, claimed he met a number of "Zen students of varying sincerity of purpose" and that "no one lasted very long as a student of Zen." According to Fuller Sasaki, many gave up when faced with the mental and physical strain of culture shock, not to mention long periods of zazen meditation. Others, she reported, were lured away by Kyoto's nightlife and wandered off when they got bored with hours of koan contemplation.[19]

The fact that so many potential students decided to give up on serious Zen study may be related to its esoteric belief system and demanding practice. Some articles written about the boom did indeed caution readers that Zen required a high level of commitment to understand fully. In a review of *Zen in the Art of Archery* on his radio show, Columbia University classics professor Gilbert Highet claimed that Zen contained "some values which we must all respect," but nevertheless he cautioned listeners that the authentic Asian Zen lifestyle would be too foreign for westerners to follow.[20] In his 1957 profile on Suzuki, Winthrop Sargeant warned readers that Zen "may appear puzzling in the light of Western thinking—or indeed in light of any systematic thinking whatever." Or, as the intellectually curious Israeli premier David Ben-Gurion more bluntly phrased it to the *New York Times*, "I don't know. . . . The more I read about [Zen], I can't understand what they want."[21] *Times* book reviewer J. Donald Adams found a race-based explanation for such difficulty, arguing that it largely stemmed from the fact that Asian ways of thinking were essentially impenetrable to the Caucasian mind. "Eastern thought of that kind demands a kind of contemplation that, for the most part, is beyond the reach of Western man." He went on to claim that an inherent Western propensity for action over quietude, as well as an ingrained Judeo-Christian worldview, would hinder most Americans from ever truly comprehending Zen.[22] In fact, most books on Zen began with the disclaimer that the author was about to explain in writing concepts that could not effectively be expressed in words, further mystifying the religion before they sought to demystify it for their readers.

However, in taking on the role of a sympathetic Western explorer of Eastern mysticism, Alan Watts was best able of all the renowned Zen proponents to successfully present an accessible form of Zen to a wider American audience. His version can be described as a worldview that emphasized intuitive understanding and provided the means for a person to connect to their inner emotions. He further claimed that westerners could enjoy its benefits without actually meditating on koans, an idea that gave his adapted Zen a strong appeal among a busy middlebrow American audience. Watts had attempted a traditional Zen regimen with Sokei-an for about eight months, but he found the experience left him "bored and angry," as well as resentful of the master/pupil roles. As he explained in his autobiography, "So far as I was concerned, the formal study of Zen was 'busy behavior.' To sit hour after hour and day after day with aching legs, to unravel Hakuin's tricky system of dealing with *koan*, to subsist on tea, pickles and brown rice . . . was—although good in its own way as learning to sail—not what I needed to know. What I saw in Zen was an intuitive way of understanding the sense of life by getting rid of silly quests and questions." Eventually he would write, "I do not even style myself a Zen Buddhist. For the aspect of Zen in which I am personally interested is nothing that can be organized, taught, transmitted, certified, or wrapped up in any kind of system."[23] For Watts, Zen was less a religion to be practiced than an ethos through which to approach life.

Many Americans latched on to his interpretation, believing that the strength of Zen philosophy stemmed from its stark contrast with typical suburban life and that its benefits included better job performance or a calmer and more contented outlook. Fuller Sasaki described the typical Zen seeker of her time as someone "said to . . . find in scientific materialism poor nourishment for their spirits, to feel that modern life, with its multitude of machines, is an exhausting and unrewarding way of life for them as human beings." While she did not necessarily approve of Nightstand Buddhists' actions, even she could sympathize with the desire to seek deeper spiritual meaning from a seemingly timeless Oriental source.[24]

Novelist Ray Bradbury discussed Zen's supposed professional benefits in a 1958 article in the magazine *Writer*. Initially intending to write an editorial condemning the boom's bandwagon spirit, he instead found himself reluctantly promoting Zen techniques to his readers. His title, "Zen and the Art of Writing," was a play on *Zen in the Art of Archery*. Written by German scholar Eugen Herrigel in 1948 and translated into English in 1953, the original book described its author's attempts to improve his archery skills by shooting spontaneously without thinking. Despite the fact that his teacher subscribed to an unorthodox archery school of his own design, and that almost no other Japanese archer drew much connection between their sport and Zen, the small book became one of the most popular introductions to Zen among Western readers.[25] Reading the book himself, Bradbury was surprised to discover that the advice he had always given for good writing—work hard, relax, and don't think too much— were basically the same techniques that Herrigel claimed lay at the heart of Zen. According to Bradbury, "Every wood-turner, every sculptor worth his marble, every ballerina practices what Zen preaches without having heard the word in all their lives."[26] In his opinion, what the Zen boom was essentially doing was taking universal common sense and packaging it as ancient Eastern wisdom. Disparaging yogis who "feed on kumquats, grapenuts and almonds beneath the banyan tree," Bradbury believed this fundamental philosophy would improve the work of any artist or creative professional, no matter how it was presented.

More commonly than seeking career advice, Americans were attracted to Zen in hopes of improving their personal well-being. William Barrett promised readers of Suzuki's essays that despite its Oriental origins, Zen's approach to the world was suited to the complex environment of the "modern age," adding that "the very premises of Buddhist thinking ... look much closer to what we moderns have to swallow" than Christian ideas.[27] In his essay "This Is IT," Watts argued that increasingly higher levels of technological "intelligence" were causing Americans anxiety by forcing them into ever-stricter mechanisms of self-control. He then claimed that Zen, in contrast, "provides a uniquely simple and classic way of recognizing and dissolving" such psychological malaise. Echoing earlier praise of Japanese culture in other forms, he added that Asian philosophies "offer release from conflict and anxiety. Their goal is a state of inner feeling in which oppositions have become mutually co-operative instead of mutually exclusive, in which there is no longer any conflict between the individual man and nature, or between intelligence and instinct."[28] Even loftier promises were made in the koan compilation *Zen Flesh, Zen Bones*, edited by Paul Reps in 1957: "It has been said that if you have Zen in your life you have no fear, no doubt, no unnecessary craving, no extreme emotion. Neither illiberal attitudes nor egotistical actions trouble you. You serve humanity humbly, fulfilling your presence in this world with loving-kindness and observing your passing as a petal falling from a flower. Serene, you enjoy life in blissful tranquility." While Reps's promotion of Zen ideas was certainly the most poetic, all three authors start from the premise that postwar America had become too stressful for its inhabitants. Western approaches to their problems were falling short, and solutions were more likely to be found in foreign philosophy with a contrasting worldview.[29]

Articles in the popular press made similar claims about Zen. Reporting on a visit with Fuller Sasaki at Ryosen-an in *Harper's Weekly*, Ruth Stephan wrote, "The Zen void, to me, seems like a bottomless garbage pail into which the unnecessary and the troublesome is dumped; what is left may be the mind's living picture of the universe, unlittered." Nancy Wilson Ross was more verbose in *Mademoiselle*. She characterized the postwar era as a time ridden with psychological peril, referring to "the modern world, ruled by conflicting theories, with global problems and personal problems forever presenting themselves for solution." But she then posited that "the individual" is still struggling "with the very same basic questions ... that [Buddhism's founder] Siddartha [*sic*] Gautama faced in the sixth century BC." She concluded that Zen appealed to "people tired of the increasing clutter and gadgetry of life" and claimed, "Something has gotten badly out of balance: the 'flow of life' has been stopped. The emphasis on fulfilling the appetite for 'things' is at an all-time high. Zen invites one to another range of experience." While Zen appeared universalistic in tackling timeless challenges, its ancient Oriental nature nevertheless enabled it to serve as an antimodern antidote not only to materialism but also to moral uncertainty, pressures toward conformity, and any other ills that plagued 1950s Americans.[30]

By the summer of 1959, so many fashionable Americans had come to try their hand at Zen that the *New Yorker* ran a fictional article parodying the phenomenon. In "Zen in the Art of Tennis," Calvin Tomkins caricatured the worst examples of middle-class pretensions to understanding Zen. He wrote of "cocktail-party guests" who "ask each other Zen *koans*" and complained that it was then impossible to "spend a whole evening talking to an old friend without having to hear about his *satori*, or having to argue the relative merits of beatnik Zen, square Zen, and ladies' Zen." Following a conversation with a fellow country club member who has his own personal roshi, the unnamed protagonist decides Zen could help his slumping tennis game as it did Herrigel's archery skills. While searching the yellow pages for tennis instructors, he finds a misplaced ad for a pet shop with the Japanese name Ashikawa. Not surprisingly, when he arrives at the store with his tennis racket asking for a lesson, a befuddled and disgruntled Ashikawa slams the door in his face. Interpreting this reaction as the typical rebuff of a Zen master requiring his student to prove his devotion before entering the monastery, he persists, and Ashikawa eventually agrees to take him on as a pupil, teaching him the duties of running a pet shop. When the narrator brings a tennis racket one day, Ashikawa asks him, "What have you got there?" which he decides must be his koan. The story goes on, with every one of the pet store owner's perplexed reactions misinterpreted as the behavior of an enigmatic sage. Ashikawa eventually puts an end to the foolishness by calling a policeman to stop this strange man from harassing him. By the story's end, the narrator seems no more enlightened for his troubles, and in fact his tennis game has gotten worse.[31]

Appearing at the height of the boom, the story suggests that the Zen dilettante had become a recognizable figure among the upper middle class, and it exposes many white Americans' presumption that Japanese Americans were racially endowed with useful Oriental wisdom. The narrator's claim to have read fifteen or sixteen books by D. T. Suzuki might be absurd, but in real life many New Yorkers had indeed picked up at least one or two and probably did fancy themselves experts on Zen after reading those paperbacks. Delivering a speech at MIT in 1958, Fuller Sasaki described a particular type of visitor to her institute who, "without having read a single primary Buddhist or Zen text, think they know all about it. How many hours have I not spent in my Kyoto temple listening to people, usually Americans recently come to Japan, tell me what Zen is!"[32] Other authors concurred. In "Seymour," J. D. Salinger wrote, "Zen is rapidly becoming a rather smutty, cultish word to the discriminating ear.... Pure Zen ... will be here even after the snobs have departed." Both, as well as Tomkins, feared that too many Americans were attracted to Zen, not primarily to attain spiritual enlightenment or personal understanding, but for its association with sophisticated urban tastes.[33] It is hard to discern to what extent such accusations would have been true, but as the media trumpeted the personal benefits of an established religion as if it were popular psychology, many Americans came to see Zen as a possible solution to their everyday troubles. But upon finding that the same foreign elements that gave it cachet in the first place also made it seem demanding and difficult to understand, their commitments tailed off and their interest waned. In such cases, upper-middle-class Americans' search for Zen knowledge may have indeed been as much a status symbol as a sincere spiritual quest.

Beat Zen: Eastern Religion Gains a Defiant Edge

Not long after it was declared, like most fads the Zen boom went bust. When snippets of Zen philosophy failed to deliver quickly on their promises of personal fulfillment, many Nightstand Buddhists became disillusioned and decided to move on. Another factor in the decline was the emergence of Beat Zen, yet another form practiced by Jack Kerouac and the rest of the Beats. They too placed Zen's origins in an unknowable Oriental past, but differed from more shibui interpretations by emphasizing Zen's spontaneity and strenuousness above its sense of quiet repose. Beat Zen was decidedly virile and masculine, like most of its practitioners, and seemed to encourage loud and rowdy behavior over dignified meditation and communing with nature. As this interpretation rose to prominence, it began to taint the more general conception of Zen in the minds of respectable American elites. Once tarnished, Zen lost a considerable number of middle-class enthusiasts, now afraid of being labeled "bohemian."

Many Americans who studied Zen were indeed fairly affluent, especially those who practiced the religion devotedly. Ruth Fuller Sasaki was born into one of Chicago's wealthiest families, and she continued to project that status even after she became a Zen priest. Gary Snyder described her as frequently wearing expensive cashmere sweaters, adding that "her hair and grooming were perfect, finished with pearl earrings." Many of her friends appeared to come from a similar economic background, some stopping by the First Zen Institute in Kyoto in the course of world tours. On some level, Fuller Sasaki felt compelled to justify her socioeconomic position in light of Suzuki's claim that Zen practice required appreciation of the simple life through poverty. In the margins of *Zen and Japanese Culture*, she defensively countered, "Poverty is no different from riches. It is no-ego egolessness that is the *true* poverty." In her mind, spiritual outlook mattered more than actual economic standing, and she was thus able to reconcile Zen's insistence on self-denial with her comfortable lifestyle.[34]

The Beats took the opposite position. Living in voluntary poverty, they were fundamentally attracted to Zen for its antimaterialist humility. Beats studied the same Zen religion as middle- and upper-class Americans, but formulated a much different interpretation. Instead of promoting quietude, intellectual contemplation, and self-restraint, they used its tenets to criticize what they perceived as the hypocrisy of middle-class material comforts, as well as to tap into their often exuberant and seemingly chaotic artistic impulses.[35] In the early 1950s the Beats emerged as a group of mostly young white male rebellious artists, living in the low rent districts of New York's Greenwich Village, San Francisco's North Beach, and Los Angeles's Venice Beach. Often credited as the forerunners of the 1960s counterculture, they rejected the established American social order, which in their opinion had become complacent, repressed, and divorced from real experience. Their main targets included industrialism, consumerism, militarism, and above all, social convention. Modern society, they argued, was overly restrictive, forcing people to suppress their instincts, emotions, and creative impulses to fit into a bland middle-class society. This desire to conform, they further believed, led bourgeois Americans to become materialistic in an effort to maintain their social status, a practice that led to mindless consumption. Zen philosophy, in contrast, denounced materialism and encouraged spontaneity.

To escape the strictures and general banality of American society, the Beats chose to engage in what they proclaimed to be more authentic and freer ways of living. Rejecting consumerism, they moved into neighborhoods that prior to their arrival had been considered ghettos, and lived in apartments with little furnishing or decoration. Some occasionally tried to escape urban society by retreating to the mountains or the desert with a backpack, riding the rails, or hitchhiking, all of which were romanticized in Jack Kerouac's quintessential 1957 Beat novel, *On the Road*. As an outlet for their creative impulses, many wrote poetry or painted, and some had a reputation for tapping into their emotions by drinking heavily or smoking marijuana. They rejected fashion trends by wearing dark, casual, often secondhand clothing. To liberate their libidos, they eschewed monogamy and celebrated casual sex. They also appreciated jazz music for its free and impulsive improvisational style. Their penchant for both jazz and marijuana (which at the time was associated with black culture), as well as the slang they adopted, were part of a larger effort among the Beats to identify with African Americans. Seeing themselves as similarly outcast, and willfully ignoring their option to rejoin white middle-class society whenever they saw fit, Beats intentionally painted themselves as a new minority and another Other.[36]

Many mainstream journalists appeared more than willing to help further such a reputation, portraying the Beats as dirty, promiscuous, shiftless, drug-addicted, self-indulgent, misguided youth. Articles would employ the derogatory term *beatniks*, assuming a core of true artistic "Beats" and a larger contingent of followers. In the *Partisan Review*, literary and cultural critic

Norman Podhoretz categorized them as anti-intellectual and solipsistic. John Ciardi of the *Saturday Review* called them "juvenile," the *Chicago Tribune* found them "phony," and novelist Nelson Algren portrayed them as self-absorbed and deluded.[37] But there were some writers and commentators who assessed the Beat movement as a serious literary and social phenomenon. The *New York Times* review for *On the Road* defended the movement's "excesses" as serving "a spiritual purpose. . . . It does not know what refuge it is seeking, but it is seeking." In his best-known work, *Growing Up Absurd*, social critic Paul Goodman denigrated the Beats' artistic output and mimicry of "Negro culture," but found their search for authenticity to be a natural response to the imposed corporatism of postwar American society. The Catholic magazines *America* and *Commonweal*, which might have been expected to bristle at the Beats' hedonistic lifestyle, instead offered impartial in-depth analyses of their roles as authors and movement leaders, with the *Commonweal* comparing the Beats to the biblical figure of "the naughty psalm-singing David."[38]

Paralleling the ambivalence of the mainstream press, many middle-class Americans responded to the movement with a combination of revulsion and attraction, fueled by a curiosity about the Beats' squalid lifestyle, unusual dress, and "hip" lingo. Regular beatnik characters appeared in the radio soap opera *Helen Trent*, the TV comedy *The Many Loves of Dobie Gillis*, and the comic strip *Popeye*. Coffee shops in cities throughout the country began branding themselves as "authentic beatnik hangouts," whether or not they attracted any real Beats. San Francisco's North Beach erected a sign declaring itself "Gateway to Beatnikland," and sponsored a best beard contest as part of a summer festival in 1959. Abraham & Straus, a New York variety store, used images of beatniks in several print ads and had its cartoon spokesmen utter such Beat sounding phrases as "Man, you've been shopping Squaresville" and "A&S is the most." Another New York department store began selling "beatnik kits" that included a beard, dark glasses, and a beret, so any American could instantly (yet temporarily) transform themselves into a Beat.[39]

At the center of this swirl of criticizing, gawking, and co-optation lay the group's pioneers and most prominent authors, Jack Kerouac and Allen Ginsburg, assumed by many both inside and outside the movement to embody the Beats' true nature and goals. Both became interested in Zen in the early 1950s; in their effort to identify with outsiders and minorities, they felt an attraction to philosophies and art forms considered foreign and unusual. Initially, Kerouac had read Henry David Thoreau's *Walden*, which makes multiple references to Indian Buddhist texts, and he was inspired to learn more about Eastern thought. He purchased a translation of *The Life of Buddha* and later discovered Dwight Goddard's *A Buddhist Bible*.[40] While neither book promoted the Zen sect in particular, both were written in the typical vein of early twentieth-century interpretations of Zen, emphasizing modernist concepts of a disordered universe and the value of direct experience over intellectual positivism. For his part, Ginsberg was enthusiastically studying Chinese painting, and he understood Buddhism to be its underlying spiritual influence. He wrote to his friend and fellow Beat, Neal Cassady, that he was on "a very beautiful kick which I invite you to share.... [I have] begun to familiarize myself with Zen Buddhism thru a book ... by one D. T. Suzuki (outstanding 89 yr. old authority now at columbia [*sic*] who I will I suppose go see for interesting talk)."[41] He went on to express his enthusiasm for the concept of the koan and how enamored he was of a religion that seemingly eschewed rationality and valued spontaneity, much as he did in his own poetry.[42]

Most aspiring Beats—as well as those interested in their lifestyle—in turn learned about Zen through Kerouac's popular novel *The Dharma Bums*, published in the midst of the boom in 1958. It tells the story of Ray Smith, a barely disguised version of the author, and his friendship with Japhy Ryder, a thinly veiled characterization of Gary Snyder. (At one point in the text, Kerouac slips and refers to his character as "Gary.")[43] Kerouac composed the book employing the same spontaneous style he famously used for *On the Road*, typing continuously on a roll of teletype paper without stopping to insert paragraph breaks or punctuation.[44] Its narrative is thus rather rambling and anecdotal, sprinkled throughout with bits and pieces of Ray/Kerouac's Asian-influenced personal philosophy. Ray and his friends live in San Francisco, making a meager living as poets and artists, and occasionally venture into the wilderness in search of spiritual enlightenment. Together they drink heavily, recite poetry, and debate philosophy with one another. On his own, Ray reads sutras and spends weeks at his family home in North Carolina meditating under a tree in imitation of the Buddha. The novel ends soon after he takes a job as a fire spotter in Oregon and finally experiences something like satori, realizing his inherent unity with God and nature, but without the use of formal koan meditation. Overall, the book portrays a discursive quest for spiritual answers by one young white American artist who borrows heavily from Buddhist thought and practice.

In formulating this spiritual outlook, Kerouac tended to incorporate only those elements from Zen belief that he found most appealing, discarding those that he viewed as overly disciplinarian or repressive.[45] As journalist Lawrence Lipton phrased it, "The Zen elements stick out in the novel like so many undigested lumps."[46] At one point, Ray denies that he is a follower of Zen, instead claiming allegiance to other forms of Buddhism as "an old-fashioned dreamy Hinayana coward of later Mahayanism."[47] He goes on to call koan training "mean" and denounces "all those Zen Masters throwing young kids in the mud because they can't answer their silly word questions."[48] He also incorporates practices from other sects, including the Tibetan practice of "yabyum," which essentially involves attaining higher spiritual consciousness through sexual congress.[49] At one point, Ray even puts forth a theory that Jesus Christ was a later incarnation of the Buddha, bringing in elements from his Catholic upbringing.[50] Kerouac was hardly concerned about practicing Zen in any authentic, strictly Japanese form. Even as he cast himself as a member of a maligned minority, he remained a privileged white American narrator with the ability to pick and choose from a seeming Oriental smorgasbord of religious practices in creating his own spiritual amalgam.

There is some question as to whether Gary Snyder, the inspiration for Ray's spiritual guide Japhy, would have approved of this conglomerating process. As a member of the First Zen Institute and close colleague of Fuller Sasaki, he embraced her strict and demanding interpretation of the religion, once writing to her that "the 'essential meaning' of Zen cannot be made available to westerners in a durable form, without some of the supporting lumber of tradition, including Zendos and Masters." Alan Watts had referred to Snyder as more "serious" than Kerouac and added, "Indeed it would be difficult to fit Snyder into any stereotype of the Bohemian underworld." Showing sincere dedication to his Zen study, Snyder learned Japanese and studied T'ang poetry in the original Chinese at the University of California, Berkeley. He went on to translate the works of poet Han Shan before heading to Ryosen-an. In the early 1950s, he wrote to Mary Farkas from Kyoto, criticizing American religious movements that sought to combine various Asian beliefs. "I have an understandable fear of [Zen] being cheapened and misinterpreted by westerners, in the manner that much Buddhist and Hindu thought has been stained by the appalling sloppiness of the Theosophists and other even less mentionable groups." Later asked to write an article on Beat Zen for the leftist magazine *Liberation* in 1959, he argued that true Zen should involve not only spiritual searching and a "respect for abandon," but also respect for "discipline" and "tradition," sounding more like Fuller Sasaki than Kerouac.[51]

Nevertheless, Snyder described the character of Japhy Rider as "a fair portrait" of himself at the time.[52] Mirroring real life, Japhy meets Ray at a Beat poetry reading, closely based on the "Six Poets at the Six Gallery" event, where Ginsberg delivered his famous debut performance of the poem "Howl." Like Snyder, Japhy lived in a small cottage filled with Oriental objects where he translated Chinese poetry, and toward the end of the novel, Japhy leaves San Francisco to study Zen in Japan. It is clear throughout the story that he has a far deeper dedication to Zen than Ray does, but in some cases, perhaps reflecting Kerouac's beliefs more than Snyder's own, Japhy does advocate a form of Beat Zen. During one conversation with Ray, he accuses his unnamed sponsor in Japan (not unlike Fuller Sasaki) of having "little sense of America and who the people are who really dig Buddhism here."[53]

Indeed, many Beats did "dig" Zen, according to academic studies conducted at the time. Psychologist Francis Rigney noted that while most Beats came from a Christian or Jewish background, many professed, like Ray, to follow a new religion of their own invention heavily influenced by Zen. Lawrence Lipton, acting as "the Boswell of the Beatniks" in his study *The Holy Barbarians*, tried to explain its appeal. Like other American Zen adherents, most Beats believed Zen offered an antidote to postwar materialism that created "the rat race of ten thousand things."[54] In *The Dharma Bums*, Japhy poetically elaborates on this idea, declaring a utopian vision of "a world full of rucksack wanderers, Dharma Bums refusing to subscribe to the general demand that they consume production and therefore have to work for the privilege of consuming all that crap they didn't really want anyway such as refrigerators, TV sets, cars, at least new fancy cars, certain hair oils and deodorants and general junk you always see a week later in the garbage anyway, all of them imprisoned in a world of work, produce, consume, work, produce, consume."[55] Here too, as for Watts and Fromm, Zen provided a foreign alternative outlook that emphasized the impermanence of material goods to combat the rampant consumerism gripping the majority of the nation. Such an interpretation appealed to Beats especially, disapproving as they were of material acquisition and social striving.

However, Beat Zen differed from other forms in its emphasis on Zen's embrace of spontaneity. While Goodman doubted that white twentieth-century youth were equipped to comprehend a religion born of a "feudal" Asian society, he nevertheless felt that Zen filled an important need for "these young men. . . . It is a theology and style of immediate experience," in contrast to the stifling corporate world of their parents.[56] Lipton noted that Beats discovered the same type of antirationality in Zen that they did in jazz, poetry, and Kerouac's writing style. Noticing that many koans offer seemingly nonsensical answers to simple questions, Beats came to believe that Zen's true essence lay in surrealistic free-form thinking. Japhy explains as he continues his speech, "I see a vision of a great rucksack revolution thousands or even millions of young Americans wandering around with rucksacks, going up to mountains to pray, making children laugh and old men glad, making young girls happy and old girls happier, all of 'em Zen Lunatics who go about writing poems that happen to appear in their heads for no reason and also by being kind and also by strange unexpected acts keep giving visions of eternal freedom to everybody and to all living creatures."[57] This sense of spontaneity could help justify the common Beat practice of trying to shock "Squares" out of their complacency. While attending a Chicago cocktail party held in their honor, Ginsberg, his partner Peter Orlovsky, and fellow poet Gregory Corso responded to a *Time* reporter's questions as if they were koans, with answers like "fried shoes," "Don't shoot the warthog," and "my mystical shears snip snip snip."[58] While "square Zen" might have emphasized quietude, their version primarily encouraged the freedom to think, say, and do whatever an individual felt from one moment to the next.

Despite Kerouac's tendency to mix various forms of Buddhism into his spiritual outlook, the Beats gained a reputation—likely with help from Watts's "Beat Zen, Square Zen" article—for practicing Zen specifically. In its review of *On the Road*, the *New York Times* listed the most prominent habits of the Beats as "drink, drugs, sexual promiscuity, driving at high speeds [and] absorbing Zen Buddhism." In 1959 novelist Franc Smith published *Harry Vernon at Prep*, which featured a self-absorbed antihero who tries his hand at the Beat lifestyle by characteristically transforming himself into an angry young writer/Zen scholar. That same year, *Time*'s review of Kerouac's film *Pull My Daisy* was punningly titled "Zen Hur." By the end of the decade, a mere mention of the word *Zen* was enough to serve as shorthand for Beat sensibilities.[59]

In keeping with their usual combination of fascination and disdain, many journalists proved critical of Beat Zen. Two *New York Times* reviews of *The Dharma Bums* found fault with the inconsistency of its characters, one criticizing "their immersion, after brief flights into the Buddhist stratosphere, in the world of pure sensation, or—to put it more explicitly—in the world of drugs, drunkenness, and aimless wandering, spiked by frequent orgies of sex in the raw." Novelist Herbert Gold characterized Kerouac's spiritual amalgam as "promiscuity in religion," and declared with wry and racist humor that "Zen Buddhism has spread like the Asian flu" in Beat communities. John Ciardi echoed such criticism: "They have raided from Zen whatever offered them an easy rationale for what they wanted to do in the first place." Making such remarks, these critics seemed to disregard the fact that most "square" Zen enthusiasts were doing the same in borrowing from Zen to suit their own ends. But dissention even arose from among the Beats' own ranks, as Beat elder statesman William Burroughs wrote to Kerouac: "I have seen nothing from those California Vedantists [i.e., Beat Buddhists] but a lot of horse shit, and I denounce them without cavil as a pack of frauds. In short [they are] a bunch of psychic retreaters from the dubious human journey." Worse than dilettantism, Burroughs accused Zen followers of losing sight of the movement's real artistic goals.[60]

Nor did many other American Zen promoters condone the Beats' interpretation. Unsurprisingly, Ruth Fuller Sasaki disapproved of Kerouac's "garbled and mistaken" Buddhism, characterizing the Beat movement as nothing more than the latest incarnation of pig-headed youthful rebellion. She wrote to Snyder, "The present day 'Dharma bums' are just the same type of boys that appear in every generation, each time with a new name and new line, but intrinsically the same 'bums.'" Thomas Merton also referenced the Beats in a 1959 letter to D. T. Suzuki: "America is now full of people who think Zen is mere yielding to irrational impulses, and who do not know the difference between satori and being dead drunk."[61] Although Watts would later reconcile with the Beats in his 1972 autobiography, in a 1959 radio broadcast he denounced the Beat movement on no uncertain terms. Admitting the existence of some "original Beats" who chose to forgo a status-seeking life in favor of doing what they loved, he criticized "beatnik hangers-on," whom he described as "just pretenders. They have the beards, the blue jeans, the jazz records, the marijuana. But they don't do anything. They just play at being Beats. They lie around all the time and are completely unproductive. They are weak people, parasites, exploiting a new cult."[62] In turn, Kerouac unfavorably caricatured Watts as the spiritually shallow Zen huckster Arthur Whane in *The Dharma Bums*, and Snyder declared in the *Liberator* that only squares write books about "Buddhism and Happiness for the masses."[63]

Watts offered his best-developed criticism of Beat Zen in "Beat Zen, Square Zen, and Zen." He characterized it as "hostile," writing that it "clangs with self-defense," then adding, "But just because Zen truly surpasses convention and its values, it has no need to say 'To hell with it,' nor to underline with violence the fact that anything goes." He took issue with a philosophy based in serenity being misused as a weapon in the arsenal of social rebellion. He further accused the Beats of employing Zen as "a pretext to license." It was true, he argued, that Zen did allow for moral relativism, as well as encourage uninhibited thought and spontaneous action, but Watts feared that in this case it was serving as "a simple rationalization," abusing the credibility of an ancient religion to justify the Beats' hedonistic lifestyle. Instead, he insisted, Zen's antirationalism was a means to the end of expanding individual consciousness, not an end in itself to be employed to shock conformists.[64]

D. T. Suzuki would eventually criticize the Beats along similar lines. At first, however, he did try to reach out to them, inviting Kerouac to his home. When Kerouac arrived, accompanied by Ginsberg and Orlovsky, Suzuki welcomed them, served them tea, and showed them his collection of Chinese paintings. However, Kerouac felt compelled to barrage Suzuki with koans, a behavior that Suzuki did not seem to appreciate. As they were leaving, Kerouac told him, perhaps facetiously, "Dr. Suzuki, I'd like to spend the rest of my life with you," to which Suzuki replied, "Sometime," as he showed them the door.[65] After this confused encounter, Suzuki made clear his disapproval of Beat Zen in the fall 1958 issue of the *Japan Quarterly*. He argued that the Beats were using Zen to justify their own immature rebellion without taking the time to fully understand it. He claimed that Beat writing contained "enough of childishness but not much of childlikeness. Spontaneity is not everything; it must be 'rooted.' These men ... must grow up as human beings to become conscious of the true roots of being and walk with human dignity." He went on to describe the sense of balance and serene inner composure that practitioners had to develop before they could follow Zen with any measure of integrity.[66]

Along with Suzuki and white American Zen experts, the Beats also engaged in debate with Japanese American Buddhists. Snyder convinced Kerouac and several other Beat poets to attend study sessions hosted by the Buddhist Churches of America (BCA) in San Francisco. However, it soon became apparent that the Beats did not have much interest in practicing Buddhism according to the strictures of organized religious doctrine. One local BCA member, a white high school religion teacher, did defend the Beats in the organization's English-language newsletter, claiming they absorbed Buddhist principles, even if they didn't practice them like most Japanese Americans. He even argued that Beats were perhaps more attuned to Buddhist doctrine than Japanese American Buddhists, knowing more about "oneness, emptiness, wisdom and compassion" than some of those born into the religion who might take these values for granted. In a later issue, one such Nisei Buddhist strongly countered his position, asserting that the Beats were fleeing Christianity to an alternative religion in search of easy answers. Doubting they had any sincere commitment to understand Buddhism as he and his family practiced it, he called Beat Zen "a nebulous concoction composed of one part Zen, one part anti-Christianity (!) and one part metaphysical gymnastics."[67] He accused the Beats of behaving like many white Orientalist interpreters of Asian culture who came before them. Despite their embrace of an outsider identity, as well as their professed sympathy with racial minorities, they nevertheless took a privileged position in utilizing Zen and other various Buddhist practices. Granting themselves authority of interpretation, they created a new philosophy to suit their own tastes by picking and choosing as they liked, rather than attempting to sincerely comprehend the viewpoint of those who lived the culture and religion as a regular part of their lives.

It seems that Watts was indeed correct in singling out the Beat interpretation of Zen as separate from other American versions circulating in the 1950s. Many white Zen enthusiasts were fairly comfortable and middle class, and they used their appreciation of Zen as a means to advance themselves socially. Meanwhile the Beats were a group of rebels who adhered to a low-rent, confrontational aesthetic and eschewed all forms of material-ism and status seeking. Whereas "Square Zen" adherents emphasized the religion's sense of reflective serenity and self-discipline, Beats would likely label such characteristics as effete or repressive. Instead they focused on elements of Zen that appeared more aggressive or liberating, turning it into an active masculine, as opposed to a subdued feminine, philosophy. In fact, rising awareness of Beat Zen brought a swifter end to the Zen boom among the middle class, making respectable suburbanites fear an interest in Zen might link them to a group of debauched artists.

Nevertheless, there remained a significant fundamental similarity among all American versions of Zen: they treated it as an esoteric, distinctly foreign, ancient Oriental way of thinking. As such, it formed a lens through which white Americans from various backgrounds could view the far away nation of Japan. Beat Zen might not have fit the State Department's image of a sub-dued compliant Japan as much as the Zen practice of more established artists and intellectuals, but the popularized version most middle-class Americans adopted did follow the Square Zen pattern of emphasizing the quietude behind the philosophy. Furthermore, all of these many interpretations, as varied as they might have been in their primary audience and underlying motives, reflected at least the fundamental power relationship between Japan and the United States at the time. Once again Japan and its culture appeared admirable in keeping with the recently reestablished alliance, but in its seeming strangeness and perpetual antiquity, it appeared out of synch with the twentieth century. For all of those Americans who engaged in the Zen boom, Japanese culture needed help from westerners to adapt, reinterpret, and update it to give Zen the power to appear relevant in this modern world.

CHAPTER 7

JAPAN FOR THE REST OF US

Non-Shibui Japanese Imports in the Postwar Era

Over the course of the two decades following World War II, the shibui understanding of Japan had become the dominant mode among circles of intellectuals, established artists, and well-traveled cultural experts, as well as cosmopolitan urbanite and fashionable suburbanite consumers. Many Americans came to view Japan as a timeless foreign land of rich traditions that promoted reflection, serenity, and a form of simplicity that shared much in common with modernist aesthetics. Japanese art, design, and philosophy were sophisticated, refined, and subtly tasteful, as were (it was assumed) those who appreciated them. To create this image, however, American tastemakers had to be selective in the types of Japanese culture they imported, a limitation that often forced them to focus on traditions that were becoming increasingly irrelevant in Japan. Few Japanese people continued to live in sho-in houses, bonsai was an old man's hobby, and Zen temples were struggling to preserve their shrinking congregations. The film *Rashomon* did not see significant box office returns in Japan until it won praise in Europe and the United States. Paradoxically, at the same time that American viewers watched the movie to better understand Japanese culture, Japanese audiences used it to learn more about Western tastes.

FIG. 13. Still from *Godzilla*, 1954. Directed by Ishiro Honda, produced by Toho Studios.

But even as the shibui version of Japanese culture gained widespread influence, it did not necessarily find fertile ground with all American consumers. Working-class people and young Americans in particular formed their own conceptions of Japan based on different forms of commercial culture. For instance, humorist Dave Barry recalled the impression he gained of Japan as a youngster in the early 1960s as that of "a weird foreign country that was for some reason under almost constant attack by giant mutated creatures. Godzilla was the most famous one, of course, but there were also hyperthyroid pterodactyls, spiders, etc., all of which regularly barged into Tokyo and committed acts of mass destruction."[1] Indeed, many Americans outside of the demographic of upwardly mobile middle-class adults were more likely to be exposed to Godzilla and other giant movie monsters than they were to see Japanese architecture or bonsai, creating an impression in their mind that differed significantly from the ancient land of cherry blossoms.

Other types of Japanese imports that did not quite conform to the shibui image were also able to slip through the filter enforced by editors, museum directors, and critics. More widespread in American stores than furnishings meant to evoke traditional Japanese aesthetics were commercial products made in Japan that resembled U.S.-produced goods, but were often lower quality and less expensive. Instead of examples of painstaking craftsmanship, they reflected an image of an industrialized Japan whose businessmen were every bit as profit-minded and materialistic as Americans. Both Japanese monster movies and Made-in-Japan merchandise challenged the dominant image of sedate, antimodern Japan by offering glimpses of a nation caught up in the loud and tacky version of modernity that the shibui trend sought to oppose. However, in the end these kinds of imports did little to besmirch the reputation of a "tasteful" Japan, in part because they were frequently enjoyed by lower-class people with less cultural influence, but more directly because their country of origin was often confused or hidden, at times intentionally so.

Made in Japan: A Label of Cheap Taste

The first major challenge to the shibui portrayal of Japan as a land that valued taste and quality was the arrival on American shores of inexpensive manufactured goods. Yet in the end, it was largely diffused by the fact that few upper middlebrow enthusiasts of the shibui aesthetic paid much attention to such low-end merchandise. Moreover, despite another kind of threat these goods posed by competing with and underselling U.S. manufacturers, many Americans viewed the purchase of "Made in Japan" goods as furthering foreign policy interests and aiding the welfare of a struggling Cold War ally.

Throughout the 1950s, imported Japanese products were a common sight on American five-and-dime store shelves, as the U.S. market absorbed an average of 21.7 percent of Japan's total exports every year.[2] Official U.S. policy, as outlined in the State Department's National Security Council document 13/2 of 1948, was to rehabilitate Japan economically, in order to strengthen the nation in the fight against communism. SCAP, and later State Department leaders, knew that Japanese manufacturers needed to sell goods abroad to survive, but were wary about allowing them to take advantage of the lucrative Chinese market after it became the communist People's Republic in 1949. Southeast Asia was a better option ideologically, but its inhabitants had little money to spend. This left policymakers with little choice but to open Western markets to Japanese exports, which they did by helping Japan become a signatory to the General Agreement on Tariffs and Trade (GATT) in 1954. However, most Western European nations, especially Great Britain, feared underselling and enacted quotas against Japanese goods. The United States was the only option left, and as a consequence Americans became Japan's biggest overseas customers.[3] President Eisenhower succinctly explained the situation to the National Editorial Association in 1954: "It becomes absolutely mandatory to us, and to our safety, that the Japanese nation does not fall under the domination of the Iron Curtain countries," otherwise, "the Pacific would become a Communist lake." But "Japan cannot remain in the free world unless something is done to allow her to make a living. Now . . . if we will not trade with her . . . what is to happen to Japan?"[4] The editors present at that meeting went on to make that message clear to their readership: buying Japanese products was an issue of national security.

Prior to World War II, Japanese exports to the United States consisted mostly of low-cost, fairly disposable items. The insignificant nature of such products reinforced most Americans' understanding of the country as diminutive and inferior. In 1947 trade between the two nations initially resumed in much the same vein. At a party in Tokyo during the occupation, Secretary of State John Foster Dulles, holding a drink in his hand, suggested to a finance ministry official that Japan rebuild its postwar economy by exporting cocktail napkins. Akio Morita, one of the founders of Sony, admitted in his memoirs that he was at first reluctant to sell his electronics in the United States because "most people . . . associated Japan with paper umbrellas . . . toys, and cheap trinkets."[5] Japan's earliest postwar exports were indeed mostly small discount store items and bore the label "Made in

Occupied Japan" to reassure patriotic American consumers they were not supporting the wartime regime. Such goods included ceramics (figurines, plates, tea sets, lamp bases, mugs, planters, salt and pepper shakers), toys (plastic dolls, wind-up toys), paper goods (umbrellas, fans, flowers), glassware (wine glasses, perfume bottles), metalware (ashtrays, serving dishes, salt cellars), and Christmas tree ornaments. Few of these products looked "Japanese" per se; more commonly they were less expensive versions of merchandise already manufactured elsewhere. Japanese factories produced ceramic figurines dressed like eighteenth-century European nobility, teapots with Chinese decorative motifs, and American-style plastic Kewpie dolls.[6]

The situation changed significantly during the Korean War. Sales of military procurements to United Nations forces provided Japan with an economic windfall that allowed its economy to recover and expand in earnest, precipitating what would later be known as Japan's "economic miracle." The war brought such a dramatic change that Prime Minister Shigeru Yoshida referred to it as "a gift from the gods." On behalf of the UN, the United States purchased goods such as clothing, shoes, small machinery, building materials, and light weaponry, as well as services such as vehicle and aircraft repair, totaling an estimated $2.3 billion.[7] As a result, Japan experienced a sudden influx of U.S. currency. Employment soared, and industrial production grew higher than it had ever been. In 1954 a newly elected government decided that the Ministry of International Trade and Industry should shift its attention to the production of consumer electronics and established JETRO to investigate foreign markets and promote Japanese goods overseas, providing stimulus to what would quickly become Japan's most lucrative industries.[8] By 1960, not only had manufacturing revived, but so too had the Japanese stock market, education system, agriculture sector, and health care standards. Japan's middle-class consumer society sparked back to life and expanded to include a larger percentage of the population than it ever had before. In the span of ten years, Japan's economy had expanded to compete with any prosperous Western nation.[9]

In the early stages of this transformation, manufactures first began to branch out into a wider variety and higher quality of household goods, including dinner sets, glassware, and silverware, as well as textiles, with dress shirts proving especially common.[10] But in doing so, they often continued the practice of offering less expensive versions of merchandise produced in the United States and Europe. By the end of the decade, American consumers began to complain about the prevalence of lower-cost Japanese products, worrying about unfair competition, and in some cases reinvoking racist images of duplicitous Asians. In 1960 an editorial letter to the *Chicago Tribune*, signed "Grandma," reported with concern that the writer had just received "stainless steel knives, forks, and spoons, and a stainless steel chafing dish—all made in Japan" as Christmas presents. The previous holiday season, "Mrs. EJK" related the shock she experienced in the moment when she discovered that nearly all the gloves and scarves she had purchased as gifts bore a "Made in Japan" label. "I love Japan," she concluded, "but this is ridiculous."[11] Some Americans began to fear these goods would undersell and unfairly compete with domestic manufacturers. The most notorious example was a "one dollar blouse" that prompted headlines in *Newsweek* warning of a "deluge" of Japanese textiles and a "flood from the East," evoking memories of the racist fears of a "Yellow Peril" wave of immigrants in the early twentieth century. In 1958 one umbrella manufacturer more explicitly revived recent wartime hatred in proclaiming, "We feel we are again being attacked, Pearl Harbor fashion."[12]

Fortunately for the postwar binational alliance, coverage of Japanese imports in the 1950s American press was often more benign and tended to resurrect the prewar image of a diminutive, harmless Japan that produced cheap and insignificant goods. The *Chicago Tribune* ran a number of articles making light of the notion that most Japanese products were cheap in both price and quality, despite the fact that Japanese companies had already begun to export the high-end cameras and electronics for which they are known today. One columnist recounted a family outing at Wrigley Field, where he bought his daughter a ballpark souvenir stamped "Made in Japan," only to hear her whine, "All my toys seem to be made in Japan." Some derived humor from the irony of "keepsakes from Brown County, Indiana, made in Japan," and the Japan-produced paper shamrocks that Chicago mayor Richard Daley proudly displayed in the city's 1960 St. Patrick's Day Parade. In 1959 a letter to the *Tribune*'s editor told the story of an American electronics salesman who discovered an ingenious new kind of TV while visiting Japan, but was afraid no Americans would take it seriously if they knew where it came from. According to the anecdote, the retailer happily obliged in hiding the set's country of origin when he shipped it, labeling it "Not Made in Japan." While the story does reveal an emerging appreciation for Japanese engineering, it also relies on race-based humor that belittled the intelligence of Japanese manufacturers, and perhaps also assuaged some Americans' fears over the threat of trade competition.[13]

The prevalence of this assumption that most Japanese products were essentially cheap was confirmed by a 1960 survey of U.S. consumers conducted by a private nonprofit group of Japanese and American businessmen known as the U.S.-Japan Trade Council. The study found that most American consumers considered Japan an exporter of "toy goods" and thought Japanese products were lower quality than their American equivalents. Even more expensive items, like sewing machines and radios, received low scores in association tests. However, the study also revealed a slight warming trend toward Japanese goods among respondents. Three out of five participants admitted that products made in Japan could sometimes provide a worthwhile bargain, agreeing with the statement, "If you know how to judge quality of a product, you can often find Japanese imports which are much less expensive and just as good as American-made products." It also found that 78 percent of respondents thought Japanese people had "good taste and an appreciation of beauty," suggesting that repeated press coverage of Japanese arts and Japan-inspired fashions was affecting how American consumers perceived the nation as a whole.[14]

In truth, 1960 marked a turning point for Japanese manufacturing, as the ensuing decade brought growing numbers of high-end Japanese electronics to American stores. Instead of appearing competitive and thereby threatening, the affluent consumers most likely to purchase such goods perceived them as further proof that the Japanese people were skilled artisans who had inherited long-standing traditions of craftsmanship. A 1959 article in *Industrial Design* magazine lamented the lack of design innovation in Japan, especially considering the nation's "highly refined philosophical system" that made "no rigid separation between utility and art." Citing the practical beauty of the tea ceremony and Kyoto's Katsura palace, author Ursula McHugh found it ironic that most Japanese manufacturers at the time were slavishly imitating American designs in producing cheap "knock-offs," as opposed to drawing on their deep pool of artistic tradition for inspiration. Yet she did credit the emerging camera industry as "a hopeful portent" where "Japanese design can hold its own in originality and technical experience," and she mentioned some electronic gadgets that did indeed show signs of innovation.[15]

At this point, as Japan's economy and industry grew in strength, Japanese cameras made significant inroads into one specialty American market, and they were soon joined by appliances like transistor radios and portable TVs manufactured by expanding companies like Sony, Toshiba, and Matsushita/Panasonic. In the early 1960s Honda motorcycles also became increasingly popular among U.S. consumers. One British manufacturer described these bikes as "made like a watch. And it isn't a copy of anything." Unlike the cheap imports of previous decades, these products were aimed at more discerning purchasers, either as part of a niche market or by carrying a higher price tag. It was likely not a coincidence that this was the same demographic as Americans most likely to appreciate more traditional shibui imports, and indeed, like McHugh, some did draw a link with Japan's long-standing reputation in the practical arts. In 1964 one advertisement for Japanese typewriters read: "Precision Engineered in the Tradition of Meticulous Japanese Craftsmanship."[16] Like art house samurai films before them, these machine-age products of modern technology paradoxically became further evidence of the strength of Japan's timeless aesthetic traditions. As the economic miracle continued to strengthen Japan's economy into the 1960s and 1970s, this reputation as a manufacturer of high-end, well-crafted merchandise would far eclipse the earlier image of an exporter of cheap imitative goods. Eventually even the products of modern industry would become at least somewhat shibui.

Godzilla and Other Giant Monsters: Japan for the Drive-in Crowd

While inexpensive Japanese imports gradually disappeared from American store shelves, even while they were plentiful they did little to affect most upper-middle-class Americans' impression of the country as a whole. Consumers who purchased cheap Japanese knock-offs were likely to be working class and highly unlikely to hold much influence in terms of middlebrow opinion. Similar divisions in social class, taste, and consumption were at work in neutralizing another threat to the image of a timeless, serene, feminized Japan. In February 1956 a group of exhibitors gathered in Boston to preview a Japanese movie "highlighting a monster 30 stories high . . . that bites railroad trains in half [and] destroys cities with a flick of its tail." According to Terry Turner, the man responsible for promoting the film to U.S. theater owners, "it was the most loathsome sight they ever saw," so naturally "they signed up at once." The movie was *Godzilla: King of the Monsters*, and while most critics harbored the same opinion of the film as Turner, it did indeed make large profits for neighborhood theater and drive-in owners across the country. In the early 1950s, most Japanese movies exhibited in American art houses were period costume dramas meant to appeal to thoughtful upper-middle-class patrons. But the latter half of the decade was dominated by cinematic giant monsters (referred to as *kaiju* among their producers) wreaking havoc in the science fiction films of Toho Studios.

The most common venue for Japanese monster movies was the drive-in theater, which enjoyed its heyday in the mid-twentieth century when Americans moved out of the cities into more spacious suburbs and purchased automobiles in larger numbers than ever before. These theaters have since earned a reputation as "passion pits," where teenagers went to escape the watchful eyes of their parents in the privacy of their cars. However, marketing studies from the time reveal that the majority of drive-in attendees were in fact middle- or working-class families with young children. Watching the movie in the car as a family did away with the need for a babysitter, and parents were often able to enjoy the film while the children slept in the backseat. Most drive-ins included playgrounds underneath the screen, where kids could wear themselves out and settle down once the movie began.[17] But while these families may have appeared more respectable than sexually misbehaving teenagers, neither resembled the typical art house clientele. Communications scholar Eric Mark Kramer referred to drive-in theaters as "intimate, local, down to earth," adding, "Whoever goes there is automatically transformed into a Grade B person."[18]

Indeed, the movies screened at these theaters were often B grade productions. Most drive-in proprietors had little choice other than to show low-budget films, since the major studios looked down on them as unwelcome upstarts and refused to rent them first-run films. As a result, many drive-ins evolved schedules that included second- or third-run large budget films during the week, marketed mostly to family audiences, with B movies on weekends, when teenagers were more likely to attend. Most patrons didn't seem to mind this low-budget selection, since they were often too distracted by their children or date to devote their full attention to what was playing on the screen. Nor did most theater owners care, assuming that their "lowbrow" patrons were unconcerned with a movie's critical reputation. One concessions manager actually preferred bad movies, telling a film executive, "The worse the pictures are, the more stuff we sell."[19]

At the time, there was no lack of cheap movies for these theaters to screen. The Supreme Court's *Paramount* decision, which broke up Hollywood's studio monopoly system, worked in favor of independent film companies in much the same way it had for foreign films. Studios and distributors like American International Pictures (AIP) and Embassy Pictures profited greatly as they rushed to fill the gap created when major studios closed their B departments.[20] Occasionally they too would distribute foreign movies, most frequently "spaghetti westerns," "sword and sandal" epics, and horror films from Italy that were thought to have a wider appeal than more "artistic" European films.[21] But the vast majority of weekend drive-in features were domestically produced "exploitation pictures." Film scholar Thomas Doherty explains that such movies exploited on three levels. First, they exploited current events, cashing in on timely subjects.

One egregious example was Roger Corman's *War of the Satellites*, which appeared in theaters only two months after the launch of Sputnik. Second, they exploited sensational themes, in other words, sex and violence, and third, they exploited the tastes of their audience, assumed to be high school aged and unsophisticated. In many ways the opposite of art house movies that were meant to appear intellectually challenging and artistically inspired, these B grade films pandered to base emotions and employed simplistic themes in an undisguised effort to make money.[22]

One particular exploitation genre that proved profitable for independent distributors in the 1950s was science fiction. Typically filled with violence and destruction, these movies would often appeal to young audiences by featuring a protagonist they could relate to, like a teenage werewolf or vampire. At other times, these movies cashed in on contemporary anxiety over the spread of nuclear weapons, a theme meant to resonate with high-schoolers accustomed to "duck and cover" drills as part of their regular routine.[23] In this subgenre, radiation produced giant monsters that would destroy the nearest city, offering a superficial critique of nuclear proliferation to overlay the movie's true attraction, which was the fear and excitement of watching modern civilization utterly decimated by freakish beasts. One of the earliest and most distinguished of these films was *The Beast from 20,000 Fathoms* (Eugene Lourie, 1953), which featured a giant dinosaur awakened by an atomic blast wreaking destruction on New York City. Another famous example was *Them!* (Gordon Douglas, 1954), in which the southwestern United States is invaded by radioactively mutated ants. Other similar titles included *It Came from beneath the Sea*, *Tarantula*, *Mole People*, *The Deadly Mantis*, *Attack of the Crab Monsters*, *The Amazing Colossal Man*, *The Monster from Green Hell*, *The Alligator People*, and *The Giant Behemoth*.[24]

Producer Tomoyuki Tanaka was allegedly contemplating *The Beast from 20,000 Fathoms* one afternoon in 1954 as he flew over the Pacific returning to Tokyo from Indonesia. He was also mulling the recent *Lucky Dragon* incident, in which a Japanese fishing boat (the *Lucky Dragon No. 5*) absorbed radioactive fallout from classified nuclear tests the United States was conducting nearby. Gazing down into the ocean's depths, he began to wonder what would happen if another bomb were to awaken a hideous monster similar to the dinosaur in Lourie's movie. He was inspired to create his own giant monster in a Japanese setting, and upon landing he set his creative team on the project. Eventually they named the creature Gojira, combining the English word *gorilla* with the Japanese word for whale, *kujira*.[25]

When the film *Gojira* was finally finished, it was a dark and serious commentary on nuclear proliferation, produced in the country that had felt its effects more directly and horrifically than any other nation in the world. Evoking the *Lucky Dragon* incident, the film begins when a prehistoric beast awakened by nuclear tests attacks a small fishing boat in the Pacific Ocean. While no country is blamed explicitly for detonating the radioactive weapon, audiences would assume the United States was at fault. Yet it is Japan that bears the brunt of the consequences when the monster destroys nearby Tokyo. One prominent scientist, Dr. Yamane, wants to preserve the creature for research, but government officials overrule him and call for the monster to be destroyed. Gojira proves so powerful that the only thing that can kill him is a prototype weapon known as the oxygen destroyer, a device more deadly than the hydrogen bomb with the potential to completely destroy humanity. To prevent such an outcome, the weapon's creator Dr. Serizawa commits suicide as he detonates the bomb, taking with him the knowledge of how to create any duplicates. The film concludes with a warning from Dr. Yamane that unless nations put an end to nuclear testing, more Gojira-like creatures could emerge. In addition to the plot's mature reflections on mankind's ability to annihilate itself, the movie includes dark, realistic shots of a burning and devastated Tokyo, as well as hospital wards filled with the injured and dying, all recalling the recent pain and destruction wrought by urban firebombing as well as atomic weapons.[26]

The film proved a box office hit of the highest order in Japan. It was received by the public as a blockbuster spectacle with top-ranking acting talent (including *Rashomon's* Takashi Shimura as Dr. Yamanae) and state-of-the-art special effects, and more than 6 million Japanese moviegoers paid to see it. With such renowned success, the movie proved popular among Japanese-speaking American audiences as well, which is how it came to the attention of independent studios in the United States. According to Alex Gordon of AIP, he and colleague Sam Arkoff first heard about the movie from a friend who suggested they attend a screening in Los Angeles's Little Tokyo neighborhood. They were so impressed by the audience reaction that they soon contacted Toho about distributing an English version of the film and were told by an LA sales representative that they could buy the rights for $12,000. Meanwhile, the Tokyo offices were carrying out their own negotiations, and they sold the rights to Joseph Levine of Embassy Pictures for $25,000, still considered a bargain price.[27] The film premiered in New York in April 1956 under the title *Godzilla: King of the Monsters*. In May it opened in Boston and Washington DC and spread to theaters throughout the country over the summer, becoming a major box office success in Los Angeles, Seattle, Kansas City, Minneapolis, and Cleveland, grossing more than $2.5 million in total.[28] After its initial run in generally respectable theaters, Embassy began treating the film like other B grade science fiction flicks and sold it to drive-ins, while theaters started to screen it in the typical exploitation venue of the matinee double feature, in this case paired (inexplicably) with Roger Corman's busty prison break caper, *Swamp Women*.[29]

After *Gojira* proved so successful both at home and abroad, Toho producers sensed there was more money to be made in a sequel and began production on *Gojira no Gyakushuu* (Gojira's Revenge) almost immediately after the first movie left theaters. Made without the original director and on a much smaller budget, it proved to be a lower quality film.[30] A new Gojira now confronts Angilus, another prehistoric monster sporting a spiny shell, and destroys the city of Osaka in the process. The monster returned a third time in 1962 at the request of an American producer. Willis O'Brien, special effects technician for the film *King Kong* (1933), had long wanted to make a sequel to his initial blockbuster by pitting his giant ape against another famous monster. Unable to obtain financing in the United States, he brought the project to Toho. Since *Gojira*'s special effects producer was inspired as a child by *King Kong*, the studio granted him the opportunity to bring one of his favorite characters to life. Director Ishiro Honda also returned to the project, this time including more laughs and less social

FIG. 14. Still from *Mothra vs. Godzilla*, 1964. Directed by Ishiro Honda, produced by Toho Studios.

commentary for an audience experiencing the happier boom times of a recovered postwar economy. The formula worked, and *King Kong vs. Gojira* became the highest grossing movie of the entire Gojira series in Japan. Both movies appeared in American drive-ins, the former under the puzzling title *Gigantis the Fire Monster*, and they were distributed by Warner Brothers and Universal Pictures, respectively.[31]

In the wake of the first Gojira movie, other giant monsters from Toho's creative team of Tanaka, Honda, and special effects producer Eiji Tsuburaya found popularity on both sides of the Pacific. *Rodan* (1956) was a giant prehistoric bird that terrorized the southern island of Kyushu. The movie offered a critique of commercial environmental exploitation. When miners dig too deep into a dormant volcano, they are terrified to uncover an army of giant prehistoric insects, which turn out to be the prey of two much larger rodans. After the monstrous birds destroy the town of Sasebo in their efforts to nest, the military successfully drives them out of their lair and

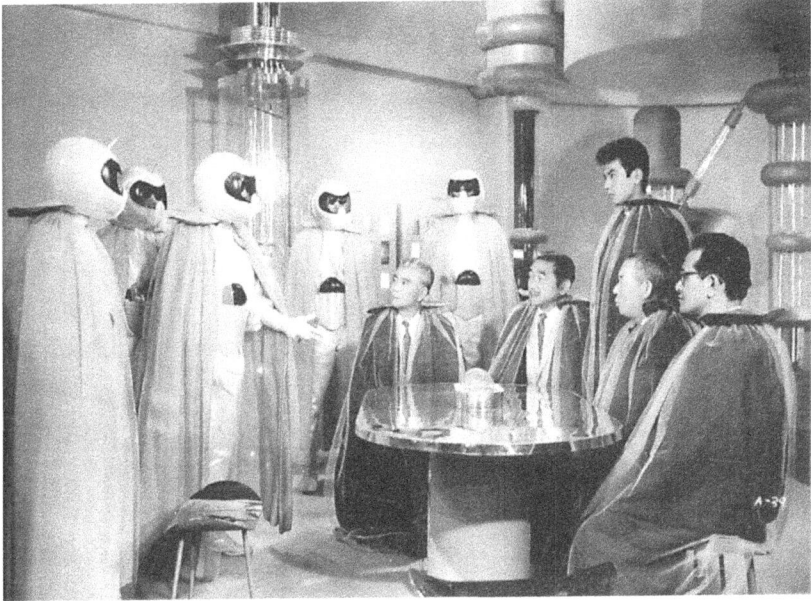

FIG. 15. Still from *The Mysterians*, 1957. Directed by Ishiro Honda, produced by Toho Studios.

leaves them to perish in the ensuing lava flow. Making a substantial profit in Japan, the film then grossed $450,000 in the United States (considerably more than art house box office champion *Gate of Hell*) while playing at seventy-nine theaters throughout the New York metro area alone.[32]

Rodan was followed by *Mothra* (1961), featuring Toho's first and only female giant monster. Sponsored by Columbia Pictures in the United States, this film had the largest budget of any Japanese monster movie to date, and thus included more scenes of giant monsters destroying meticulously detailed model sets than had previous films.

The movie also took on an international scope. Mothra herself was more accurately a goddess from a primitive South Pacific island, and the villain in this case is a human hailing from the fictional country of Rolisica, a combination of the Japanese names for Russia and America. A greedy theater producer, he kidnaps the two tiny priestesses who serve Mothra and puts them on display in Tokyo, which Mothra subsequently ransacks in an effort to recover them. The chaotic action then moves to New Kirk City, Rolisica, where the scheming producer flees. In the end, the day is saved when an intrepid Japanese reporter, his spirited female photographer, and an innovative scientist come up with a plan to reunite Mothra with the twins so all three can return home safely. The movie thus not only addressed the universal sin of greed but also reflected Japan's geopolitical position at the time, promoting its own sense of nationalism while offering subtle critiques of other nations. In addition to the movie's jabs against Cold War superpowers, Southeast Asian islanders appear backward and childlike with echoes of Japan's World War II rhetoric, when the would-be colonial power exerted its own form of Orientalism in painting South Pacific peoples as requiring Japanese guidance and governance.[33] If examined closely, *Mothra*'s Japan appears neither geopolitically weak nor unquestioningly compliant, yet admittedly few of its American viewers would have subjected the movie to such a close reading.

Along with these *kaiju* movies, Toho released other science fiction films directed by Honda and featuring Tsuburaya's special effects. Two of them, *The Mysterians* (1957) and *Battle in Outer Space* (1959), featured a race of men from the planet Mysteroid who sought to conquer Earth after their planet had been destroyed by nuclear fallout.

Other monsters emerged from Toho Studios, but none had the success or popularity of Godzilla, Rodan, or Mothra, with some failing to even reach the drive-in circuit. Instead they were relegated exclusively to late night television screenings.

Importing any of these films, regardless of quality, required American distributors to alter them in certain ways to suit their new audience. Translation is of course an issue for any foreign language film, and in this case Gojira even got an entirely new pronunciation of his name after one romanization system spelled out the Japanese *ji* syllable as *dzi* in English. But while foreign languages and cultures might have been a draw to intellectually minded art house patrons seeking a challenge, drive-in owners felt exoticism would more likely alienate their audiences. Japanese science fiction films were adapted accordingly, often in keeping with the already familiar giant radioactive monster genre. Instead of playing up their foreign attributes to provide an alternative to American popular culture, distributors like AIP and Embassy tried to make them appear like typical American low-budget science fiction movies of the era.

The most basic issue any importer of foreign films faced was translating their dialogue for an English-speaking audience. Art house distributors frequently resolved the issue by providing subtitles, as few of their patrons seemed to mind making the extra effort to "read a movie." In contrast, exploitation movie distributors assumed that their young or working-class audiences would not have the ability or the patience for subtitles, especially with a car's windshield potentially obscuring the bottom of the screen. But according to a 1955 *Variety* article by Peter Riethof, president of the American Dubbing Company, "Whereas a good foreign film can earn money only in the art theaters, an English-speaking version can be shown everywhere." As a result, all Japanese science fiction movies were dubbed into English.[34]

While the presence of subtitles on the screen draws attention to the act of translation, dubbing masks it, allowing viewers to forget that another original dialogue track and script exist. According to Riethof, this is precisely why attention to quality was so crucial in the dubbing process. "The directing of the actors is . . . difficult, as the director of a dub job has to guide his actors to express the same emotions in exactly the same way as the original cast and in lip synch. It is therefore not surprising that compromises, and attempts to get by with quick and cheap dubbings, seldom pay off."[35] Among the Toho movies, the quality of translated scripts and voice dubbing varied greatly. In *Mothra* the characters' lines and delivery seem fairly natural and appropriate to the flow of their conversations with close lip-synching. The same cannot be said of *Gigantis the Fire Monster*, where characters occasionally make statements that have little relevance to the previous line, and at one point the hero utters the archaic expletive "Ah, banana oil!" There are also cases where joking verbal repartee in the Japanese version is played straight in the American version, without any humor at all.[36] Most English-speaking audiences who saw the film probably assumed its script writing was bizarre, dull, or downright poor, lowering their impression of the movie as a whole.

In addition to translating scripts, dubbing also involved hiring English-speaking actors to read those lines. Here again, Reithof warned that dubbing "calls for very careful casting, so that the English voice blends perfectly with the face and characteristics of the actor of the original version. This writer has sometimes spent weeks and even months before he could find the actor whose voice corresponded in an ideal way." Some kaiju movie voice actors were indeed quite talented, including *Star Trek*'s George Takei, as well as Daws Butler and Paul Frees, best known for voicing cartoon characters Yogi Bear and Boris Badenov, respectively.[37] But frequently actors were second-rate performers asked to speak in Japanese accents, mimicking Asian stereotypes with pidgin pronunciation. As a result, the quality of acting in these dubbed films often sounded far worse than it had been in their original versions. For example, a *New York Times* critic declared that no one in *The Mysterians* could act, despite the fact that like *Godzilla*, it featured Takashi Shimura.[38] Shimura, featured as a prominent actor in many of Kurosawa's films in addition to playing the woodcutter in *Rashomon*, could in fact act very well, but the same probably could not be said for the voice actor making him sound like an aging Charlie Chan.

In contrast to some of his colleagues, Joe Levine, American producer of the original *Godzilla*, devoted great care to adapting his film in terms of translation. He devised a creative solution to avoid the cheap feel of dialogue dubbing, hiring director Terry Morse to shoot new material for English-speaking viewers. These scenes starred Raymond Burr as newspaper correspondent Steve Martin, who covered the Godzilla story from Tokyo with the help of a translator, played by Japanese American actor Frank Iwanaga. Morse then spliced these scenes into the Japanese footage, with Burr occasionally conducting conversations in English with Japanese characters whose backs were turned to the camera. For the few scenes in which Burr did not appear, the Japanese actors' voices were indeed dubbed, but the new scenes successfully minimized use of the technique.[39]

Levine and Morse's editing did more than make the movie comprehensible to an American audience. It also toned down the film's critique of nuclear testing. Aware that many members of the movie's target working-class audience still held negative memories of the war, they knew that any hint of criticism toward U.S. military efforts might cause viewers to bristle at the film's content. The production staff deleted references in the dialogue to Hiroshima, Nagasaki, and bomb shelters, as well as Yamane's prophetic final line: "If we keep on conducting nuclear tests, it's possible that another Godzilla might appear somewhere in the world again." Also missing is a dark and painful scene where a child wails as her dead mother is taken away on a stretcher, and the line spoken by a mother clasping her children in the path of Gojira's destruction: "We will be joining your father in just a moment." Given the context of the time, it is likely "father" had died fighting U.S. troops.[40] Yet in keeping with the well-tested themes of previous American giant monster movies, the presence of a diffuse nuclear threat was allowed to remain. This effective blunting of the original film's political message was made clear by one *New York Times* review of the movie. "One might remotely regard [*Godzilla*]," critic Bosley Crowther wrote, "as a symbol of Japanese hate for the destruction that came out of nowhere and descended upon Hiroshima one pleasant August morn. But we assure you that the quality of the picture and the childishness of the whole idea do not indicate such calculation. Godzilla was simply meant to scare people."[41] In coming to America, *Gojira* lost its critical dark side and was rendered simple entertainment.

Subsequent Godzilla movies were also edited to make them easier for American drive-in audiences to understand, but without as much attention to quality. In *King Kong vs. Godzilla*, Universal Pictures copied the technique of adding new English-language footage, this time news reports about the rampaging Godzilla and King Kong. However, these scenes were clearly shot on a much lower budget than the original blockbuster film, and mostly feature newsmen talking directly to the camera with paper maps tacked to the walls behind them. The edited versions of both Godzilla sequels also removed renowned Japanese composer Akrira Ifukube's score, replacing it with stock soundtracks, on the assumption that the original music would sound "too Oriental" to American ears.[42]

The choice to alter these movies to appear less Asian and more American was undoubtedly influenced by the nature of their target audience.

Exploitation movie producers reasoned that teenagers and working-class families would avoid a foreign movie that challenged their worldview. Instead of trusting a film's artistic quality to attract viewers, they relied on the cheap thrills of fantasy and violence, and therefore no scene of a monster attacking a city or otherwise engaging in acts of battle or destruction was ever cut from a *kaiju* movie. Moreover, the films were marketed using the hyperbolic rhetoric common in exploitation movie advertising, promising lots of titillating excitement and employing plenty of exclamation points. Posters advertising *Godzilla* read, "It's Alive! Raging through the World on a Rampage of Destruction!" and "See it crush ... See it kill ... A mighty city of 8 million wiped out by its death ray blasts! Enjoy the thrill of your life!!" When *Rodan* arrived in American theaters, it was double-billed at some drive-ins with *Gigantis* as "the mammoth monster show of the century!" Mothra, the only feminine monster, was duly softened, but only somewhat: "The Mightiest Monster in All Creation! Ravishing a Universe for Love!"[43]

Some advertising campaigns also attempted to disguise the fact that the movies were foreign. Lobby cards promoting *Godzilla* listed Raymond Burr as the star and gave directorial credit to Morse in larger letters than Honda. Posters for *Rodan* similarly listed the distributors, the King Brothers, in much bigger typeface than Toho Studios, with some featuring a dragonlike creature that looks nothing like the actual Rodan and white people fleeing a city in terror.[44] As a consequence, most theater patrons heading out to see a giant monster movie, especially children, had no idea they were going to watch a Japanese film. One Godzilla fan later recalled his surprise at seeing the monster for the first time: "I was really confused. Why were all the people Japanese, and why were their mouths moving so weirdly?"[45] In contrast to Japanese art house films, where foreign origins were seen as a selling point, Toho's sci-fi films were marketed to look as much as possible like other American B movies for an audience they assumed had no desire to experience challenging new perspectives at the movies.

Through the combination of all of these techniques of adaptation and translation, films that had been at worst middling action movies, and at best big-budget blockbusters in Japan, were reduced to low-grade, second-class flicks by the time they were widely distributed in the United States. Nevertheless, they proved to be incredibly popular among their intended audiences, especially youth, with the *New York Times* declaring Godzilla a "household word" in 1963.[46] Yet it is hard to know exactly what appealed to viewers so much about giant monsters, since average working-class Americans, let alone children, rarely leave accessible records of their day-to-day feelings and opinions. An academic conference "In Godzilla's Footsteps: Japanese Pop Culture Icons on the Global Stage" held in October 2004 at the University of Kansas attempted to answer this question. One theory, offered by Japanese studies professor Susan Napier, was that the monster served to embody and resolve fears of an encroaching Oriental Other. But most other scholars posited a more universal appeal to Godzilla. Anthropologist Theodore Bestor theorized that the destruction of civilization and the symbols of its progress is a spectacle fraught with both terror and possibility in all cultures. Literary scholar Joyce Boss offered the idea that Godzilla acts as mythical trickster figure, functioning as both punisher and educator. Many conference participants came to agree that perhaps he is so popular because he resists any one definition of what he symbolizes.[47]

One group that was able to register their reactions to these movies was contemporary movie reviewers, who often hailed from more educated affluent backgrounds than the monsters' biggest fans. As such, their reaction proved largely negative. In fact, few critics condescended to even review this type of B movie in the first place. Crowther called *Godzilla: King of the Monsters* "an incredibly awful film" and said the monster itself looked like "a miniature of a dinosaur made of gum shoes" smashing "about $20 worth of toy buildings and electric trains." *Newsweek* described him as "a 400-foot-high plucked chicken" who "cannot act his way out of a paper bag," and with a notable lack of foresight argued the movie was vastly inferior to Universal Studios' now forgotten *The Creature Walks among Us*. A *Chicago Tribune* review of *Rodan* was titled "Horror—Poorly Done." *Variety* called *Mothra* "a ludicrously written, haphazardly executed monster picture," adding "exploitation measures are bound to lure thrill-seekers who flock indiscriminately to monster films, but even cinemutation buffs should wince at this one." Arthur Knight speculated in the *Saturday Review*, "Perhaps only a glutton for punishment would go to see *King Kong vs. Godzilla*," to which Crowther added, "Viewers who attend the ridiculous melodrama . . . should know exactly what to expect, and they get what they deserve." To these same critics who had adulated Japanese art house films, sci-fi movies seemed to be more in keeping with other shoddy merchandise made in Japan: exported primarily for commercial purposes, they were similarly dismissible as cheap and trashy.[48]

But some reviewers did value these movies for their commercial potential. Trade magazine *Variety* claimed that *Godzilla's* shortcomings, like its thin story line and Raymond Burr's mediocre acting (both the fault of American translation), were "more than offset by the startling special effects which obviously lend themselves to strong promotion." They recommended the film to "houses geared to bally product" and even more upscale "deluxers harassed by the current product shortage." Other critics saw signs of quality as well as marketability in these movies. Philip T. Hartung of the Catholic magazine *Commonweal* applauded *Rodan's* antinuclear message and praised scenes in *The Mysterians* that portrayed the United Nations coming together to preserve world peace. In keeping with Japanese studios' established reputation for producing beautifully artistic camera work, some critics admired the movies' visual effects. A *New York Times* review for *Battle in Outer Space* claimed, "The most attractive thing about this Toho production is the décor—the clean, bright color, and a fetching assortment of obvious, but effective, miniature settings and backgrounds." Two years later, another review included a similar comment about *Mothra*. "There's that color, as pretty as can be, that now and then smites the eye with some genuinely artistic panoramas and décor designs," adding, "Several of the special effects shots are brilliant." At least some critics were able to put aside their prejudices toward drive-in movies and recognize the results of Toho's big budgets along with Tsuburaya's efforts.[49]

However lukewarm their critical reception may have been, it was audience appreciation that mattered more in the long run, and indeed, most of these movies enjoyed a life span far beyond their initial runs at the drive-in. Most were given added longevity through the medium of television, which is how countless American children would encounter Godzilla for the first time. In the early days of TV, many local stations desperate for content wanted to fill air time with movies, but the major studios rebuffed them, considering television a competitive threat. At first, only British studios and independent distributors were willing to rent any movies to TV stations. In the mid-1950s, Hollywood relented, but made only their pre-1948 catalogs available. Therefore any movie airing on television at the time was by necessity either English, B grade, or old. In this context, popular independently distributed movies were a boon to many station owners. This explains why, in the late 1950s, *Godzilla* and *Rodan* were both selected as New York station WOR's "Million Dollar Movie," and were run twice a night for an entire week.[50]

Propelled by such exposure, Godzilla has become the most recognizable Japanese import in America. Parodied in sitcoms and on commercials, depicted in countless toys and merchandise, and even featured in his own rock song, he has become inextricably woven into the fabric of American culture.[51] Yet in his own time he was largely ignored by the mainstream press, most likely because he did not conform to the notion of Japan crystallized in the minds of most movie critics and other journalists. In contrast to other examples of Japanese culture circulating within the United States in the 1950s, Godzilla's foreign characteristics were never recruited in the service of international relations, nor did he ever serve as a refined, sophisticated, or spiritual alternative to mainstream America. American film producers did all they could to hide his foreign origins so as not to alienate potential ticket buyers, and tastemakers made no effort to link him to a supposedly unique Japanese essence. As opposed to promoting serenity and self-restraint, Godzilla engendered panic and chaos, creating an indulgent spectacle in the process. Far from minimalist, he can better be described as "maximalist," not only in that he towers above major cities and emits deafening roars, but in that each of his subsequent films upped the ante to offer more creatures for him to duel and more locations for them all to destroy. Whereas a person who studied shibui arts could come across as a sophisticated seeker of something deeper than banal American culture, attending a Toho monster flick at a drive-in would mark them as part of the tasteless unwashed masses who enjoyed kitsch. But then, most true fans of these movies were probably too young or too far removed from the social circles of midtown Manhattan to even care; as far as they were concerned, they were having fun experiencing the action.

Inexpensive Japanese goods and monster movies both demonstrate how Americans from different socioeconomic backgrounds can form different images of the same foreign country by consuming different exports from that nation. Both of these examples posed potential challenges to the shibui image of Japan by suggesting that Japanese culture didn't have to be austere, restrained, bound by tradition, or in any way elitist, and might in fact be as loud, cheap, and modern as the United States. Such images might have been problematic for policymakers, as they implied that Japan was perfectly well attuned to the twentieth-century world, could have the power to act on its own in that world, and do so in a way that was at least aggressive, if not outright critical of U.S. actions. But those same class distinctions that allowed these alternative viewpoints to exist in the first place could simultaneously neutralize their threat. The opinions of most lower-class consumers rarely seem to carry much weight in determining the contours of upper middlebrow American taste and fashion, let alone strongly influence foreign policy. In an era when increasing numbers of suburbanites were seeking upward mobility by attempting to conform and appear more respectable, other voices such as these were often pushed to the margins.

Moreover, it is unclear how often American commentators and consumers even thought of these imports as Japanese. The producers of Japanese merchandise and monster movies attempted to hide any hint of exoticism in their products in order to appeal to a wide variety of patrons and make as much money as they could. Made-in-Japan products may have had their origin directly stamped on them, but they were designed to serve as less expensive versions of familiar American-made goods. Promoters of monster movies took deliberate steps to disguise their films' Japanese roots, removing their soundtracks (both voice and music) and hiding Japanese names on promotional posters. In dodging or disguising their origins, none of these commercial imports upset the diplomatically useful image of Japan as a compliant nation whose timeless culture promoted refined taste and a peaceful and cooperative worldview. Over time, high-end merchandise even enhanced such depictions by appearing shibui itself. Nevertheless, as commercial products of an industrialized nation, Japanese goods and science fiction movies did offer glimpses of a truly dynamic and modernized nation, if Americans made the effort to notice them.

CONCLUSION

Conducting research in Ryosen-an in 2008, the immediate impression I had of the temple was of an institution whose best days lay behind it. While the library, zendo, and abbots' quarters remain open and well kept, the Zuin-ken dormitory is gone and, with it, the platoon of Zen scholars who lived there in the 1950s and 1960s. The fall I was there, the temple's sole inhabitants consisted of an elderly roshi and one Zen student from London who slept on the library floor. The subtemple's affiliation with the First Zen Institute of America has been discontinued, but a hand-painted sign at the front gate announces meditation sessions conducted in English. Ruth Fuller Sasaki's vast collection of books on Buddhism is also still available for perusal to those who make appointments to visit the library. While currently a shadow of its postwar self, Ryosen-an pushes onward, serving as a resource for a markedly reduced community of English speakers wanting to study and practice Zen in Japan. In many ways, the current condition of the temple is emblematic of the present state of rinzai Zen in the United States. The First Zen Institute is still in operation in Manhattan, but has scaled back to a scope of operations similar to the 1930s, minus a resident roshi.[1] The vogue of koan contemplation and minimalist sumi-e brush paintings faded as the 1960s progressed, and the emerging counterculture built its spirituality off a fondness for LSD and art that exploded with color. Tibetan Buddhism with its complex vibrant mandalas and legions of fantastical bodhisattvas seemed to fit these new tastes better than the staid abstraction of Zen. When self-appointed acid guru Timothy Leary created a guide to tripping based on the *Tibetan Book of the Dead* in 1968, it became clear that American interest in Buddhism had shifted to another geographic locus.[2]

Similarly, the word *shibui* itself is one few Americans recognize in the twenty-first century. However, the terms *wabi* and *sabi*, used by Suzuki in *Zen and Japanese Culture* to denote a similar aesthetic, are still in circulation among interior designers, and in May 2014 I heard the host of a gardening show on Mississippi Public Radio describe the concept of *shibumi* (noun form of *shibui*) to his listeners. The idea of Japanese-style beauty in simplicity still lingers, but is now confined to a smaller niche audience.[3] Japan-inspired architecture tends to look dated in the twenty-first century, as American tastes have long since rebelled against the bland functionalism of modernist designs and their almost complete lack of ornamentation. New suburban houses sport columned entryways and bay windows that evoke familiar American building traditions, attempting to create an air of hominess as opposed to efficiency.

Ikebana, too, has been in decline since the 1960s. In 1969 Ikebana International showed a net financial loss for the first time, and from the late 1970s onward, more chapters opened outside the United States than within. Some members attempted to change with the times. In her introduction to a 1975 book written by Allie Uyehara, Ruth Gordon Allen insisted, "MODERN TIMES TOO AFFECT OUR FLOWER ARRANGEMENTS" and "our responsibility is to create flower arrangements for OUR DAY."[4] Nevertheless, when II sponsored an exhibit at the National Arboretum in Washington DC in 2008, staff at the facility described arrangers as an impressively talented group of "old ladies."[5] It has become a pastime with an aging following and few new recruits.

Meanwhile, bonsai has fared somewhat better and Japanese cinema perhaps best of all. Bonsai cultivation no longer attracts enough enthusiasts to fill nine separate societies in one city, but the American Bonsai Society continues to list a substantial number of clubs on its website.[6] Although it discontinued its regular bonsai classes decades ago, the Brooklyn Botanic Garden maintains a permanent exhibit of the tiny trees. Meanwhile, many of Kurosawa's works are now considered canonical by American film scholars, and English-language critical analysis of both his and Mizoguchi's films is plentiful. Even the works of Yasujiro Ozu, whose films were previously dismissed as "too Japanese," have become highly admired among Western film scholars. But while both of these arts have remained popular, they are interpreted in different ways and valued for different reasons than they had been circa 1960. Instead of grouping Japanese directors together as part of a national oeuvre, scholars are today more likely to look for individual, personalized style in Kurosawa and Mizoguchi's films, treating them as universally appealing, as opposed to being a window into Japanese culture. Bonsai still looks fashionable and sophisticated, but is just as likely to be associated with meticulousness and precision as with spiritual serenity. For instance, in a 2010 television commercial for Cheetos, an office drone gets revenge on a "neat freak" coworker by smearing orange snack food crumbs on his desk. The markers of his anal-retentiveness include hand sanitizer, pencils placed perfectly parallel, and a well-manicured bonsai.

The fading of both the term and the concept of *shibui* are due in large part to radical shifts in American popular culture that began in the late 1960s. In addition to psychedelic colors overtaking modernist minimalism, the country has also experienced a shift from formal to casual modes of dress and deportment, a reprioritizing of youth over the culture of the wealthy, and increasing sensitivity toward the rights and basic humanity of nonwhite people.[7] In such an environment, an aesthetic that uses simplified designs to promote upper-class tastefulness while at times borrowing from Asian stereotypes would not gain as much traction as it once did. Meanwhile, the Vietnam War rekindled other, more virulent racial stereotypes, as the United States was once again confronted by an Asian enemy. Throughout the conflict, the American media often made firm distinctions between "good" and "bad" Asians, often painting in broad strokes images of embattled Catholic democratic South Vietnamese versus sadistic godless communist North Vietnamese. For the most part, Japanese people continued to remain on the positive side of that divide, but for some veterans, at least, all Asian "gooks" began to look alike. One reported feeling sick while walking Tokyo's Ginza on R and R leave, besieged by "all the slant eyes." As the war dragged on and efforts to win Asian "hearts and minds" appeared increasingly misguided, so too did the general trope of eager pupils seeking democratic tutelage from the United States.[8] Meanwhile, other changes were taking place in Japan, as the nation's economy and industrial output surpassed prewar levels. The image of Japan as a quaint country preserving a timeless past in opposition to the onslaught of modernity became increasingly more difficult to sustain once Japanese manufacturers began exporting enough cameras, transistor radios, television sets, and automobiles to rival, and conceivably overtake, the United States.

Beginning in the 1970s, new popular cultural imports from Japan better suited to the times also began to appear in the United States. Much more in the mold of Godzilla than ikebana or shoji screens, they were often fantastical, aimed at a youth audience, and ambiguous about their country of origin. The Gojira movies themselves began to target a younger audience in Japan as the series continued into the 1960s and '70s. Filmmakers literally softened the monster's sharp edges, rounding out his fangs and spikes, and even gave him a cute reptilian toddler son.[9] By that point, Eiji Tsubaraya had left Toho to open his own production studio, where he created *Ultraman*, a television show in which a hero in a space age suit would battle a new city-stomping giant monster every week. A syndicated, English-dubbed version aired in the United States in late afternoon timeslots and proved popular among children arriving home from school.

The live action *Ultraman* was joined by Japanese cartoon series over the course of the 1960s, '70s, and '80s. These included *Astro Boy*, *Battle of the Planets*, *Speed Racer*, *Voltron*, and *Sailor Moon*. While none achieved the success of the most popular American-made cartoon shows, they were typically inexpensive to import and therefore still profitable for their distributors. Like Toho's science fiction movies, these shows were translated and dubbed as well as edited to make them more age-appropriate to their juvenile audience. The American producers of *Battle of the Planets* in fact spoke no Japanese and invented their own scenarios and dialogue to match the animated action. They also added a robot narrator to explain the plot, not unlike Raymond Burr in the first *Godzilla*. In Japan, these shows had been aimed at a general audience and contained scenes Americans parents would consider too dark or violent for children. Producers removed depictions of characters being killed or maimed, as well as episode endings that left the "good guys" losing.[10] In the 1970s, instead of creating serene art forms for the consumption of fashionable and sophisticated adults, Japan was now primarily an exporter of action shows for kids.

Over the following decades, more fantastic characters would continue to emerge from modern Japan's popular culture industry, but they would increasingly be geared toward adolescents and adults. One transitional figure was Hello Kitty; initially the creation of the Sanrio Toy Company, she eventually appealed to large numbers of adult U.S. women as well as children.[11] Arriving around the same time were icons in the world of video games, including Pac Man, Super Mario, and Sonic the Hedgehog. While such games are often marketed to teenagers, they tend to be enjoyed by a significant number of adults as well. But one aspect all of these late twentieth-century imports shared—cartoons, toys, and game characters alike—is that Americans did not necessarily associate them with Japan. Their country of origin was never prominently displayed, nor did they appear distinctly Japanese to American audiences. To borrow a concept from cultural scholar Koichi Iwabuchi in his exploration of the late twentieth-century globalization of Japanese popular culture, they were "culturally odorless." As opposed to exports from the 1950s and '60s that carried a positive association or "fragrance" of Japan, these new artistic creations did not seem to evoke the essence of any nation. Cartoon characters appeared racially indistinct and spoke English in American accents to U.S. audiences. The only video game characters with a specified ethnicity were Mario and Luigi, and they were Italian. Kitty has hardly any facial features, save two abstracted eyes, and Pac Man had hardly any physical features whatsoever. Completely deracialized, such figures took on a status similar to Godzilla, sidestepping Orientalist stereotypes to become transcendent international icons.[12]

But this is not to say that such characters led Americans to forget about Japan's supposedly unique traditions or think of their culture as indistinguishable from the West. In the U.S. press, Japan continued to appear as a land with an exotic and mysterious past, but that supposedly timeless past took on new meanings in the last decades of the twentieth century. Beginning in the 1970s, Japanese manufactured products offered stiff competition to American brands, at the same time that U.S. factory workers began losing their jobs. Instead of examining loose quality controls, a lack of investment in innovation and development, or a decline in labor union strength to explain rising unemployment and stagnant wages, most commentators leaped to the conclusion that sneaky and underhanded Japanese business practices were to blame. The Japanese government's tight relationship with corporations was assumed by many American experts to be rooted in Japanese feudal traditions. James Clavell's best-selling novel *Shogun*, which later became a television miniseries, painted a portrait of a heartless Tokugawa era society that presumably gave direct rise to ruthless business practices after World War II. Michael Crichton's novel (and later movie) *Rising Sun* made similar arguments in the 1990s, suggesting that hierarchical standards of etiquette and the *bushido* "way of the sword" served as the foundation for contemporary Japanese corporate culture.[13] Traditions had reemerged, but against the backdrop of economic conflict, the Japanese now appeared menacing in their stoicism instead of pacifist; the chrysanthemum had turned back into the sword.

The most recent wave of Japanese cultural imports arrived in earnest in the late 1990s, after Japan's economic recession made it appear less threatening as an economic adversary. Anime cartoon series and manga comic books resembled the earlier giant monsters and cartoon series in that they frequently fit the science fiction or fantasy genre and were treated as contemporary, as opposed to traditional art forms. However, they differed not only in that they were aimed at adults, but also in that they were actively promoted as Japanese. Translated, but not censored, anime books and manga films often deal frankly with sex, violence, and death, as befitting their adult audiences. Moreover, Manga comic books in the United States are printed in their original right-to-left layouts, keeping the original artwork exactly as it was first produced and drawing attention to the comics' foreign origin (much like subtitles in an art house film). While the appeal of both anime and manga are still being explored and highly debated by cultural scholars, their attraction may lie in their appearance as foreign and transgressive, giving them an outsider status, not unlike Beat Zen before them. Finding American cartoons and comic books too childish, banal, or dishonest, many anime and manga enthusiasts seek out alternatives that offer frank portrayals of complex themes and find them in the pens of Asian artists.[14]

In addition to treating Japanese culture as a fascinating Eastern alternative to the American mainstream, anime and manga further resemble cultural imports from the 1950s in that they serve as signifiers of social distinction, albeit a much different type of distinction. Instead of marking consumers as the most stylish members of the mainstream, appreciation for these newer art forms suggests inclusion in a particular subgroup. *Otaku*—as they call themselves, borrowing another Japanese term[15]—form a diverse but close-knit community organized around fan conventions, newsletters, and clubs. Many participate in *cosplay*, a shorthand term for dressing up in costume as favorite characters and acting out well-known scenes from books and movies. Some even create and circulate homemade manga, placing established characters in plots of their own invention, a practice that remains notably unregulated by Japanese copyright enforcement. Often viewing themselves as stepping outside mainstream American tastes, otaku bond over their enthusiasm for cultural forms that few of their fellow countrymen appreciate. While most members of this group tend to be young, white, and male, none of these are hard and fast demographic rules. Instead, manga and anime's fan base transcends lines of class, gender, geography, and education. Discovering new commonalities to bind themselves together, often revolving around insider familiarity with plots, characters, and lingo, these newer Japan enthusiasts create their own social distinction.[16]

All of these fantastical imports, from Godzilla through the present day, differ from shibui culture in that they break the Orientalist mode of treating Japan as timeless and ancient. But even these latter-day exports have rarely translated into political influence or substantial "soft power" for Japan vis-à-vis the West, and the nation is still hardly on equal footing with the United States.[17] While Japan may have caught up to, or even slightly surpassed, the United States in terms of technology, the Japanese people are still typically treated as strange and curious in American media. Today Japan appears as both an exporter of quality cutting-edge gadgets and a society where sexually repressed businessmen and socially awkward engineers rely on escapist comic books to transport them beyond their overworked existence. The latter image in particular often makes Japanese men appear adolescent and, for lack of a better term, nerdy. Widespread rumors of vending machines that sell schoolgirls' used panties suggest a frustrated and emasculated culture, where men have to rely on technology for sexual gratification. So too does a January 12, 2010, *Colbert Report* joke about an intriguing new development from a New Jersey laboratory: "Someone has invented a sex robot, and amazingly it wasn't the Japanese." Although this new image of Japan may be more accurate than the shibui portrait in that it admits the nation's competency of the modern era, the country nevertheless maintains its "junior partner" status, as Japanese men are denied the same strong, capable qualities as their American counterparts.

While the pull of the Cold War is no longer a factor making an alliance with Japan seem as desperately necessary as it was in the late 1940s, the United States still views Japan as an important ally. The United States continues to maintain a large network of military bases on Japanese soil, and the fact that Japan is the world's third largest economy makes it a significant player on the global stage.[18] Yet the nation with by far the largest economy and military in the world is the United States. The mid-twentieth-century hierarchy has remained intact with only a few adjustments. Japan is still a worthy ally, but now this is due to its technical competence rather than its ancient wisdom. Instead of a nation filled with effete artists and antiquities specialists, it more frequently appears as a country largely populated by weird gadget developers, hardworking techies who spend their spare time creating square watermelons or other *chindogu* (useless inventions), or perfecting their entrants for the upcoming robot marathon.[19]

In the postwar era, Americans characterized Japan through the respectable but emasculated figures of the graceful geisha and the aging Zen master. Today Japan's export of video games and cartoons with offbeat niche appeal make it more closely resemble a repressed technology geek: a highly intelligent and successful man with some admirable qualities, but nevertheless an odd duck who could use some guidance and aid from an American with more savvy and virility. This recent restructuring of Japan's image serves to reinforce the wider point that arts and culture—commercial or otherwise—still hold the power to mold Americans' opinions of overseas nations "far more than foreign policies and white papers ever could." Consuming Japanese culture continues to cast the nation as a friendly ally, yet one that is subordinate by nature of its seeming inability to comfortably conform to the Western values and culture that continue to dominate the globe politically and economically. By reading a human interest story on an offbeat Tokyo trend, watching one of Kurosawa's films, visiting an exhibit on *ukiyo-e* prints, or purchasing a Japanese-inspired objet d'art for their living room, Americans from 1945 to the present have been able to feel like they are peering through a small window into a fascinating foreign land. The vision of Japan they saw may have varied with the times, but maintained the underlying characteristic of appearing sympathetic on some level while exotic and unfamiliar on another, providing an artistic, wise, or possibly quirky alternative to everyday middle-class life in the United States.

NOTES

INTRODUCTION

1. Donald Keene, "West Goes East—East Goes West," *New York Times Magazine*, March 27, 1960, 27.
2. For examples, see Hoganson, *Consumer's Imperium*.
3. For general discussion of the concept of "cultural imperialism," see Gienow-Hecht, "Shame on U.S.?" For examples of literature, see Wagnleitner, *Coca-colonization and the Cold War*; Wagnleitner and May, *Here, There, and Everywhere*; de Grazia, *Irresistible Empire*; and Perez, *On Becoming Cuban*.
4. Dower, *War without Mercy*; Shibusawa, *America's Geisha Ally*.
5. Dower, *War without Mercy*, 77–93.
6. Quoted in Iwamura, *Virtual Orientalism*, 28.
7. "'Teahouse Geisha' Is Giving Thanks in Modern Kimono," *Portland Evening Star-Telegraph*, April 9, 1954, Museum of Modern Art Public Information Scrapbook, microfilm reel 5073, frame 525.
8. Imada, *Aloha America*; Kirsten, *Tiki Pop*. I noticed these trends myself while conducting research for this project, flipping through the same magazines that featured shibui fads.
9. Brandt, *Kingdom of Beauty*.
10. Klein, *Cold War Orientalism*, 16; McAlister, *Epic Encounters*, 12.
11. McClintock, *Imperial Leather*, 40–42.
12. Benedict, *Chrysanthemum and the Sword*.

13. See Reischauer and Auslin, *Japan Society*; *History of the Japan Society of San Francisco*, pamphlet available at Japan Society of Northern California, San Francisco; Lancaster, *Japanese Influence in America*; Henning, *Outposts of Civilization*; Auslin, *Pacific Cosmopolitans*; Yoshihara, *Embracing the East*; Converse Brown, "The Japanese Taste"; Meech-Pekarik, *Frank Lloyd Wright and the Art of Japan*; and Harris, "All the World a Melting Pot?"

14. For more exact numbers, see LaFeber, *The Clash*, 316–17.

15. See Kovner, *Occupying Power*; Lark, "They Challenged Two Nations"; Koshiro, *Trans-Pacific Racisms*; and Berthiaume Shukert and Smith Scibetta, *War Brides of World War II*.

16. For more on military wives and children serving in diplomatic roles, see Alvah, *Unofficial Ambassadors*.

17. John S. Robinson, "Seattle, Where Far East and Northwest Meet," *New York Times*, May 15, 1960.

18. I was first informed of this usage by my friend and colleague at Iowa, Yuka Kishida, and later had it confirmed by Professor Masumi Izumi's seminar of cultural studies students at Doshisha University, Kyoto.

19. Harada, *Lesson of Japanese Architecture*; Drexler, *Architecture of Japan*, 74.

20. Illini Ceramic Service ad, *Chicago Daily Tribune*, August 13, 1961, N A2; Martin Senor Paints ad, *House Beautiful*, September 1960; Weibolt's State Street department store ad, *Chicago Daily Tribune*, November 19, 1964, 11; Weibolt's State Street ad, *Chicago Daily Tribune*, May 17, 1964, W8; Gatelys department store ad, *Chicago Daily Tribune*, September 24, 1964, IND4. Rather appropriately, the logo for Shibui women's underwear is the Japanese character for female (女) rotated slightly to the right.

21. For examples, see Shibusawa, *America's Geisha Ally*, as well as the army training film *Our Job in Japan* available at https://archive.org/details/OurJobInJapan1945.

22. See Said, *Orientalism*, as well as Hammond, introduction to *Cultural Difference, Media Memories*.

23. Gallup Poll Index, vol. 3 (April 28, 1961). When asked to choose words from a list that best described the Japanese people, 47 percent of American respondents picked "hardworking," 36 percent "artistic," 35 percent "practical," 24 percent "sly," and 24 percent "progressive."

24. Shibusawa, *America's Geisha Ally*.

25. Iwamura, *Virtual Orientalism*.

26. Adeney Thomas, *Reconfiguring Modernity*.

27. Chaplin quoted in Kurashige, *Japanese American Celebration*, 42.

28. Koestler, *Lotus and the Robot*; Keene, "West Goes East," SM86.

1. Klein, *Cold War Orientalism*, 23, 54.

2. In addition to Klein, *Cold War Orientalism*, see Johnson and Colligan, *Fulbright Program*; Bu, *Making the World Like Us*; Scott-Smith, *Networks of Empire*; and Loayza, "'A Curative and Creative Force.'"

3. Borgwardt, *New Deal for the World*, 267.

4. See Bu, *Making the World Like Us*, 210–15, and Scott-Smith, *Networks of Empire*, 403–24.

5. Rockefeller quoted in foreword to Schwantes, *Japanese and Americans*, ix.

6. Matsuda, *Soft Power and Its Perils*, 5

7. Editorial note (meeting between Ambassador Dulles and Sir Avery Gascoigne), January 29, 1951, Foreign Relations of the United States (FRUS), *Asia and the Pacific*, pt. 1, 1951, doc. 486.

8. Abel, *International Minimum*, 81–107. See also Schlichtmann, *Japan in the World*.

9. Dower quoted in foreword to Schwantes, *Japanese and Americans*, xiv.

10. Matsuda, *Soft Power and Its Perils*, 228.

11. Dower, *Embracing Defeat*; Schaller, *Altered States*; Shibusawa, *America's Geisha Ally*; Koshiro, *Trans-Pacific Racisms*; Johnson, *Japanese through American Eyes*; and Chiba, "From Enemy to Ally."

12. For a primary source example, see Gorer, "Themes in Japanese Culture." For historical analysis, see Dower, *War without Mercy*, 118–46, and Shibusawa, *America's Geisha Ally*, 54–95.

13. Dower, *Embracing Defeat*, 203–5, quotation on 550.

14. George Kennan memorandum to John Foster Dulles, July 20, 1950, FRUS, 1950, *East Asia and the Pacific*, vol. 6.

15. Herndon Crockett, *Popcorn on the Ginza*, 4. For her often condescending comic interpretation of Japanese attempts to mimic American taste, see 238–46.

16. For further examples and analysis, see Shibusawa, *America's Geisha Ally*, 13–53.

17. Akiyuki, "American *Hijiki*."

18. See Schaller, *Altered States,* 127–62, and LaFeber, *The Clash*, 314–24.

19. Bourdieu, *Distinction*, 6, 173.

20. Reprinted in Horowitz, *American Social Classes*. Pages 191–95 feature a gallery of cartoons and advertisements illustrating both the popularity of Packard's book and the prevalence of class consciousness in the postwar era.

21. Russel Lynes, "Highbrow, Lowbrow, Middlebrow," *Harper's*, February 1949, 19–28; "High-brow, Low-brow, Middle-brow," *Life*, April 11, 1949, 100–101.

22. Morton, *Home and Its Furnishings*, 184. For more on the concept of modernism, see General Motors' 1958 film *American Look* available on YouTube at www.youtube.com/watch?v=gS6HZv4GXj8. At one point the narrator asserts, "The modern

designer creates beauty through simplicity." See also Smith, *Making the Modern*; Castillo, *Cold War on the Home Front*; and Kaufmann, *What Is Modern Design?*

23. Nelson, *Problems of Design*, 186–87.

24. Riesman, Glazer, and Denney, *Lonely Crowd*, 336–37.

25. For more on the general history of Japanese Americans, see Azuma, *Between Two Empires*; Takaki, *Strangers from a Different Shore*; and Daniels, *Asian America*.

26. For examples, see Justice Robert A. Jackson's dissent in *Korematsu vs. United States* and Dower, *War without Mercy*, 3–32.

27. For accounts of camp life, see Daniels, *Prisoners without Trial*; Okubo, *Citizen 13660*; and Kikuchi, *Kikuchi Diary*, as well as the Japanese American Evacuation and Resettlement Study led by Dorothy Swaine Thomas and published as *The Spoilage* and *The Salvage*.

28. See Daniels, *Asian America*, 280–82.

29. For more on the Chicago resettlers, see Swaine Thomas, *Salvage*; Wu, *Color of Success*, 16–42; and Chung Simpson, *Absent Presence*.

30. Brooks, *Alien Neighbors, Foreign Friends*, 159–93; Kurashige, *Shifting Grounds of Race*, 186–204. For more on "model minority" status, see Wu, *Color of Success*, as well as Ogawa, *From Japs to Japanese*. For one of the earliest examples of this discourse, see William Petersen, "Success Story, Japanese-American Style," *New York Times Magazine*, January 9, 1966, 180.

31. "The Encounter," *The Twilight Zone*, season 5, episode 31, CBS, May 1, 1964, written by Martin Goldsmith, directed by Robert Butler.

32. See interviews with relocated internees collected by Swaine Thomas in *The Salvage* and also Oda, *Gateway to the Pacific*, 22–23.

33. For instance, Mrs. Kaoru Ito of Stockton, California, taught ikebana classes while interned in Rohwer. Interview with Kaoru Ito, December 4, 1997, JACL/CSUS Oral History Project, tape 1, side B. For other examples, see Takaki, *Strangers from a Different Shore*, 395, and Daniels, *Prisoners without Trial*, 70–71.

34. See Wu, *Color of Success*; Kurashige, *Shifting Grounds of Race*; Chung Simpson, *Absent Presence*; Robinson, *After Camp*; and Yoo, *Growing Up Nisei*.

35. Kurashige, *Japanese American Celebration*, 119–50; Oda, "Rebuilding Japantown."

2. SAMURAI AT THE SURE SEATERS

1. A. H. Weiler, "Random Observations on Pictures and People," *New York Times*, December 16, 1951, 113.

2. Falk, *Upstaging the Cold War*, 12.

3. Figures taken from a chart provided to the author by Lary May at the 2008 American Historical Association annual conference. For contemporary discussion of the trend, see "Foreign Films 'Arrive,'" *Variety*, January 30, 1957, 1.

4. See Wilinsky, *Sure Seaters*, 65–69; Doherty, *Teenagers and Teenpics*, 18–24.

5. See Leff and Simmons, *Dame in the Kimono*; Baumann, *Hollywood Highbrow*, 101–5.

6. "Cautious U.S. Exhibitors Raise Wall between Foreign Pix and U.S. Public," *Variety*, October 12, 1955, 7.

7. "Film Chain Finds Cure for Box-Office Blues," *Business Week*, March 22, 1958, 72; Doherty, *Teenagers and Teenpics*, 32; A. H. Weiler, "Noted on the Local Screen Scene," *New York Times*, July 15, 1956, 69. For a complete list of art house theaters in the United States by location as of 1965, see appendix to Mayer, *Foreign Films on American Screens*, xiv.

8. "Film Chain Finds Cure for Box-Office Blues," 75; Stanley Frank, "Sure-Seaters Discover an Audience," *Nation's Business*, January 1952, 37.

9. See Falk, *Upstaging the Cold War*, 86–118, and Sbardellati, *J. Edgar Hoover Goes to the Movies*.

10. "Film Chain Finds Cure for Box-Office Blues," 75; Stanley Frank, "Sure-Seaters Discover an Audience," *Nation's Business*, January 1952, 37. See also Wilinsky, *Sure Seaters*, 80–127, and Baumann, *Hollywood Highbrow*, 161–78.

11. De Valck, *Film Festivals*, 47–53.

12. Richie, *Films of Akira Kurosawa*, 79–80.

13. Ray Falk, "Japan's 'Rasho-Mon' Rings the Bell," *New York Times*, October 21, 1951, 100.

14. Galbraith, *Emperor and the Wolf*, 129.

15. At the 1980 San Francisco Film Festival, Kurosawa did reveal to audience members, "Probably the person closest to the truth was the woodcutter, but he's lying, too." Stone, "Akira Kurosawa," 162.

16. Wilinsky, *Sure Seaters*, 105–6; Gomery, *Shared Pleasures*, 187; "Of Local Origin," *New York Times*, December 24, 1951, 9; *Rashomon* ad, *Variety*, March 5, 1952, 13.

17. "'Rashomon' Doing Sock, RKO Nabs Israeli Film," *Variety*, January 16, 1952, 5; A. H. Weiler, "By Way of Report," *New York Times* (Saturday supplement), February 3, 1952, X5; "National Board of Review Names 'Place in the Sun' Year's Best Movie," *NYT*, December 18, 1951, 41; "Humphrey Bogart Wins Movie 'Oscar,'" *NYT*, March 21, 1952, 25; Thomas M. Pryor, "Warners to Make 27 Films in Color," *NYT*, May 19, 1952, 12; "'Streetcar' Wins Film Critics' Nod," *NYT*, December 28, 1951, 18. The film was also rereleased in Japan where it became a runaway hit thanks to its newfound international prestige.

18. Eleanor Jewett, "Fascinating Oriental Art Is Exhibited," *Chicago Tribune*, September 20, 1953, E4; "Of Local Origin," *New York Times*, August 20, 1955, 20; "Tyler Speaks on Film Tonight," *NYT*, April 27, 1956, 24; "From the Theater Screens to 16mm," *NYT*, May 10, 1959, X7. For a contemporary profile of one repertory theater, see "Bleeker Cinema Plans Revivals," *NYT*, June 8, 1963, 15. Listings of *Rashomon* screenings at such theaters include "Midtown Houses List New Movies," *NYT*, October 28, 1959, 40; Ascot theater ad, *NYT*, December 2, 1959, 55; Thalia theater ad, *NYT*, December 4, 1959, 36; Eugene Archer, "Maria Schell Set for Role Abroad," *NYT*, July 16, 1960, 9; Howard Thompson, "British Director Plans 2 Pictures," *NYT*, November 25, 1961, 26.

19. Akutogawa, *Rashomon and Other Stories*; James Kelly, "No Jade, No Peonies," *New York Times*, November 30, 1952, BR47; "And Bear in Mind," *NYT*, December 28, 1952, BR8; Liveright Publishers ad, *NYT*, May 3, 1953, BR28; Seymour Peck, "'Rashomon' from the Screen to the Stage," *NYT*, January 18, 1959, XI; Claudia Cassidy, "On the Aisle," *Chicago Tribune*, January 29, 1959, C1; Larry Glenn, "Hollywood New Look," *New York Times*, January 19, 1964, X9; A. H. Weiler, "Paul Newman Starred in 'The Outrage,'" *NYT*, October 8, 1964, 48; Swank Company ad, *NYT*, November 15, 1959, SM3.

20. Richie and Anderson, *Japanese Film*, 212.

21. "Japanese Winner at Venice to Harrison," *Variety*, June 30, 1954, 16; "Iguchi at Premier," *New York Times*, September 8, 1954, 40; "Of Local Origin," *NYT*, September 15, 1954, 39; John Goodspeed, "It's Cool . . . but Too Long," *Baltimore Sun*, October 6, 1963, D11. For examples of ten best list inclusions, see "Take Ten!" *Saturday Review*, January 1, 1955, 63; "Choice for 1954," *Time*, January 3, 1955. For other art house and reparatory listings of the film, see "Playhouse Owner Marks 40 Years of Movie Trade," *Chicago Tribune*, December 5, 1954, F3; "Camera Club Notes," *CT*, February 1, 1962, N8; "IIT Series Will Begin with 1928 Russian Movie," *CT*, September 15, 1963, S1; The Hyde Park theater ad, *CT*, November 4, 1960, B18; "Series at Fordham," *New York Times*, January 28, 1960, 26; Eugene Archer, "Movie 'Failures' Will Be Revived," *NYT*, May 31, 1961, 26; "Modern Museum Sets Film Series," *NYT*, May 1, 1962, 34; "Of Local Origin," *NYT*, August 25, 1961, 17; Howard Thompson, "Six Imports Scheduled," *NYT*, May 19, 1962, 18; Bleeker St. theater ad, *NYT*, September 15, 1963, 135.

22. "Japan Society Film Premier," *New York Times*, December 12, 1954, 134; "Film Board Votes for 'Waterfront,'" *NYT*, December 21, 1954, 31; "'Gate of Hell' Gets Burstyn Film Prize," *NYT*, December 28, 1954, 20; A. H. Weiler, "Critics' 'Best' Goes to 'Waterfront,'" *NYT*, December 29, 1954, 18; "Film Critics Here Present Awards," *NYT*, January 23, 1955, 86; "Of Local Origin," *NYT*, March 19, 1955, 12;

Thomas M. Pryor, "'Waterfront,' Brando, Grace Kelly Win 'Oscars,'" *NYT*, March 31, 1955, 23; and "Hollywood TV Tiff," *NYT*, February 20, 1955, X5.

23. Wilinsky, *Sure Seaters*, 110–11. The movie first broke the Guild's attendance record in February 1955, with 125,000 ("Of Local Origin," *New York Times*, February 23, 1955, 24). It next broke the record for the longest running film at the Guild in April ("Of Local Origin," *NYT*, April 12, 1955, 25). It finally closed on November 6, 1955, after premiering on December 13, 1954 ("Of Local Origin," *NYT*, November 5, 1955, 22); "Japanese 'Gate of Hell' Exceeds 'Queen' and 'Luther' 10-Week Grosses," *Variety*, March 2, 1955, 7; "'Deck' Hep $19,000 Frisco; 'Hell' 7 1/2G," *Variety*, March 9, 1955, 8; "Chi Strong . . . 'Hell' Hot 16G . . ." *Variety*, March 9, 1955, 9.

24. Segrave, *Drive-in Theaters*, 36; Beekman, Vogue, Symphony, and Little Neck theater ads, *New York Times*, December 26, 1955, 22; Symphony, Beekman, Vogue, Center, and Ascot theater ads, *NYT*, December 27, 1955, 30; "Japanese Film," *Chicago Tribune*, February 27, 1955, J19; "Japanese Film," *CT*, March 27, 1955, K3; Lakeside, Hyde Park, Irving, and Stanley Warner theater ads, *CT*, July 24, 1955, E10; "Newsreel," *Time*, June 13, 1955. The film also found continued success in repertory theaters. See *Chicago Tribune*, March 23, 1962, B16; "Film Openings Listed," *NYT*, October 27, 1962, 14; Bleeker St. theater ad, *NYT*, August 25, 1963, X8; Thalia theater ad, *NYT*, December 26, 1963, 37.

25. For more on this practice, see Mayer, *Foreign Films on American Screens*; Philips and Stringer, *Japanese Cinema: Texts and Contexts*, 10–11; Yoshimoto, *Kurosawa: Film Studies and Japanese Cinema*, 9–19.

26. Richie, "A Personal Record," 20–21.

27. Sato, *Kenji Mizoguchi and the Art of Japanese Cinema*, 56; McDonald, *Mizoguchi*; Deleuze, "Figures, or The Transformation of Forms," 78.

28. Richie, *A Hundred Years of Japanese Film*, 272.

29. "Rashomon," *Time*, January 7, 1952, 82; "New Picture," *Time*, September 20, 1954; "The Year in Films," *Time*, January 3, 1955; Robert Hatch, "Films," *Nation*, December 11, 1954, 516; Bosley Crowther, "This Week: Ugetsu," *New York Times*, September 12, 1954, X1; Richie, "A Personal Record," 28; John McCarten, "The Current Cinema: What Happened in Those Woods?" *New Yorker*, December 29, 1951, 60–61.

30. Example borrowed from LeFanu, *Mizoguchi and Japan*, 149.

31. "Miss Kyo's Smudges," *New York Times*, May 15, 1955, SM7; Robert Bingham, "Movies: Ghosts and Flesh," *Reporter*, September 24, 1954, 41.

32. McCarten, "The Current Cinema: What Happened in Those Woods?" 60, and "The Current Cinema: The Potter's Saturday Night," *New Yorker*, September 18, 1954, 62; "Film," *New Republic*, January 14, 1952, 22; Robert Bingham, "Movies: 3 Loves Gone Wrong," *Reporter*, August 11, 1955, 54.

33. Richie, *Films of Akira Kurosawa*, 79; Galbraith, *The Emperor and the Wolf*, 130–32.

34. Aline B. Saarinen, "Our Cultural Pattern 1929–and Today," *New York Times*, October 17, 1954, SM24; Parker Tyler, "*Rashomon* as Modern Art," 151.

35. "Rashomon," *Newsweek*, January 7, 1952, 59; "Ugetsu," *Newsweek*, September 20, 1954, 100; "New Picture," *Time*, September 20, 1954; "The New Pictures," *Time*, December 13, 1954; Arthur Knight, "Japan's Film Revolution," *Saturday Review*, December 1, 1954, 26; McCarten, "The Potter's Saturday Night," 62.

36. Knight, "Japan's Film Revolution," 26–27; Hatch, "Films," 517; "Universal Samurai," *Newsweek*, December 13, 1954, 98.

37. Richie and Anderson, "Traditional Theater and the Film of Japan."

38. Bosley Crowther, "The Screen in Review," *New York Times*, December 27, 1951, 37, and "Gem from Japan," *NYT*, January 6, 1952, X1; "Ugetsu," *Newsweek*, September 20, 1954, 98; "Rashomon," *Newsweek*, 59; McCarten, "The Current Cinema: The Potter's Saturday Night," 6.

39. Hatch, "Films," 516; "The New Pictures," *Time*, December 13, 1954; Bosley Crowther, "Under the Wire," *New York Times*, December 19, 1954, X3.

40. "Rashomon," *Newsweek*, January 7, 1952, 59.

41. Crowther, "The Screen in Review," 31; Knight, "Japan's Film Revolution," 26; "Universal Samurai," 98.

42. "Ugetsu," *Newsweek*, 98. For another example, see the review of the film in the *Saturday Review*.

43. "Japanese Films' Big Nip-Up," *Variety*, November 17, 1954, 7; "The Year in Films," *Time*, January 3, 1955; "Foreign Film Fare," *New York Times*, March 6, 1955, SM26.

44. "Daiei Copper of Prizes, Topper of Jap Profits," *Variety*, April 20, 1955, 3; "Japan Exports Soar 19% over '55," *Variety*, August 15, 1956, 16.

45. Thomas M. Pryor, "Hollywood Annual," *New York Times*, March 18, 1956, 131; "Manhattan's Japanese Film Festival," *Variety*, January 30, 1957, 7. Other mini festivals were subsequently held at art house and repertory theaters. A. H. Weiler, "By Way of Report," *NYT*, December 6, 1959, X9; Bleeker St. theater ad, *NYT*, October 24, 1962, 44; "Of Local Origin," *NYT*, November 14, 1962, 43; Bleeker St. theater ad, *NYT*, April 7, 1964, 28.

46. Galbraith, *Emperor and the Wolf*, 296–98; Bosley Crowther, "Screen: Film from Japan," *New York Times*, January 23, 1963, 5.

47. "A Domestic Film Festival," *Saturday Review*, September 11, 1954, 44; "Heyward, Wayne Head Movie Poll," *New York Times*, February 15, 1953, 79; "Japanese Circuits Make Own Films; Calls Von Sternberg Unmeaning Comic," *Variety*, June 23, 1954, 4; "Of Local Origin," *NYT*, July 27, 1955, 15; A. H. Weiler, "By Way of Report," *NYT*, September 25, 1955, X5.

48. Richie and Anderson, *Japanese Film*, 337.
49. Richie, *Films of Akira Kurosawa*, 80; Ray Falk, "Introducing Japan's Top Director" and "Akira Kurosawa: Japan's Poet Laureate of Film." For examples of critics who seek western themes in Kurosawa's work, see Andre Bazin, "*Rashomon*" in Goodwin, *Perspectives on Kurosawa*, 113–14; Goodwin, *Akira Kurosawa and Intertextual Cinema*. For examples of scholars who react to these by arguing instead for Kurosawa's Japaneseness, see Prince, *Warrior's Camera* and "Zen and Selfhood: Patterns of Eastern Thought in Kurosawa's Films." For a critical discussion of the persistence of the debate over Kurosawa's Western-ness versus his Eastern-ness, see Yoshimoto, *Kurosawa*.
50. Richie and Anderson, *Japanese Film*, 229–33; Richie, "A Personal Record," 27. For more on the postwar *chanbara* genre and its comparison to westerns, see Yoshimoto, *Kurosawa*, 227–34.
51. Akira Kurosawa, foreword to Richie and Anderson, *Japanese Film*, 13.
52. Richie, "The Later Films of Yasujiro Ozu," 18. One technical explanation why Ozu's films seemed too Japanese is that he refused to employ eyeline matching in the same way as most Western directors. See Burch, "Akira Kurosawa," 241.
53. Richie and Anderson, *Japanese Film*, 228; "Yuji Ito, Designer for the Theater," *New York Times*, November 4, 1963, 35.
54. Crowther, "Under the Wire," x3; John McCarten, "The Current Cinema: Japanese Passion, English Satire," *New Yorker*, January 8, 1955, 70.
55. Richie and Anderson, *Japanese Film*, 245–50; Galbraith, *Emperor and the Wolf*, 271–74; Ray Falk, "Designed in Japan for the U.S.A.," *New York Times*, March 6, 1960, X9; "On a Japanese 'Flight,'" *NYT*, October 14, 1962, 131; A. M. Rosenthal, "'Buddha' Faces Camera," *NYT*, August 13, 1961, X7; "The Zen Commandments," *Time*, August 11, 1961.
56. "The New Pictures," *Time*, April 25, 1955.
57. Bosley Crowther, "Screen: Nasty Politics in Old Nippon," *New York Times*, March 23, 1955, 27; "Just an Ol' Samurai," *NYT*, January 22, 1956, 93; and "Screen: 'Hidden Fortress' from Japan," *NYT*, January 24, 1962, 24. Dates provided are those of their U.S., as opposed to Japanese, releases.
58. Bosley Crowther, "Screen: Oriental Western," *New York Times*, October 16, 1962, 34; "Screen: Japanese Import," *NYT*, November 20, 1956, 45; and "Eastern Western," *NYT*, November 25, 1956, 145.
59. Galbraith, *Emperor and the Wolf*, 203–6, 249; "Manhattan's Japanese Film Festival"; Robert F. Hawkins, "Politics Plagues Venice Showing—Edinburgh Expands Its Lists," *New York Times*, September 18, 1955, X7; "Cannes Close-Up," *NYT*, May 20, 1956, 119.

60. Bosley Crowther, "Screen: Japanese Cycle," *New York Times*, December 16, 1959, 56.

61. Howard Thompson, "Japanese Film Has Debut at Victoria," *New York Times*, January 11, 1960, 35; Bosley Crowther, "Screen: Change in Scene," NYT, November 23, 1961, 50.

62. Crowther, "Screen: Japanese Cycle," 56; "Screen: Change in Scene," *New York Times*, November 23, 1961, 50; "Screen: Chinese Legend," NYT, September 11, 1956, 41, and "The Screen: From Japan," NYT, June 5, 1959, 17.

63. Philips and Stringer, *Japanese Cinema*, 9.

3. FRIENDSHIP THROUGH FLOWERS

1. Dower, *Embracing Defeat*, 204–13.

2. Hume and Annarino, *When We Get Back Home from Japan*, 2, 8. A copy can be found in the University of Iowa Special Collections.

3. See Alvah, *Unofficial Ambassadors*, 167–97.

4. Ohi, *History of Ikebana*, 4.

5. Ashton, *Delicate Thread*, 142, and "Ikebana International Presents Our Flower Master Advisors," *Ikebana International Magazine*, Spring 1957, 47, archived at the National Arboretum.

6. Edith Weigle, "Japanese Close-Ups," *Chicago Daily Tribune*, February 6, 1955, 16; Makoto Kakao, "Ikebana International Reprints from *Tokyo Monthly* 'Art around Town,'" *Ikebana International Magazine*, Spring 1957, 36; "Art: Grass Moon Master," *Time*, July 11, 1955.

7. See Edith Wiegle, "Japanese Artist to Lecture on Flower Arranging," *Chicago Tribune*, March 3, 1960, C4; B. Altman & Co ad, *New York Times*, September 14, 1961, 9; "Garden Club Plans Exhibit of 'Ikebana,'" CT, October 26, 1961, 58; "Courses and Shows on Schedule," NYT, September 24, 1961, X28; "Events Offered to Homemaker," NYT, October 21, 1961, 14; "Alumnae Club Will See Flower Arranging Art," CT, April 3, 1963, B3.

8. Helen van Pelt Wilson, "Flower Arrangement Trends for 1960," *Flower Grower*, January 1960, 88; Edith Weigle, "You Too Can Learn the Art of Flowers," *Chicago Tribune*, August 4, 1963, G8.

9. Ellen Gordon Allen, "The Magic Carpet of Ikebana International," in *Ikebana International: Our Founders Story and History of Chapter #1*, pamphlet published by Ikebana International, Chapter #1, Washington DC, 1976; and Ferretti, *Friendship through Flowers: The Ikebana International Story*, 25–36.

10. Fay Kramer, "From My Ikebana Notebook," *Ikebana International Magazine*, Spring 1960, 22–23, 42.

11. For a complete list of chapters, see index in Feretti, *Friendship through Flowers*, 109–11, and DeB Longbotham, "Ikebana International Reports a Triumphant Tour," *Ikebana International Magazine*, Spring 1957, 49. See also "Ikebana International: A Resume" and Ruth Dillon "What's Your Querie, Dearie?" (immediately following), *Ikebana International Magazine*, Fall 1959, 44–49.

12. A lot of the correspondence in the regular feature "Ikebana International Reprints Letters from Abroad" in *Ikebana International Magazine* recounts stories like this. For examples, see Spring 1957 issue, 52–53, issue no. 2 (n.d.), 44–45, and April 1959 issue, 10–11.

13. Longbotham, "Ikebana International Reports a Triumphant Tour," 49; "Ikebana International: Our Founders' Story and History of Chapter #1"; "The Week's Events," *New York Times*, July 27, 1958, X39; "Japanese Ikebana Show Opens," *Chicago Tribune*, August 6, 1964, S2; "Master of Floral Arrangement Here for Two Programs," *CT*, August 16, 1960, B2; "Japanese Flower Arrangers to Display Their Ancient Art," *CT*, November 5, 1961, SW A4; "Floral Displays in Westchester Will Be Viewed," *NYT*, May 13, 1962, 99; Kayla Costenoble, "Ogawa Sensei Makes Third Trip to America," *Ikebana International Magazine*, April 1959, 8–9; Ruth Dillon, "Around the World with Houn Ohara," *Ikebana International Magazine*, April 1959, 4–7; Costenoble, "The U.S. Meets the Sparnons," *Ikebana International Magazine*, Spring 1961, 30–31.

14. Fae Huttenlocher, "Summit Meeting of Flower Arrangers," *Better Homes & Gardens*, October 1959, 76–77, 124.

15. Ellen Gordon Allen, "Ideas on Establishing an International Ikebana Association" and "A Tribute," in *Our Founder's Story and History of Chapter #1*, 36, 47; Merrill Dillon, ed., "Ikebana International Reprints Notes from Abroad," *Ikebana International Magazine* 1, no. 2, 44, 1, no. 3, 36; Douglas MacArthur II, "100 Years of Friendship," *Ikebana International Magazine*, Fall 1960, 9.

16. "Arranging," *New Yorker*, April 16, 1960, 33; William Kistler, letter in "Ikebana International Reprints Notes from Abroad," *Ikebana International Magazine*, no. 3 (n.d.), 37. Since the man in question was the director of the American Floral Art School, there is little doubt that he was indeed accepted; Allie Uyehara, e-mail to the author, January 18, 2008; Sparnon, *Japanese Flower Arrangement*, 29.

17. Allie Uyehara, e-mail, January 18, 2008. It should also be noted that Mrs. Uyehara herself fits the typical profile of an International Ikebana member as a white middle-class woman. Her husband is of Japanese ancestry, and she uses his last name. "Museum to Start Class in Floral Art," *New York Times*, March 16, 1960, 41; "Arranging," 33. All currency calculations derived by the U.S. Bureau of Labor Statistics' Inflation Calculator at http://data.bls.gov/cgi-bin/cpicalc.pl.

18. For examples of members of Asian ancestry, see the chapter reports in *Ikebana International Magazine*, Spring 1960, 33–43.

19. *Rafu Shimpo* Collection. Unfortunately, captions do not specify whether the displays were organized by the International Ikebana or Japanese American ikebana clubs.

20. "Chicago Chapter," *Ikebana International Magazine*, Spring 1960, 38; Johnson's Wax advertisement, *Sunset*, November 1959, 119; Ruth MacKay, "American Born Japanese Girl Achieves Success as a Businesswoman and Artist," *Chicago Tribune*, March 2, 1951, A2; Anne Douglas, "Ancient Japanese Art Inspires Flower Arrangement: A Talented Girl Wins New Fame," CT, December 26, 1954, NB; "Jap-American Center Opened on Ellis Ave," CT, March 7, 1948, S2. For more on Chicago Nisei and assimilation, see Wu, *Color of Success*, 16–42.

21. Sanae Yamazaki for *Pacific Stars and Stripes*, reprinted in *Ikebana International Magazine*, Fall 1959, 24.

22. Clark Powell, *Japanese Flower Arrangement for Beginners*, 84; Rachel E. Carr, "Japanese Arrangers Are Masters of Line, Balance, Form, Harmony," *Flower Grower*, August 1961, 36.

23. Gordon Allen, *Japanese Flower Arrangement in a Nutshell*, 52; Webb, *An Easy Guide to Japanese Flower Arrangement Styles*, 139.

24. "Flower Arrangements in Japan Complex," *New York Times*, July 4, 1953, 8; "A Visit with Madame Arai," *Flower Grower*, November 1959, 38.

25. Rachel Carr, "1-2-3 of Japanese Arrangements," *New York Times*, X26; "The Art of Ikebana Explained," NYT, March 29, 1964, X24; "A Japanese Art," NYT, October 23, 1960, X42.

26. Gordon Allen, *Japanese Flower Arrangement in a Nutshell*, 9; Cleveland, *It's Better with Your Shoes Off*, 41–46; van Pelt Wilson, "Flower Arrangement Trends for 1960," *Flower Grower*, January 1960, 91–92; Rachel Carr, "A Japanese Art," *New York Times*, October 23, 1960; X42.

27. "Ikebana International Presents Our Flower Master Advisors," and Margaret Cromer, "My Sensei Tomoyuki Minomura," *Ikebana International Magazine* 1, no. 3 (1957?): 40–41.

28. Ashton, *Delicate Thread*; "Flower Arranging in Japan Complex," *New York Times*, July 4, 1953, 8; "Ikebana International Presents Our Flower Master Advisors," 5.

29. Report from Houston chapter, *Ikebana International Magazine*, April 1959, 42.

30. See Rachel Carr, "1-2-3 of Japanese Arrangements," *New York Times*, May 4, 1958, X26; Webb, *An Easy Guide to Japanese Flower Arrangement Styles*; Uyehara, *Ten Keys to Japanese Flower Arrangements*, 1–14.

31. Rachel Carr, "New Directions in Japanese Floral Art," *New York Times*, September 23, 1962, 151, and "New Dimensions," *Flower Grower*, August 1963, 35–37.

32. David Anderson, "Ikebana Experts Show Skill Here," *New York Times*, February 22, 1964, 46.

33. Rachel Carr, "New Directions in Japanese Floral Art," *New York Times*, September 23, 1962, 151; van Pelt Wilson, "Flower Arrangement Trends for 1960," *Flower Grower*, January 1960, 88.

34. Sanae Yamazaki for *Pacific Stars and Stripes*, reprinted in *Ikebana International Magazine*, April 1959, 55; Robert C. Cherry, "More Flowers, Please," *New York Times*, February 16, 1964, X23.

35. Kan Yashiroda, "The Amateur Bonsai Fancier," in *Handbook on Dwarfed Potted Trees*, 1975, 81.

36. Yoshimura and Halford, *Japanese Art of Miniature Trees and Landscapes*, 21.

37. "Tiny Trees," *New Yorker*, January 12, 1963, 22.

38. "Kyuzo Murata: The Father of Modern Bonsai" originally found at http://www .users.qwest.net/~rjbphx/Kmurata.html. While the website no longer exists, a copy of this article remains in the BBG; *Handbook on Dwarfed Potted Trees*, 1953, 221; Gertrude H. Stewart, "Yuji Yoshimura Authors Book on Bonsai," *Ikebana International Magazine* 1, no. 2 (n.d.): 50.

39. Elizabeth Scholtz, "Accentuate the Positive" (original publication and date unknown), BBG; "Bonsai," *Brooklyn Botanic Garden Annual Report 1961–1964*, 14–16; Robert Hubert, "Frank Okamura: Bonsaiman and Teacher" (original publication and date unknown); Thad McGar "Bonsai at BBG: Eighty Years of Tender Loving Care," *Brooklyn Botanic Garden Volunteer and Staff Newsletter*, April 2005, 4, 24, all available in BBG.

40. *Handbook on Dwarfed Potted Trees*, 56; "Orchids in the South—Other Activities," *New York Times*, January 17, 1954, X21.

41. Hubert, "Frank Okamura"; McGar, "Bonsai at BBG"; Stuart Lavietes, "Frank Okamura, Bonsai Expert, Is Dead at 94," *New York Times*, January 14, 2006; interview with Elizabeth Scholtz, former BBG director of adult education, Brooklyn Botanic Garden, Brooklyn NY, July 15, 2008.

42. George S. Avery Jr., "Intriguing Subject—Intriguing Teacher," *New York Times*, August 7, 1955, X36.

43. Elias, "History of the Introduction and Establishment of Bonsai in the Western World," 75–76; Yoshimura and Halford, *Japanese Art of Miniature Trees and Landscapes*, 1; "Courses, Lectures and Other Notes," *New York Times*, January 11, 1959, X46; "Tours, Courses and Lectures," *NYT*, April 26, 1957, G7.

44. Hull, *Bonsai for Americans*, 33–36; interview with Elizabeth Scholtz, July 15, 2008; Robert G. Breen, "Dwarf Trees Grown 'Traditionally,'" *Baltimore Sun*, March 4, 1959, 16D; Cherrill Anson, "Devotees of a 1,000-Year-Old Oriental Art," *BS*, March 12, 1961, SM 12.

45. "Dwarf Trees Grown 'Traditionally,'" 16D; "How to Share the Bonsai Hobby," *Sunset*, March 1964, 236; Robert E. Atkinson, "Bonsai in One Day," *Flower Grower*, October 1963, 51; "The Charm and the Art of Bonsai," *American Home*, November 1964, 96.

46. Yashiroda, "The Amateur Bonsai Fancier," 82; Stewart, "Yuji Yoshimura Authors Book on Bonsai," 39; "Tiny Trees," 23; Scholtz interview. I was also assured by Prof. Masumi Izumi's cultural studies seminar at Doshisha University in December 2008 that bonsai continues to be a hobby associated with older retired men.

47. Kobayashi, *Bonsai*, 126; Neal Boenzi, "Study Is Planned in a Japanese Art," *New York Times*, February 2, 1957, 21; Kan Yashiroda, "Caring for 'House Plant' Bonsai," *NYT*, December 1, 1963, 217; Hubert, "Frank Okamura," 1; Zeko Nakamura, "Miniature Bonsai," *Handbook on Dwarfed Potted Trees*, 1953, 46.

48. Yashiroda, "The Amateur Bonsai Fancier," 82; Pomona Tile advertisement, *Sunset*, July 1959, 165.

49. Joanna May Thach, "Japanese Bonsai," *New York Times*, March 29, 1959, X45; Hull, *Bonsai for Americans*, 14–16; "We Tell the 'Secret of Bonsai,'" *Popular Gardening*, January 1963, 28; Yoshimura and Halford, *Japanese Art of Miniature Trees and Landscapes*, 14–19, 172; "Tiny Trees," 23; Scholtz interview.

50. Kobayashi, *Bonsai*, 72–75; Yashiroda, "The Amateur Bonsai Fancier," 83–84, 90; Neal Boenzi, "Study Is Planned in a Japanese Art," *New York Times*, February 2, 1957, 21.

51. "We Tell the 'Secret' of Bonsai," 42; "A Simpler Way to Grow Dwarfs," *Sunset*, April 1954, 276; "Quick Bonsai—by Air Layering," *Sunset*, January 1963, 146–47; "Shopping with an Eye for Plant Structure," *Sunset*, October 1957, 66–67; "It's an 'Adapted' Bonsai," *Sunset*, March 1957, 233.

52. Tatsuo Ishimoto, "Grow Miniature Trees in Less than One Year," *Flower Grower*, November 1959, 26–27; George F. Hull, "Practical Shortcuts to Decorative Bonsai," *New York Times*, December 1, 1963, 217; Mary Alice Roche, "Do-It-Yourself Bonsai," *American Home*, May 1963, 94; Atkinson, 50; "Bonsai Briefs: How to Collect, Care for, Create Your Own," *House & Garden*, November 1963, 306.

53. Kan Yashiroda, "For Bonsai Beginners," *Handbook on Dwarfed Potted Trees*, 1953, 173. This passage criticizing some aspects of American enthusiasm for bonsai was removed in later editions.

54. Miniature Forests Inc. ad, *New York Times*, February 9, 1958, X45.

55. Joanna May Thach, "Japanese Bonsai," *New York Times*, March 29, 1959, X45; Hull, *Bonsai for Americans*, 14–16; "We Tell the 'Secret of Bonsai,'" 28; Yoshimura and Halford, *Japanese Art of Miniature Trees and Landscapes*, 14–19, 172; "Tiny Trees," 23; Scholtz interview; Yashiroda, "The Amateur Bonsai Fancier," 82.

4. HOW TO BE AMERICAN WITH SHIBUI THINGS

1. "The Warmth of Oriental for a Modern House," *Better Homes & Gardens*, February 1959, 39–40; "How Americans Are Using Japanese Ideas," *House Beautiful*, September 1960, 126–36, 177–78.

2. Min, "Japanese/American Architecture," 274.

3. Lancaster, *Japanese Influence in America*, 47–48, 78–83, 97–103, 139; Yoshihara, *Embracing the East*; Harris, "All The World a Melting Pot?"

4. Nute, "Frank Lloyd Wright and *Japanese Homes*," 75. Also see Lancaster, *Japanese Influence in America*, 84–89, and Meech-Pekarik, *Frank Lloyd Wright and the Art of Japan*.

5. For a more detailed discussion of this tendency, see McNeil, "Myths of Modernism," 281–94.

6. See Sand, *House and Home in Modern Japan*, and Waswo, *Housing in Postwar Japan*.

7. Morse quoted in Nute, "Frank Lloyd Wright and *Japanese Homes*," 75; Wright quoted in Lancaster, *Japanese Influence in America*, 88; also Meech-Pekarik, *Frank Lloyd Wright and the Art of Japan*, 263–70.

8. Nelson, "The Japanese House" in *Problems of Design*, 127–31.

9. As an example, see Frank Capra's *Know Your Enemy: Japan*.

10. Nelson, "The Japanese House," 127–31.

11. Lancaster, *Japanese Influence in America*, 172.

12. For a brief history of the planning and sponsorship of the MOMA Japanese house, see *Bulletin of the America-Japan Society*, July–August 1954, MOMA Scrapbook microfilm, reel 5073, frames 628–31.

13. Paul V. Beckly, "Japanese House Here in Crates" *New York Herald Tribune*, March 16, 1954, MOMA Scrapbook microfilm, reel 5074, frame 523; Margaret Parton "Japanese Home Seen at Museum," *New York Herald Tribune*, June 21, 1954, MOMA Scrapbook microfilm, reel 5073, frame 530.

14. The text of this pamphlet was reprinted in *Bulletin of the America-Japan Society*, July–August 1954, MOMA Scrapbook microfilm, reel 5073, frames 626–28.

15. See MOMA Scrapbook, reel 5073, frames 661 and 693, also http://www.shofuso.com. Figure quoted in *Christian Science Monitor*, October 15, 1954, MOMA Scrapbook microfilm, reel 5073, frame 547.

16. Lewis Mumford "Windows and Gardens," *New Yorker*, October 2, 1954, 122–29.

17. Margaret Parton, "Japanese Home Seen at Museum," *New York Herald Tribune*, June 21, 1954, MOMA Scrapbook, reel 5073, frame 530.

18. "A Style of Home Adapted by West," *Life*, December 31, 1951, 61; "Jersey Home's Octagonal Rooms Lend Atmosphere of the Exotic," *New York Times*, May 8, 1960, R1; Curtis Besinger, "Lessons We Are Learning from Japan," *House Beautiful*, September 1960, 121.

19. "Announcing the Award Winners of the Second Biennial Round of the American Institute of Architects–Sunset Magazine Western Home Awards," *Sunset*, September 1959, 65. For an excellent example, see the AIA award-winning house featured on page 75 of the same issue.

20. Elizabeth Rannells, "The Japanese Touch in a Rural Home," *New York Times*, July 18, 1954, C24; Cynthia Kellogg, "Translated from the Japanese," *NYT*, February 23, 1958, SM48; Kathryn Geraghty, "Oriental Décor in a Baltimore Split-Level," *Baltimore Sun*, July 10, 1960, 194; "A Bit of Japan on the Magothy," *BS*, June 24, 1962, SM20; Pauline Graves, "Try This for a Unique Vacation House," *Chicago Tribune*, July 7, 1963, SW18. For other examples, see General Motors, *American Look*, 1958.

21. For examples, see "Long Island Home Blends Oriental Styling with Contemporary Open Plan," *New York Times*, June 22, 1958, R1, and "Shows Ranch Home in Japan Motif," *Chicago Tribune*, September 15, 1962.

22. "4 Model Homes in Settings That Fit Imported Names," *Chicago Tribune*, June 30, 1962, N10. The "shoji room" is mentioned in Cherry Hill ad, *CT*, June 3, 1962, H25. Unfortunately, the ad provides no explanation as to what exactly this feature would entail.

23. See Lancaster, *Japanese Influence in America*, 51–64; Converse Brown, "The Japanese Taste"; Yoshihara, *Embracing the East*; and Hoganson, *Consumer's Imperium*, 36.

24. "What Japan Can Contribute to Your Way of Life," *House Beautiful*, August 1960, 54–56, 119; Anthony West, "What Japan Has That We May Profitably Borrow," *House Beautiful*, August 1960, 118.

25. "How to Be *Shibui* with American Things," *House Beautiful*, September 1960, 149; Elizabeth Gordon "New Home Furnishings with the *Shibui* Concept of Beauty," *House Beautiful*, September 1960, 159.

26. Engel, *Japanese Gardens for Today*, 6; Mori, *Typical Japanese Gardens*, 6.

27. Engel admired his finished product so much that he even took the stones from the garden back to his New Jersey residence following the exhibit. "Precious Stones from Japan Will Adorn Princeton Pond," *Trenton NJ Times*, August 8, 1958, and "Japanese Stones to Adorn Garden near Princeton," *Princeton Packet*, August 8, 1958, MOMA Scrapbook microfilm, reel 5073, frame 723.

28. "In Golden Gate Park, Cherry Trees Are Ready to Blossom," *Sunset*, March 1959, 3; "The New Harvest Shrine," in Brooklyn Botanic Garden report "The First 50 Years," 1938 Annual Report of the BBG, 24–25, both in the BBG Collection; "Seattle's Japanese Garden," *Ikebana International Magazine*, Fall 1960, 52, National Arboretum.

29. June Meehan, "In Japan You Will Find the Most Meaningful Gardens in the World," *House Beautiful*, January 1962, 82–83, 120–21; David Engel, "Translating

the Japanese Garden into American Terms," *House Beautiful*, September 1960, 161–63, 191–96.

30. Mori, *Typical Japanese Gardens*, 8, 155.
31. "Intimate Garden . . . in the Japanese Manner," *Sunset*, January 1955, 100; "Gardens in the Japanese Manner," *Sunset*, May 1962, 118–23.
32. "The Japanese Influence in American Gardens," *Flower Grower*, November 1959, 29.
33. "New York Flower Show Preview," *New York Times*, February 23, 1958, X41; "Flower Shows Start This Week," *NYT*, March 4, 1962, 127; "World Gardens Imported for Chicago Flower Show," *Chicago Tribune*, January 8, 1961, SB; Mary Merryfield, "City Gardens Import Illusion," *CT*, May 21, 1961, F7.
34. George Avery to "Dear Member," July 1961, BBG; "Ryoanji Stone Garden," in Brooklyn Botanic Garden Report 1961–1964, 37, BBG.
35. "A Quiet Place: Japanese Stone Garden at the Port of New York," *Via the Port of New York*, date unknown, BBG; George Avery to "Dear Member," July 1961, BBG; interview with Elizabeth Scholtz, July 15, 2008, Brooklyn Botanic Garden, Brooklyn NY.
36. "Garden?" *New Yorker*, September 7, 1963, 28; interview with Elizabeth Scholtz, July 15, 2008.
37. Ryoanji Temple Stone Garden brochure, Brooklyn Botanic Garden, 1963, BBG; Susan E. Sargoy, "Stone Garden to Be Dedicated in Brooklyn," *New York Times*, May 26, 1963, 119.
38. Kaoru Ito mentions the phenomenon of Japanese American men becoming gardeners following the war in her interview, tape 1, side B, JACL/CSUS; see also Ogawa, *From Japs to Japanese*.
39. Kikuchi, *Kikuchi Diary*, 132–33.
40. For a blow-by-blow account of their arguments, see Ashton, *Noguchi: East and West*, 146–47.
41. For more on Noguchi's biracial, bicultural, and ultimately transcendent status, see Ashton, *Noguchi: East and West*; Lyford, *Isamu Noguchi's Modernism*; Duus, *Life of Isamu Noguchi*; Winther-Tamaki, *Art in the Encounter of Nations*; Fletcher, *Isamu Noguchi: Master Sculptor*; Apostolos-Cappadona and Altshuler, *Isamu Noguchi: Essays and Conversations*.
42. T. H. Parker, "West 54th Meet East," *Hartford Courant*, July 4, 1954, MoMA Scrapbook microfilm reel 5073, frame 541; Tom Donnelly, "Pardon Me While I Push This Wall Away," *Washington DC News*, July 6, MoMA Scrapbook microfilm reel 5073, frame 541; Betty Pepis, "Japanese House Gets Praise Here," *New York Times*, August 9, MoMA Scrapbook microfilm reel 5073, frame 535.

43. "Zen Grows in Brooklyn," *Newsweek*, June 10, 1963, 69; interview with Elizabeth Scholtz, July 15, 2008.

44. Auslander, *Taste and Power*, 11–12.

45. Horowitz, *American Social Classes in the 1950s*, 61–62.

46. Morton, *Home and Its Furnishings*, 262–64.

47. Gordon, "New Home Furnishings with the Shibui Concept of Beauty," *House Beautiful*, September 1960, 159.

48. For more on the content and readership of postwar women's magazines, see Walker, *Shaping Our Mother's World* and *Women's Magazines, 1940–1960*.

49. Mary McCarthy "Up the Ladder from *Charm* to *Vogue*," *Reporter*, July 18, 1950, reprinted in *Women's Magazines, 1940–1960*, 248.

50. Yamazaki, *We Loved Every Minute*.

51. Virtue Brother Manufacturing ad, *Sunset*, May 1959, 253.

52. Betty Pepis, "'Tradition' Theme of New Furniture," *New York Times*, January 8, 1954, 24.

53. Betty Pepis, "From the Far East," *New York Times*, December 14, 1952, SM46; Gloria Emerson, "Japanese Works on Sale in Profusion Here," *NYT*, October 24, 1960, 23; Cynthia Kellogg, "Oriental Fad in the House Due to Last," *NYT*, April 14, 1958, 14.

54. "Samurai's Meeting Place Imported for Sale Here," *New York Times*, October 7, 1960, 39; According to http://www.bls.gov/data/inflation_calculator.htm, the house would have cost about $65,000 in 2015. Unfortunately, figures on how many prefab teahouses were actually sold are unavailable.

55. Johnson, *MITI and the Japanese Miracle*, 228–32.

56. "Washington HFL Foreign Promotion Award to Japan," *Retailing Daily*, May 4, 1954, MoMA Scrapbook microfilm, reel 5073, frame 529. Accepting the award on behalf of Japan was Junzo Yoshimura. "Japanese Furniture, Fabrics Are Shown at Trade Center," *New York Times*, January 15, 1958, 33.

57. Gloria Emerson, "Japanese Specialty Store to Open on Fifth Avenue" *New York Times*, June 27, 1958, 22; Takashimaya department store ad, *NYT*, March 10, 1960, 8; Takashimaya department store ad, *NYT*, August 12, 1961, 7.

58. Cynthia Kellogg, "Home Furnishings Report: Background Story," *New York Times*, September 25, 1960, SMA9; "Esquire" ad, *NYT*, September 26, 1956, 43; "Shoji Screen's Popularity," *NYT*, October 29, 1957, 26; Carson Pririe Scott department store ad, *Chicago Tribune*, October 19, 1959, A7.

59. See Bloomingdale's department store ad, *New York Times*, September 21, 1958, 63; Gimbel's department store ad, *New York Times*, July 13, 1958, 20; and Macy's department store ad, *NYT*, April 12, 1959, 40. Price in current dollars determined using the Bureau of Labor Statistics' Inflation Calculator at http://data.bls.gov/cgi-bin/cpicalc.pl.

60. "Other Chapters in Action," *Ikebana International Magazine*, Spring 1960, 49.

61. Betty Pepis, "Solving Built-in Problems," *New York Times*, September 2, 1956, SM26; "Easy Way to Divide: Use Screen," *Chicago Tribune*, May 7, 1959, N A15.

62. Kellogg, "Oriental Fad in the House Due to Last," 14; "Easy Way to Divide: Use Screen," N A15; Mandel Bros. department store ad, *Chicago Tribune*, March 1, 1959, 26; Bernard Gladstone, "Shoji Screen," *New York Times*, August 28, 1960, X36

63. "Style Trends in Furniture Are on View," *New York Times*, July 11, 1958, 27; B. Altman & Co. department store ad, NYT, November 27, 1960, 125; Pauline Graves, "Make Your Own Outlook," *Chicago Tribune*, March 29, 1959, G32; "Readers Help Put More Comfort, Charm into Home" CT, September 10, 1960, N A3.

64. "Japanese Hibachi Cooking: New in American Living Rooms," *Vogue*, May 1, 1954, 154; Poppy Cannon, "The Pace Setter House Introduces the Hibachi," *House Beautiful*, November 1953, 322.

65. Patricia Rile, "Her Hobby: Cooking and Serving Foreign Food," *Chicago Tribune*, March 21, 1958, B3; Frieda Zylstra, "Harriet Lee Finds Cooking Exciting, Satisfying Hobby," CT, August 19, 1960, B9; Frieda Zylstra, "His Guests Do the Cooking," CT, August 17, 1962, B9; Mary Meade "Foods to Fix on Hibachi," CT, February 3, 1960, B3, and "Fix Franks on the Hibachi," CT, February 10, 1960, B3.

66. For more on Japanese architects' use of Western styles and modernist Japanese architecture more generally, see Stewart, *Making of a Modern Japanese Architecture*, 186–218.

5. SATORI IN AMERICA

1. "Professor Phillips to Keynote Conference on Zen Buddhism," *Campus* (student newspaper), April 17, 1959, Sarah Lawrence College. Records from the college's archives do not reveal the reasons why they decided to host such an event, but it appears that the school gave ongoing support to those interested in Zen outside of the conference. Beginning in 1936, Zen-inspired psychologist Erich Fromm conducted research there, and in 1949 the college hosted a guest lecture by Zen-influenced author J. D. Salinger.

2. Anita Silvers, "Zen Conference Notes Found at Site of Unearthed College," *Campus*, April 24, 1959, Sarah Lawrence College.

3. For examples see introductions to Sparnon, *Japanese Flower Arrangement* and Hull, *Bonsai for Americans,* and "Garden?" *New Yorker*, September 7, 1963, 28.

4. This general overview of Zen belief is constructed from the numerous books on the subject footnoted throughout the chapter. All were written for either European or American audiences, published in English (if not initially then

at least in translation), and produced by those who followed Soyen's school of thought.

5. Sharf, "The Zen of Japanese Nationalism."

6. For a thorough and now canonical account of this movement, see Hughes, *Consciousness and Society.* For a concise summary of cultural relativism, see Perry, *Intellectual Life in America,* 319–24.

7. McMahan, *Making of Buddhist Modernism,* 3–25.

8. For an excellent synopsis of the koan training process, see "Zen Training" in First Zen Institute of America, *Cat's Yawn,* 31–32.

9. Fields, *How the Swans Came to the Lake,* 119–29.

10. See Hearn, *Japan's Religions,* 240, and *Gleanings in Buddha Fields,* 223–29.

11. Sharf, "The Zen of Japanese Nationalism," 14–18. See also Verhoeven, "Americanizing the Buddha: Paul Carus and the Transformation of Asian Thought."

12. For more on Sokei-an's life, see Sasaki, *Holding the Lotus to the Rock.*

13. McMahan, *Making of Modern Buddhism*; Graebner, *Age of Doubt,* 19–68, 121–43.

14. Watts, *Way of Zen,* x.

15. See reprint in Stirling, *Zen Pioneer,* 179–246.

16. "The Zen Priest," *Time,* May 26, 1958, 65; Ruth Stephan, "The Zen Priests and Their Six Persimmons," *Harper's Magazine,* June 1962, 48.

17. Stirling, *Zen Pioneer,* 131–58; "The Zen Priest," 65; Ruth Fuller Sasaki, "Letter from Kyoto," *Zen Notes,* March 4, 1957, and "Letter from Kyoto," *Zen Notes,* August 3, 1957, First Zen Institute.

18. Tea and Queries Notes, November 25, 1962, and Zazenkai Meeting Notes, August 27, 1961, November 26, 1962, First Zen Institute.

19. Stephan, "The Zen Priests and Their Six Persimmons," 47.

20. Daisetz Teitaro Suzuki, "Early Memories," manuscript available at First Zen Institute; Abe, *A Zen Life.*

21. See Sharf, "The Zen of Japanese Nationalism." Also see Christmas Humphries, preface to Suzuki, *Living by Zen.*

22. Fields, *How the Swans Came to the Lake,* 196; "People Are Talking About," *Vogue,* January 15, 1957, 98; NBC television network ad, *New York Times,* April 1, 1959, 74.

23. Fromm, "Memories of Dr. D. T. Suzuki"; Winthrop Sargeant, "Profiles: Great Simplicity," *New Yorker,* August 31, 1957, 36; Merton, "D. T. Suzuki: The Man and His Work," in *Zen and the Birds of Appetite,* 61.

24. See Iwamura, *Virtual Orientalism,* 25–32; Daniel J. Bronstein, "Search for Inner Truth," *Saturday Review,* November 16, 1957, 23; Sargeant, "Profiles: Great Simplicity," 34.

25. Watts, "Zen and Control," in *This Is IT,* 61–75.

26. See Keightley, *Into Every Life a Little Zen Must Fall*; Clark, *Pantheism of Alan Watts.*

27. Furlong, *Zen Effects*; Watts, *In My Own Way*; Watts, *Zen and the Beat Way*.

28. Sasaki, *Holding the Lotus to the Rock*, 156; Ruth Fuller Sasaki to "Everyone," July 5, 1951, First Zen Institute. Ruth Fuller Sasaki's annotated personal copies of Watts's *This Is IT*, Suzuki's *Essence of Buddhism*, and Suzuki's *Zen and Japanese Culture* can still be found in the library at Ryosen-an, Kyoto.

29. Watts, *In My Own Way*, 143; D. T. Suzuki, "Zadankai: Zen no kokusai-sei ni tsuite," *Zen Bunka* 1963, quoted in Yamada, *Shots in the Dark*, 222.

30. "The Real Spirit of Zen?" *Newsweek*, September 21, 1959, 121–22; Berg, "Beating the Drum with Gary," 383; "Zensation," *Time*, February 23, 1959, 52. Suzuki in particular was responsible for promoting the connection between Zen and dying an honorable death in battle. See Victoria, "Zen as a Cult of Death in the Wartime Writings of D. T. Suzuki."

31. Masatsugu, "Beyond This World of Transiency and Impermanence." Quotation from Watts first appeared in Alan Watts, "A Program for Buddhism in America," *Berkeley Bussei*, 1952, 21.

32. Jackson MacLow interview with Peter Dickinson, in Dickinson, *Cage Talk*, 95.

33. "Art: Contemporaries Abroad," *Time*, July 22, 1957, 56–57.

34. Tobey, "Japanese Traditions in American Art," 157.

35. Kass, "The Art of Morris Graves: Meditation on Nature," and *Morris Graves*, 20.

36. Wight, *Morris Graves*, 19; Kass, "The Art of Morris Graves," 24.

37. Nicholls, *John Cage*, 31–36; Earle Brown interview with Peter Dickinson in *Cage Talk*, 138; Wehr, "Mark Tobey: A Dialogue between Painting and Music," 34.

38. Quoted in Shultis, *Silencing the Sounded Self*, 93.

39. For a more complete discussion of all the characteristics of Cage's music listed above and how they relate to Zen, see Pauline Oliveros's interview with Peter Dickinson in *Cage Talk*, 172–73. For examples, see Shultis, *Silencing the Sounded Self*, 85–126; various interviews in *Cage Talk*; Roger Maren, "The Musical Numbers Game," *Reporter*, March 6, 1958, 39; Edward Downes, "4 Pianists Play Tense Silences," *New York Times*, May 1, 1957, 42; Harold C. Schonberg, "The Far-Out Pianist," *Harper's Magazine*, June 1960, 49–54.

40. Watts, *This Is IT*, 94–95.

41. Nicholls, *John Cage*, 59; Schonberg, "The Far-Out Pianist," 49.

42. See Herzogenrath and Kreul, *Sounds of the Inner Eye*, as well as Graves, *Drawings of Morris Graves with Comments by the Artist*.

43. Watts, *This Is IT*, 97

44. Howard Devree, "News about Art and Artists," *New York Times*, February 29, 1956, 27, "Symbol and Image," NYT, March 4, 1956, X14, and "Award at Venice," NYT, June 22, 1958, X15; "American Art Award Winner Named," NYT, December 3,

1958, 12; Ross Parmenter, "Music: Experimenter," *NYT*, May 16, 1958, 20. According to Schonberg, disagreement was still prevalent over Cage's work as a number of audience members whistled and catcalled from the balcony.

45. Alexander, *Salinger*; Ranchan, *An Adventure in Vedanta*; "Sonny: An Introduction," *Time*, September 15, 1961; "The Mysterious J. D. Salinger . . . His Woodsy, Secluded Life," *Newsweek*, May 30, 1960, 93.

46. Salinger, *Franny and Zooey*, 65.

47. See essays collected in Grunwald, *Salinger: A Critical and Personal Portrait*: quotation taken from Ihab Hassan, "The Rare Quixotic Gesture," 153. See also Leslie Fiedler, "Up from Adolescence," 56–62; George Steiner, "The Salinger Industry," 82–85; Frederick L. Gwynn and Joseph L. Blotner, "One Hand Clapping," 102–14.

48. See Hale, *Rise and Crisis of Psychoanalysis in the United States*; Shorter, *A History of Psychiatry*, 145–89; Grob, *Mad among Us*, 223–48.

49. Ruth Fuller Sasaki to "Dear Everyone," July 5, 1951, and "Rinzai Zen Study for Foreigners in Japan," 1960, reprinted in Stirling, *Zen Pioneer*, 188; Watts, "Zen and Control" in *This Is IT*. See also McMahan, *Making of Buddhist Modernism*, 192–94. The psychology shelf still exists at the Ryosen-an library. It is largely dominated by the works of Carl Jung, but also contains several books by Erich Fromm.

50. Alan Watts, "The Ways of the Mind," *New York Times*, October 16, 1960, BR35.

51. Fader, "D. T. Suzuki's Contribution to the West," 102–4.

52. Akihisa Kondoo, "The Stone Bridge of Joshu," and "Zen in Psychotherapy: The Virtue of Sitting," *Chicago Review* 12, no. 2 (1958): 57–64.

53. Funk, *Erich Fromm*; Burston, *Legacy of Erich Fromm*; Fader, "D. T. Suzuki's Contribution to the West," 102.

54. Fromm, Suzuki, and DeMartino, *Zen Buddhism and Psychoanalysis*, 79.

55. Jacobs, *America's Miracle Man in Vietnam*, 189–94.

56. Peter Fingesten, "Beat and Buddhist," *Christian Century*, February 25, 1959, 227.

57. For information on the National Council of Churches, see Wuthnow, *Restructuring of American Religion*, 81–82; for more on the World Council of Churches, see Fitzgerald, *Ecumenical Movement*, 103–26. For examples of ecumenical thinkers reaching out to other faiths, see Kinnamon and Cope, *Ecumenical Movement: An Anthology*. The Catholic Church did not become involved in the ecumenical movement until the 1960s and was thus not part of the original NCC.

58. Wuthnow, *Restructuring of American Religion*, 94; Fitzgerald, *Ecumenical Movement*, 127–44; Second Vatican Council, "Declaration on the Relation of the Church to Non-Christian Religions," 399.

59. Sales figure taken from "Religion: The Mountain," *Time*, April 11, 1949. For more on the life of Thomas Merton, see Forest, *Living with Wisdom*; Furlong, *Merton: A Biography*; Maltis, *Solitary Explorer*; Merton, *Seven Story Mountain*.

60. Thomas Merton, diary entry, July 10, 1964, printed in Daggy, *Encounter*, 89–90.

61. See Daggy, *Encounter*; Maltis, *Solitary Explorer*, 104–13; Thomas Merton, "Wisdom in Emptiness" in *Zen and the Birds of Appetite*, 99–138; Thomas Merton, "Zen: Sense and Sensibility," *America*, May 25, 1963, 752. For a further explication of this notion of melding Zen with Catholicism, see Graham, *Zen Catholicism*.

62. Snyder, "Spring *Sesshin* at Shokoku-ji."

6. ZEN GOES "BOOM"

1. "Zen," *Time*, February 4, 1957, 65.

2. Nancy Wilson Ross, "What Is Zen?" *Mademoiselle*, January 1958, 64; Ruth Fuller Sasaki, "Rinzai Zen Study for Foreigners in Japan," 182.

3. Watts, "Beat Zen, Square Zen & Zen."

4. Lamport, *Scrap Irony*, 73.

5. Dorothy Barclay, "Summer Vacations for Many Parents End 2 Weeks Sooner than for Young," *New York Times*, August 22, 1958, 24.

6. "Macrobiotics," *New Yorker*, August 25, 1962, 22; Tea and Queries notes, July 30, 1961 and September 30, 1962, First Zen Institute. According to Mary Farkas, Mr. Ohsawa had never studied Zen, nor was he a member of any Zen organization. It seemed to be the consensus among Institute members that the diet was mainly a scam to make money, without any real association with the Zen religion.

7. Watts, *Way of Zen*, ix.

8. The book also came to be admired among prominent Nazis. See Victoria, "A Zen Nazi in Wartime Japan."

9. Chang, *Practice of Zen*, xi.

10. I hesitate to draw any kind of Cold War–based conclusions about this fact. For example, Americans did not use the word *ch'an* because of possible associations with Red China. At the same time, Americans were using the Chinese terms *yin* and *yang* as opposed to the Japanese *in* and *yo*. It seems that the issue of which language English speakers borrowed from in creating such neologisms was simply a matter of which country they heard the term from first.

11. Ruth Fuller Sasaki made this point forcefully herself, by taking issue with many of Suzuki's assertions in the margins of her copy of his book. Sasaki, marginalia in Suzuki, *Zen and Japanese Culture*, Ryosen-an.

12. Example suggested in Yamada, *Shots in the Dark*, 22.

13. "Zensation," *Time*, February 23, 1959, 52.

14. David Robbins, "Something for Everyone," *New York Times*, June 14, 1959, BR37.

15. Gay Talese, "Zen Selling Better than Sodas, 'Village' Store Scraps Fountain," *New York Times*, September 12, 1959, 11.

16. Tweed, "Nightstand Buddhists and Other Creatures: Sympathizers, Adherents, and the Study of Religion," 74–75.

17. Chang, *Practice of Zen*, 115; William Barrett, introduction to Suzuki, *Zen Buddhism*, xx.

18. Tea and Queries Notes, November 25, 1962, Zazenkai Meeting Notes, August 27, 1961, November 26, 1962, and Annual Meeting, November 25, 1962, First Zen Institute.

19. Gary Snyder, foreword to Stirling, *Zen Pioneer*, xii; Yampolsky, "Kyoto, Zen, Snyder," 67; Fuller Sasaki, "Rinzai Zen Study for Foreigners in Japan." For an example of a Western adherent abandoning Zen study, see the conclusion of van de Wetering, *Empty Mirror*. In this fictionalized memoir, the author gives up Zen study after he is confounded by his koan, exhausted by monastery routine, and discouraged by the lack of progress he feels he is making.

20. Stephan, "The Zen Priests and Their Six Persimmons," 47–53; Highet, *Talents and Geniuses*, 315–21.

21. Sargeant, "Profiles: Great Simplicity," 42; "The Afternoon of a Book Lover," *New York Times*, March 16, 1960, 19.

22. J. Donald Adams, "Speaking of Books," *New York Times*, November 16, 1958, BR2.

23. Furlong, *Zen Effects*, 76–77; Watts, *In My Own Way*, 262–63, and *This Is IT*, 79.

24. Ruth Fuller Sasaki, "Zen: A Method for Religious Awakening," 1959, reprinted in Stirling, *Zen Pioneer*, 176.

25. Herrigel, *Zen in the Art of Archery*. For a discussion of the authenticity of the techniques described in Herrigel's account, see Yamada, *Shots in the Dark*, 43–74.

26. Ray Bradbury, "Zen and the Art of Writing," *Writer*, October 1958, 10. Bradbury later reused this title for a collection of essays published in the 1980s.

27. Barrett, introduction to Suzuki, *Zen Buddhism*, x.

28. Watts, *This Is TI*, 29, 48, 67.

29. Reps and Senzaki, *Zen Flesh, Zen Bones*, 18.

30. Stephan, "The Zen Priests and Their Six Persimmons," 51; Wilson Ross, "What Is Zen?" 116–17.

31. Calvin Tomkins, "Zen in the Art of Tennis," *New Yorker*, August 8, 1959, 24.

32. Fuller Sasaki, "Zen: A Method for Religious Awakening," 163.

33. Salinger, *Seymour: An Introduction*, 242.

34. Snyder, foreword to Stirling, *Zen Pioneer*, xii; Ruth Fuller Sasaki, "Dear Every-one," November 5, 1956, First Zen Institute and marginalia in Suzuki, *Zen and Japanese Culture*, 253, Ryosen-an library.

35. For an excellent Beat tirade against middle-class materialist striving, see Krim, "Making It!"

36. See Lipton, *Holy Barbarians*; Rigney, *Real Bohemia*; Prothero, *Big Sky Mind*; Belgrad, *Culture of Spontaneity*.

37. Podhoretz, "The Know-Nothing Bohemians"; John Ciardi, "Epitaph for the Dead Beats," *Saturday Review*, February 6, 1960, 11; Stuart Mitchner, "Those Phony Beatniks!" *Chicago Tribune*, November 8, 1959, E47; Nelson Algren, "Chicago Is a Wose," *Nation*, February 28, 1959, 191. For overview and analysis of the press coverage on the Beats, see Rigney, *Real Bohemia*, 151–61.

38. Gilbert Millstein, "Books of the Times," *New York Times*, September 5, 1957, 27; Goodman, *Growing Up Absurd*, 155–72; Wolfgang B. Fleishmann, "Those 'Beat' Writers," *America*, September 26, 1959, 766–68; L. J. Hines, "Stephenson and the Beats," *Commonweal*, September 9, 1960, 466.

39. Paul O'Neil, "The Only Rebellion Around," *Life*, November 30, 1959, 116, 126–29; Lawrence E. Davies, "Coast Bohemians Feeling Less Beat," *New York Times*, June 14, 1959, 75; Abraham & Straus department store ad, NYT, August 2, 1959, 26; Abraham & Straus department store ad, NYT, January 3, 1960, 48; "Movement" *New Yorker*, April 16, 1960.

40. See Friedrich, *Gita within Walden*, esp. 83–111, which discusses both books' conceptions of "reality and being."

41. Allen Ginsberg, letter to Neal Cassady, May 14, 1953, reprinted in *Big Sky Mind*.

42. For more detailed information on how Kerouac and other Beat writers first encountered Zen, as well as their personal Buddhist practices, see Masatsugu, "Reorienting the Pure Land."

43. Kerouac, *Dharma Bums*, 161.

44. Aronowitz, "St. Jack."

45. For a discussion of the breadth of Kerouac's Buddhist understanding, see Giamo, *Kerouac, the Word and the Way*, 131–48.

46. Lipton, *Holy Barbarians*, 252.

47. Zen falls under the umbrella of Mahayanism. Such a label as Kerouac gives himself would have in fact been highly unlikely, considering Mahayana Buddhism arose as a movement to reform Hinayana. Most likely he means to imply that he is a holdover from the old school, which he believed valued enlightenment and

mercy over disciplined instruction. See Yoshihito and Vardaman, *Talking about Buddhism*, 73–75, and Berrigan, "The Art of Fiction: Jack Kerouac," 67.

48. Kerouac, *Dharma Bums*, 13.

49. Kerouac, *Dharma Bums*, 28–29. In the book's description of the practice, Japhy demonstrates yabyum by sitting naked while his girlfriend, Princess, also naked, straddles his lap and looks deep into his eyes.

50. Kerouac, *Dharma Bums*, 202. For more on Kerouac's ties to Catholicism, see Giamo, *Kerouac, the Word and the Way*.

51. Gary Snyder to Ruth Fuller Sasaki, May 3, 1953, First Zen Institute; Watts, *This Is IT*, 100; Fields, *How the Swans Came to the Lake*, 213–15; Snyder to Mary Farkas, April 16, 1952, First Zen Institute; Snyder, "Note on Religious Tendencies."

52. Dodge, "Ten Snyder Stories," 143.

53. Kerouac, *Dharma Bums*, 204–5.

54. Rigney, *Real Bohemia*, 33–39; Lipton, *Holy Barbarians*, 169; Harry T. Moore, "Cool Cats Don't Dig the Squares," *New York Times*, May 24, 1959, BR1; Julian Messner Publishing ad, *NYT*, July 1, 1959, 29.

55. Kerouac, *Dharma Bums*, 97–98.

56. Goodman, *Growing Up Absurd*, 113.

57. Kerouac, *Dharma Bums*, 97–98.

58. "Manners & Morals: Fried Shoes," *Time*, February 9, 1959.

59. Millstein, "Books of the Times," 27; Talese, "Zen Selling Better than Sodas," 11; Charles Poore, "Books of the Times," *New York Times*, February 28, 1959, 17; "Zen Hur," *Time*, December 14, 1959, 66.

60. J. Donald Adams, "Speaking of Books," *New York Times*, October 26, 1958, BR2; Charles Poore, "Books of the Times," *NYT*, October 2, 1958, 35; Herbert Gold, "The Beat Mystique," in *The Beats*, 161; Ciardi, "Epitaph for the Dead Beats," 12; Burroughs quoted in Jack Kerouac letter to Allen Ginsberg, August 23, 1954, reprinted in *Big Sky Mind*, 295.

61. Stirling, *Zen Pioneer*, 101; Thomas Merton to D. T. Suzuki, October 24, 1959, reprinted in Daggy, *Encounter*, 42.

62. Watts, *In My Own Way*, 309, and "The Beat Way of Life," originally delivered as a radio broadcast, August 11, 1959, transcribed in Watts, *Zen and the Beat Way*, 19.

63. Kerouac, *Dharma Bums*, 195; Snyder, "Note on Religious Tendencies," 148.

64. Watts, *Beat Zen, Square Zen & Zen*, 10–15.

65. Alfred J. Aronowitz, "The Yen for Zen," excerpted in *Big Sky Mind*, 82.

66. Suzuki, "Zen in the Modern World," 454.

67. Masatsugu, ""Beyond This World of Transiency and Impermanence,"" quotes taken from pp. 423 and 450.

7. JAPAN FOR THE REST OF US

1. Barry, *Dave Barry Does Japan*, 7. Also, the "Hyperthyroid Pterodactyls" would be a great name for a rock band.
2. Hunsburger, "Japanese Exports and the American Market," 131.
3. For more on the U.S. decision and struggle to include Japan in GATT, see Shimizu, *Creating People of Plenty*.
4. Editorial note (Eisenhower's speech to the National Editorial Association), June 22, 1954, FRUS, *China and Japan*, part 2, 1952–54, doc 772.
5. Dower, *Embracing Defeat*, 536–37; Morita, *Made in Japan*, 77.
6. For an extensive catalog of Japanese items imported to the United States in the years 1947–52, see Klamkin, *Made in Occupied Japan*; Florence, *Occupied Japan Collectibles*.
7. Dower, *Embracing Defeat*, 541–42.
8. LaFeber, *The Clash*, 293–94; Johnson, *MITI and the Japanese Miracle*, 228–32.
9. Peter F. Drucker, "Japan Tries for a Second Miracle," *Reader's Digest*, June 63, 182–84. For more on the actual reemergence of Japan's economy and consumer market, see Partner, *Assembled in Japan*.
10. See Bidwell, *What the Tariff Means to American Industries*; McHugh, "Made in Japan."
11. Grandma, "Made in Japan," *Chicago Tribune*, January 9, 1960, 10; Mrs. EJK, "She Loves Japan, but . . . ," *CT*, December 25, 1960, 10.
12. "Made in Japan: The Deluge," *Newsweek*, August 1, 1960, 65; "Textiles: Flood from the East," *Newsweek*, July 2, 1956, 66; "When Goods from Abroad Hurt Businesses at Home," *U.S. News and World Report*, March 7, 1958, 43.
13. David Condon, "In the Wake of the News," *Chicago Tribune*, June 4, 1958, C1; William W. Yates, "From a Travel Log," *CT*, August 14, 1960, F7; Herb Lyon, "Tower Ticker," *CT*, March 9, 1960, B2; Max, "You Must Be Joking Dept.," *CT*, May 9, 1959, 12.
14. "Buying Japanese," *Business Week*, September 19, 1959, 150.
15. McHugh, "Made in Japan," 57, 60.
16. "Precision on Wheels," *Time*, August 25, 1961, 61; "Japanese Plan Big Campaign to Sell Typewriters in the U.S.," *New York Times*, February 22, 1964, 45. For more on Japan's transition as an exporter of cheap goods to an exporter of high-end electronics, see Warner Mettler, "Gimcracks, Dollar Blouses, and Transistors," 202–30.
17. Segrave, *Drive-in Theaters*, 78–88, 142–47.
18. Eric Mark Kramer, "Who's Afraid of the Virgin Wolf Man? or, The Other Meaning of Auto-Eroticism," 21.
19. Anthony Downs, "Where the Drive-in Fits into the Movie Industry"; Segrave, *Drive-in Theaters*, 73, 147.
20. Doherty, *Teenagers and Teenpics*, 13–31.

21. See Wagstaff, "Italian Genre Films in the World Market"; Karola, "Italian Cinema Goes to the Drive-in: The Intercultural Horrors of Mario Bava."
22. Doherty, *Teenagers and Teenpics*, 1–12.
23. For more on nuclear anxiety, see Elaine Tyler May, "Explosive Issues: Sex, Women, and the Bomb"; Rose, *One Nation Underground*.
24. Sayuri Shimizu, "Lost in Translation and Morphed in Transit: Godzilla in Cold War America," 56; Kalat, *A Critical History and Filmography of Toho's Godzilla Series*, 13.
25. Ragone, *Eiji Tsuburaya*, 34–35.
26. For scholarly interpretations of Gojira's meaning in his original Japanese context, see Igarashi, *Bodies of Memory*, 114–22; Inuhiko, "The Menace from the South Seas: Honda Ishiro's *Godzilla*."
27. Gordon, "Godzilla, King of the Monsters"; Shimizu, "Lost in Translation," 52, 54.
28. Shimizu, "Lost in Translation," 52; see "Picture Grosses," in *Variety*, May 2, 1956, 9; May 9, 1956, 8; June 18, 1956, 9; July 25, 1956, 11; August 15, 1956, 13; August 29, 1956, 8; September 26, 1956, 18.
29. Bosley Crowther refers to the Loew's State as "respectable" in "Screen: Horror Import," *New York Times*, April 28, 1956, 11; "'Godzilla' 250 Day-Daters," *Variety*, June 27, 1956, 4. For examples of *Godzilla* in matinee double features, see Englewood, Maryland, Starlite, and Valencia theater ads, *Chicago Tribune*, August 3, 1956, A9.
30. Ragone, *Eiji Tsuburaya*, 44–47; Kalat, *Toho's Godzilla Series*, 35–41.
31. Ragone *Eiji Tsuburarya*, 66–70; Kalat, *Toho's Godzilla Series*, 42–48; Morton, *King Kong*, 118–31.
32. A. H. Weiler, "Passing Picture Scene," *New York Times*, March 23, 1958, X5.
33. For more on the infantalization of the natives of "Infant Island" in *Mothra*, see Yoshikuni Igarashi, "Mothra's Gigantic Egg: Consuming the South Pacific in 1960s Japan."
34. Peter Reithof, "Future of the Dubbed Film," *Variety*, January 12, 1955, 24. On the choice between dubbing and subtitling, see Ascheid, "Speaking in Tongues," 34.
35. Ascheid, "Speaking in Tongues," 35–38; Reithof, "Future of the Dubbed Film," 24.
36. The Toho Master Collection edition DVD of the film (here titled *Godzilla Raids Again*) includes the Japanese version of the film with English subtitles, as well as the American version, allowing viewers to make such comparisons.
37. Reithof, "Future of the Dubbed Film," 24; Kalat, *Toho's Godzilla Series*, 24–25.
38. HHT, "Screen: A Double Bill," *New York Times*, July 2, 1959, 15.
39. Kalat, *Toho's Godzilla Series*, 24–34.
40. Igarashi, *Bodies of Memory*, 116; Tsutsui, *Godzilla on My Mind*, 31, 36–37, 40. The removal of material deemed to be potentially offensive from foreign films by exploitative movie distributors, through either reediting or dubbing, was in fact

common practice. More typically, it was used to cover sexual themes. See Karola, "Italian Cinema Goes to the Drive-in," 226.

41. Bosley Crowther, "Monsters Again," *New York Times*, May 6, 1956, 129.

42. See Ragone, *Eiji Tsuburarya*, 66–70; Kalat, *Toho's Godzilla Series*, 42–48; Morton, *King Kong*, 118–31.

43. J. Rocky Colavito, "Naked! Screaming! Terror! The Rhetoric of Hype and Drive-in Movie Trailers"; Shimizu, "Lost in Translation," 53; RKO theaters ad, *New York Times*, June 24, 1959, 36.

44. Ragone, *Eiji Tsuburaya*, 17, 50, 52.

45. Kalat, *Toho's Godzilla Series*, 28.

46. Charles Poore, "Books of the Times," *New York Times*, July 16, 1963, 29.

47. See essays in *In Godzilla's Footsteps*: Napier "When Godzilla Speaks," Boss, "Hybridity and Negotiated Identity in Japanese Popular Culture," and Bestor, "Epilogue: He Did the Stomp, He Did the Monster Stomp."

48. Crowther, "Screen: Horror Import," 11, and "Screen: Wartime Adventures of President Kennedy," *New York Times*, June 27, 1963, 23; "Fair Warning," *Newsweek*, May 14, 1956, 126; Mae Tinee, "Horror—Poorly Done," *Chicago Tribune*, January 29, 1958, A3; "Mothra," *Variety*, May 16, 1962, 19; Arthur Knight, "True Confessions," *Saturday Review*, July 27, 1963, 34.

49. "Godzilla: King of the Monsters," *Variety*, April 24, 1956, 6; Philip T. Hartung, "The Screen," *Commonweal*, December 13, 1957, 288, and May 29, 1959, 232; Howard Thompson, "Screen: Moon Is Warned," *New York Times*, July 9, 1960, 10; A. H. Weiler, "Screen: Hatari! Captures the Drama of Taganyika Wildlife," *New York Times*, June 12, 1962, 19.

50. Gomery, *Shared Pleasures*, 247–48; "Television Programs," *New York Times*, October 12, 1958, X14; "Television," *New York Times*, October 10, 1960, 63.

51. Examples include episodes of *Saturday Night Live*, *The Simpsons*, *South Park*, and *Chapelle's Show*, as well as advertisements for Dr. Pepper, Nike, and Subway, and the Blue Oyster Cult song "Godzilla." For more examples of late twentieth-century Godzilla references, see Tsutsui, *Godzilla on My Mind*, chapter 4.

CONCLUSION

1. To learn more about their current activities, visit the Institute's website at www .firstzen.org.

2. Fields, *How the Swans Came to the Lake*, 304–58.

3. Evidence in this case is admittedly informal. In a class of fifteen students studying Japanese history at the University of Mississippi, not one had heard the word *shibui*. Typing the search term *wabi sabi* into amazon.com retrieves a

significant number of matches. The radio host who used the term *shibumi* was Felder Rushing on Mississippi Public Radio's *Gestalt Gardener*.

4. Ferretti, *Friendship through Flowers*, 82–87, and Appendix: Chronological Listing of Events; Uyehara, *Ten Keys to Modern Japanese Flower Arranging*, v–vi.

5. Impressions gained from conversations with arboretum staff during a research visit in July 2008.

6. See http://www.absbonsai.org/american-clubs.

7. See O'Neill, *Coming Apart*; Matusow, *Unraveling of America*; Farber, *Age of Great Dreams*; Frank, *Conquest of Cool*; Schulman, *The Seventies*.

8. Interview with Steve Harper in Polner, *No Victory Parades*, 26. For more on media depictions of good versus bad Vietnamese, see Jacobs, *America's Miracle Man in Vietnam*.

9. Tsutsui, *Godzilla on My Mind*, 43–80, 113–40.

10. Kelts, *Japanamerica*, 9–34.

11. Yano, "Monsterizing the Japanese Cute: Pink Globalization and Its Critics Abroad." Intriguingly, Kitty has a disproportionately large following among Latina women.

12. Iwabuchi, *Recentering Globalization*, 24–32, 94–95.

13. Johnson, *Japanese through American Eyes*, 111–44.

14. See essays in Allen and Sakamoto, *Popular Culture, Globalization, and Japan*; Craig, *Japan Pop!*

15. See Kelts, *Japanamerica*, esp. 156–57. The term *otaku* is actually an honorific form of second-person address in Japanese. In 1980s Japan, anime fans who met up with one another at conventions without knowing others' names would simply refer to one another as "otaku." This began the joke in Japan that all fans were named Otaku, a meaning that has been entirely transformed in its American context to mean "Japanese pop culture geek."

16. See Kelts, *Japanamerica*, 145–76; Hirofumi Katsuno, "Kikaida for Life: Cult Fandom in a Japanese Live-Action TV Show in Hawai'i," and Yulia Mikhailova, "Apocalypse in Fantasy and Reality: Japanese Pop Culture in Contemporary Russia," in *In Godzilla's Footsteps*, 167–80, 181–200.

17. Joseph Nye, in the process of initially defining the term *soft power* in 1990, wrote of the discrepancy between the relative positions of Japan and the United States. *Bound to Lead*, 29–35.

18. See LaFeber, *The Clash*, 359–406.

19. Kawakami, *101 Unuseless Japanese Inventions*.

BIBLIOGRAPHY

ARCHIVES/MANUSCRIPT MATERIALS

Brooklyn Botanic Garden Library, Brooklyn (BBG)

First Zen Institute of America Archives, New York

First Zen Institute of America Library, Kyoto

Foreign Relations of the United States (FRUS)

The Japan-America Society of Washington DC

The Japan Society of Northern California, San Francisco

Museum of Modern Art Public Information Scrapbook, New York (MOMA)

National Arboretum Library, Washington DC

North Central Valley JACL/CSUS Oral History Project, Sacramento

Rafu Shimpo Newspaper Collection, Japanese American National Museum, San Francisco, and online at http://www.janm.org/collections/toyo-miyatake-studio-rafu-shimpo-collection/

Sarah Lawrence College Archives, Bronxville NY

University of Iowa Special Collections, Iowa City

PUBLISHED WORKS

Abe, Masao, ed. *A Zen Life: D. T. Suzuki Remembered*. New York: Weatherhill, 1986.

Abel, Jessamyn. *The International Minimum: Creativity and Contradiction in Japan's Global Engagement, 1933–1964*. Honolulu: University of Hawai'i Press, 2015.

Adeney Thomas, Julia. *Reconfiguring Modernity: Concepts of Nature in Japanese Political Ideology*. Berkeley: University of California Press, 2002.

Akiyuki, Nosaka. "American *Hijiki*." In *Contemporary Japanese Literature: An Anthology of Fiction, Film, and Other Writing since 1945*, edited by Howard Hibbett, 435–68. New York: Alfred A. Knopf, 1977.

Akutogawa, Ryunosuke. *Rashomon and Other Stories*. Translated by Takashi Kojina. New York: Liveright, 1952.

Alexander, Paul. *Salinger: A Biography*. Los Angeles: Renaissance Books, 1999.

Allen, Matthew, and Rumi Sakamoto, eds. *Popular Culture, Globalization and Japan*. New York: Routledge, 2006.

Alvah, Donna. *Unofficial Ambassadors: American Military Families Overseas and the Cold War, 1946–1965*. New York: New York University Press, 2007.

Apostolos-Cappadona, Diane, and Bruce Altshuler, eds. *Isamu Noguchi: Essays and Conversations*. New York: Harry N. Abrams, 1994.

Aronowitz, Alfred J. "St. Jack." In *Conversations with Jack Kerouac*, edited by Kevin Hayes, 33–35. Jackson: University Press of Mississippi, 2005.

———. "The Yen for Zen." Excerpted in *Big Sky Mind*, ed. Stephen Prothero, 82–88. New York: Riverhead Books, 1995.

Ascheid, Atje. "Speaking in Tongues: Voice Dubbing in the Cinema as Cultural Ventriloquism." *Velvet Light Trap* 40 (1997): 32–42.

Ashton, Dore. *The Delicate Thread: Teshigahara's Life in Art*. New York: Kodansha International, 1997.

———. *Noguchi: East and West*. Berkeley: University of California Press, 1992.

Auslander, Leora. *Taste and Power: Furnishing Modern France*. Berkeley: University of California Press, 1996.

Auslin, Michael R. *Pacific Cosmopolitans: A Cultural History of U.S.–Japan Relations*. Cambridge MA: Harvard University Press, 2011.

Azuma, Eiichiro. *Between Two Empires: Race, History, and Transnationalism in Japanese America.* New York: Oxford University Press, 2005.

Barry, Dave. *Dave Barry Does Japan*. New York: Random House, 1992.

Baumann, Shyon. *Hollywood Highbrow: From Entertainment to Art*. Princeton: Princeton University Press, 2007.

Belgrad, Daniel. *The Culture of Spontaneity: Improvisation and the Arts in Postwar America*. Chicago: University of Chicago Press, 1998.

Benedict, Ruth. *The Chrysanthemum and the Sword: Patterns of Japanese Culture*. Boston: Houghton Mifflin, 1946.

Berg, Peter. "Beating the Drum with Gary." In *Gary Snyder: Dimensions of a Life*, edited by Jon Halper, 376–91. San Francisco: Sierra Club Books, 1991.

Berrigan, Ted. "The Art of Fiction: Jack Kerouac." In *Conversations with Jack Kerouac*, edited by Kevin Hayes, 55–81. Jackson: University Press of Mississippi, 2005. Originally published in *Paris Review*, 1968.

Bestor, Theodore C. "Epilogue: He Did the Stomp, He Did the Monster Stomp." In *In Godzilla's Footsteps*, edited by William M. Tsutsui and Michiko Ito, 201–4. New York: Palgrave Macmillan, 2006.

Bidwell, Percy W. *What the Tariff Means to American Industries*. New York: Harper, 1956.

Borgwardt, Elizabeth. *A New Deal for the World: America's Vision for Human Rights*. Cambridge: Belknap Press, 2005.

Boss, Joyce E. "Hybridity and Negotiated Identity in Japanese Popular Culture." In *In Godzilla's Footsteps*, edited by William M. Tsutsui and Michiko Ito, 103–10. New York: Palgrave Macmillan, 2006.

Bourdieu, Pierre. *Distinction: A Social Critique of the Judgment of Taste*. Translated by Richard Nice. Cambridge MA: Harvard University Press, 1984.

Bradbury, Ray. *Zen in the Art of Writing*. Santa Barbara: Joshua Odell, 1989.

Brandt, Kim. *Kingdom of Beauty: Mingei and the Politics of Folk Art in Imperial Japan*. Durham NC: Duke University Press, 2007.

Brooks, Charlotte. *Alien Neighbors, Foreign Friends: Asian Americans, Housing, and the Transformation of Urban California*. Chicago: University of Chicago Press, 2009.

Bu, Liping. *Making the World Like Us: Education, Cultural Expansion, and the American Century*. Westport CT: Praeger, 2003.

Burch, Noel. "Akira Kurosawa." In *Perspectives on Akira Kurosawa*, edited by James Goodwin, 241–45. New York: Macmillan, 1994.

Burston, Daniel. *The Legacy of Erich Fromm*. Cambridge: Harvard University Press, 1991.

Capra, Frank. *Know Your Enemy: Japan*. Documentary. U.S. War Department, 1945.

Castillo, Greg. *Cold War on the Home Front: The Soft Power of Midcentury Design*. Minneapolis: University of Minnesota Press, 2010.

Chang, Chen-Chi. *The Practice of Zen*. Westport CT: Greenwood Press, 1959.

Chiba, Hiromi. "From Enemy to Ally: American Public Opinion and Perceptions about Japan, 1945-1950." PhD diss., University of Hawaii, 1990.

Chung Simpson, Caroline. *An Absent Presence: Japanese Americans in Postwar American Culture, 1945–1960*. Durham: Duke University Press, 2001.

Clark, David K. *The Pantheism of Alan Watts*. Downers Grove IL: Inter-Varsity Press, 1978.

Clark Powell, Nina. *Japanese Flower Arrangement for Beginners*. New York: Charles Scribner's Sons, 1962.

Cleveland, Anne. *It's Better with Your Shoes Off*. Tokyo: Charles E. Tuttle, 1955.

Colavito, J. Rocky. "Naked! Screaming! Terror! The Rhetoric of Hype and Drive-In Movie Trailers." In *Horror at the Drive-In*, edited by Gary D. Rhodes, 41–52. Jefferson NC: McFarland, 2003.

Converse Brown, Jane. "The Japanese Taste: Its Role in the Mission of the American Home and in the Family's Presentation of Itself to the Public as Expressed in Published Sources–1876–1916." PhD diss., University of Wisconsin, Madison, 1987.

Craig, Timothy J., ed. *Japan Pop! Inside the World of Japanese Popular Culture*. Armonk NY: M. E. Sharpe, 2000.

Daggy, Robert E., ed. *Encounter: Thomas Merton and D. T. Suzuki*. Monterey KY: Larkspur Press, 1988.

Daniels, Roger. *Asian America: Chinese and Japanese in the United States since 1850*. Seattle: University of Washington Press, 1988.

———. *Prisoners without Trial: Japanese Americans in World War II*. New York: Hill and Wang, 1993.

de Grazia, Victoria. *Irresistible Empire: America's Advance through Twentieth-Century Europe*. Cambridge: Belknap Press, 2005.

de Valck, Marijke. *Film Festivals: From European Geopolitics to Global Cinema*. Amsterdam: Amsterdam University Press, 2007.

Deleuze, Gilles. "Figures, or The Transformation of Forms." In *Perspectives on Akira Kurosawa*, edited by James Goodwin, 246–50. New York: Macmillan, 1994.

Dickinson, Peter, ed. *Cage Talk: Dialogues with and about John Cage*. Rochester: University of Rochester Press, 2006.

Dodge, Jim. "Ten Snyder Stories." In *Gary Snyder: Dimensions of a Life*, edited by Jon Halper, 143–57. San Francisco: Sierra Club Books, 1991.

Doherty, Thomas. *Teenagers and Teenpics: The Juvenilization of American Movies in the 1950s*. Boston: Unwin Hyman, 1988.

Dower, John. *Embracing Defeat: Japan in the Wake of World War II*. New York: W. W. Norton, 1999.

———. *War without Mercy: Race and Power in the Pacific War*. New York: Pantheon, 1986.

Downs, Anthony. "Where the Drive-in Fits into the Movie Industry" (1953). In *Exhibition: The Film Reader*, edited by Ina Rae Hark, 123–26. New York: Routledge, 2002.

Drexler, Arthur. *The Architecture of Japan*. New York: Museum of Modern Art, 1955.

Duus, Masayo. *The Life of Isamu Noguchi: Journey without Borders*. Translated by Peter Duus. Princeton: Princeton University Press, 2004.

Elias, Thomas S. "History of the Introduction and Establishment of Bonsai in the Western World." *National Bonsai Foundation Bulletin* 17, no. 3 (2006): 1–86

Engel, David H. *Japanese Gardens for Today*. Rutland VT: Charles E. Tuttle, 1959.

Fader, Larry A. "D. T. Suzuki's Contribution to the West." In *A Zen Life*, edited by Masao Abe, 95–108. New York: Weatherhill, 1986.

Falk, Andrew J. *Upstaging the Cold War: American Dissent and Cultural Diplomacy, 1940–1960.* Amherst: University of Massachusetts Press, 2010.

Falk, Ray. "Akira Kurosawa: Japan's Poet Laureate of Film." In *Akira Kurosawa Interviews*, edited by Bert Cardullo, 20–23. Jackson: University of Mississippi Press, 2008.

———. "Introducing Japan's Top Director." In *Akira Kurosawa Interviews*, edited by Bert Cardullo, 3–5. Jackson: University of Mississippi Press, 2008.

Farber, David. *The Age of Great Dreams: America in the 1960s.* New York: Hill & Wang, 1994.

The First Zen Institute of America. *Cat's Yawn.* New York: The First Zen Institute of America, 1947.

Ferretti, Hollistar. *Friendship through Flowers: The Ikebana International Story.* Tokyo: Ikebana International, 1986.

Fields, Rick. *How The Swans Came to the Lake: A Narrative History of Buddhism in America.* Boulder: Shambhala, 1981.

Fitzgerald, Thomas E. *The Ecumenical Movement: An Introductory History.* Westport CT: Praeger, 2004.

Fletcher, Valerie J. *Isamu Noguchi: Master Sculptor.* London: Scala, 2004.

Florence, Gene. *Occupied Japan Collectibles: Identification and Value Guide.* Paducah KY: Collector Books, 2001.

Forest, Jim. *Living with Wisdom: A Life of Thomas Merton.* Maryknoll NY: Orbis Books, 2008.

Frank, Thomas. *The Conquest of Cool: Business Culture, Counterculture, and the Rise of Hip Consumerism.* Chicago: University of Chicago Press, 1998.

Friedrich, Paul. *The Gita within Walden.* Walden. Albany: SUNY Press, 2008.

Fromm, Erich. "Memories of Dr. D. T. Suzuki." In *A Zen Life*, edited by Masao Abe, 127–30. New York: Weatherhill, 1986.

Fromm, Erich, D. T. Suzuki, and Richard DeMartino. *Zen Buddhism and Psychoanalysis.* New York: Harper & Row, 1960.

Funk, Rainer. *Erich Fromm: His Life and Ideas.* New York: Continuum, 2000.

Furlong, Monica. *Merton: A Biography.* London: SPCK, 1995.

———. *Zen Effects: The Life of Alan Watts.* Boston: Houghton Mifflin, 1986.

Galbraith, Stuart, IV. *The Emperor and the Wolf: The Lives and Films of Akira Kurosawa and Toshiro Mifune.* New York: Faber & Faber, 2001.

Giamo, Ben. *Kerouac, the Word and the Way: Prose Artist as Spiritual Quester.* Carbondale: Southern Illinois University Press, 2000.

Gienow-Hecht, Jessica C. E. "Shame on U.S.? Academics, Cultural Transfer, and the Cold War: A Critical Review." *Diplomatic History* 24, no. 3 (2000): 465–94.

Gomery, Douglas. *Shared Pleasures: A History of Movie Presentation in the United States.* Madison: University of Wisconsin Press, 1992.

Goodman, Paul. *Growing Up Absurd: Problems of Youth in the Organized System.* New York: Random House, 1960.

Goodwin, James. *Akira Kurosawa and Intertextual Cinema.* Baltimore: Johns Hopkins University Press, 1994.

———, ed. *Perspectives on Akira Kurosawa.* New York: Macmillan, 1994.

Gordon, Alex. "Godzilla, King of the Monsters" *Fangoria* 72 (March 1988): 58.

Gordon Allen, Ellen. *Japanese Flower Arrangement in a Nutshell.* Rutland VT: Charles E. Tuttle, 1955.

Gorer, Geoffrey. "Themes in Japanese Culture." In *Personal Character and Cultural Milieu,* edited by Douglas Haring, 272–91. Syracuse: Syracuse University Press, 1948.

Graebner, William. *The Age of Doubt: American Thought and Culture in the 1940s.* Boston: Twayne, 1991.

Graham, Dom Aelred. *Zen Catholicism.* New York: Harcourt, Brace & World, 1963.

Graves, Morris. *The Drawings of Morris Graves with Comments by the Artist.* New York: New York Graphic Society, 1974.

Grob, Gerald. *The Mad among Us: A History of the Care of America's Mentally Ill.* Cambridge: Harvard University Press, 1995.

Grunwald, Henry Anatole, ed. *Salinger: A Critical and Personal Portrait.* New York: Harper Collins, 1962.

Hale, Nathan G., Jr. *The Rise and Crisis of Psychoanalysis in the United States: Freud and the Americans, 1917–1985.* New York: Oxford University Press, 1995.

Hammond, Phil, ed. *Cultural Difference, Media Memories: Anglo-American Images of Japan.* Washington DC: Cassell, 1997.

Harada, Jiro. *The Lesson of Japanese Architecture.* New York: Studio Publications, 1936.

Harris, Neil. "All the World a Melting Pot? Japan at American Fairs, 1876–1904." In *Cultural Excursions: Marketing Appetites and Cultural Tastes in Modern America,* edited by Neil Harris, 29–55. Chicago: University of Chicago Press, 1990.

Hearn, Lafcadio. *Gleanings in Buddha Fields: Studies of Hand and Soul in the Far East.* Boston: Houghton, Mifflin, 1897.

———. *Japan's Religions: Shinto and Buddhism.* Compiled by Kato Kazumitsu. New Hyde Park NY: University Books, 1966.

Henning, Joseph. *Outposts of Civilization: Race, Religion, and the Formative Years of American-Japanese Relations.* New York: New York University Press, 2000.

Herndon Crockett, Lucy. *Popcorn on the Ginza: An Informal Portrait of Postwar Japan.* New York: William Sloane, 1949.

Herrigel, Eugen. *Zen in the Art of Archery*. New York: Pantheon Books, 1953.

Herzogenrath, Wulf, and Andreas Kreul, eds. *Sounds of the Inner Eye: John Cage, Mark Tobey, Morris Graves*. Bremen: Kunsthalle Bremen, 2002.

Highet, Gilbert, ed. *Talents and Geniuses: The Pleasures of Appreciation*. New York: Oxford University Press, 1957.

Hoganson, Kristin. *Consumer's Imperium: The Global Production of American Domesticity, 1865–1920*. Chapel Hill: University of North Carolina Press, 2007.

Horowitz, Daniel, ed. *American Social Classes in the 1950s: Selections from Vance Packard's* The Status Seekers. 1959. Boston: Bedford St. Martin's, 1995.

Hughes, H. Stuart. *Consciousness and Society: The Reorientation of European Social Thought, 1890–1930*. New York: Vintage Books, 1958.

Hull, George F. *Bonsai for Americans: A Practical Guide to the Creation and Care of Miniature Potted Trees*. Garden City NY: Doubleday, 1964.

Hume, Bill, and John Annarino. *When We Get Back Home from Japan*. Tokyo: Pacific Stars and Stripes, 1953.

Hunsburger, Warren S. "Japanese Exports and the American Market." *Far Eastern Survey* 26, no. 9 (1957): 129–40.

Igarashi, Yoshikuni. *Bodies of Memory: Narratives of War in Postwar Japanese Culture, 1945–1970*. Princeton: Princeton University Press, 2000.

———. "Mothra's Gigantic Egg: Consuming the South Pacific in 1960s Japan." In *In Godzilla's Footsteps*, edited by William M. Tsutsui and Michiko Ito, 83–102. New York: Palgrave Macmillan, 2006.

"Ikebana International: Our Founders Story and History of Chapter #1." Pamphlet published by Ikebana International, Chapter #1, Washington DC, 1976.

Imada, Adria L. *Aloha America: Hula Circuits through the U.S. Empire*. Durham: Duke University Press, 2012.

Inuhiko, Yomota. "The Menace from the South Seas: Honda Ishiro's *Godzilla.*" In *Japanese Cinema: Texts and Contexts*, 102–11.

Iwabuchi, Koichi. *Recentering Globalization: Popular Culture and Japanese Transnationalism*. Durham: Duke University Press, 2002.

Iwamura, Jane Naomi. *Virtual Orientalism: Asian Religions and American Popular Culture*. New York: Oxford University Press, 2011.

Jacobs, Seth, *America's Miracle Man in Vietnam: Ngo Dinh Diem, Religion, Race, and U.S. Intervention in Southeast Asia*. Durham: Duke University Press, 2005.

Johnson, Chalmers. MITI *and the Japanese Miracle: The Growth of Industrial Policy, 1925–1975*. Stanford: Stanford University Press, 1982.

Johnson, Sheila K. *The Japanese through American Eyes*. Stanford: Stanford University Press, 1988.

Johnson, Walter, and Francis J. Colligan. *The Fulbright Program: A History*. Chicago: University of Chicago Press, 1965.

Kalat, David. *A Critical History and Filmography of Toho's Godzilla Series*. Jefferson NC: McFarland, 1997.

Karola, "Italian Cinema Goes to the Drive-in: The Intercultural Horrors of Mario Bava." In *Horror at the Drive-in*, edited by Gary D. Rhodes, 211–37. Jefferson NC: McFarland, 2003.

Kass, Ray. "The Art of Morris Graves: Meditation on Nature." In *Sounds of the Inner Eye*, edited by Wulf Herzogenrath and Andreas Kreul, 38–53. Bremen: Kunsthalle Bremen, 2002.

———. *Morris Graves: Vision of the Inner Eye*. New York: George Braziller, 1983.

Katsuno, Hirofumi. "Kikaida for Life: Cult Fandom in a Japanese Live-Action TV Show in Hawai'i." In *In Godzilla's Footsteps*, edited by William M. Tsutsui and Michiko Ito, 167–80. New York: Palgrave Macmillan, 2006.

Kaufmann, Edgar Jr. *What Is Modern Design?* New York: Museum of Modern Art, 1950.

Kawakami, Kenji. *101 Unuseless Japanese Inventions*. New York: Norton, 2000.

Keightley, Alan. *Into Every Life a Little Zen Must Fall: A Christian Philosopher Looks to Alan Watts and the East*. London: Wisdom Publications, 1986.

Kelts, Roland. *Japanamerica: How Japanese Pop Culture Had Invaded the U.S.* New York: Palgrave Macmillan, 2006.

Kerouac, Jack. *The Dharma Bums*. New York: Penguin Books, 1958, 1986.

Kikuchi, Charles. *The Kikuchi Diary: Chronicle from an American Concentration Camp*. Edited by John Modell. Urbana: University of Illinois Press, 1973.

Kinnamon, Michael, and Brian E. Cope, eds. *The Ecumenical Movement: An Anthology of Key Texts and Voices*. Geneva: WCC Publications, 1997.

Kirsten, Sven. *Tiki Pop: America Imagines Its Own Polynesian Paradise*. Cologne: Taschen, 2014.

Klamkin, Marian. *Made in Occupied Japan: A Collector's Guide*. New York: Crown, 1976.

Klein, Christina. *Cold War Orientalism: Asia in the Middlebrow Imagination, 1945–1961*. Berkeley: University of California Press, 2003.

Kobayashi, Norio. *Bonsai: Miniature Potted Trees*. Tokyo: Japan Travel Bureau, 1950.

Koestler, Arthur. *The Lotus and the Robot*. London: Hutchinson, 1960.

Kondoo, Akihisa. "The Stone Bridge of Joshu." In *A Zen Life*, edited by Masao Abe. New York: Weatherhill, 1986.

———. "Zen in Psychotherapy: The Virtue of Sitting." *Chicago Review* 12, no. 2 (1958): 57–64.

Koshiro, Yukiko. *Trans-Pacific Racisms and the U.S. Occupation of Japan.* New York: Columbia University Press, 1999.

Kramer, Eric Mark. "Who's Afraid of the Virgin Wolf Man? or, The Other Meaning of Auto-Eroticism." In *Horror at the Drive-in*, edited by Gary D. Rhodes, 9–23. Jefferson NC: McFarland, 2003.

Krim, Seymour, ed. *The Beats.* Greenwich CT: Fawcett, 1960.

———. "Making It!" In *The Beat Scene*, edited by Elias Wilentz, 75–83. New York: Corinth Books, 1960.

Kurashige, Lon. *Japanese American Celebration and Conflict: A History of Ethnic Identity and Festival, 1934–1990.* Berkeley: University of California Press, 2002.

Kurashige, Scott. *The Shifting Grounds of Race: Black and Japanese Americans in the Making of Multiethnic Los Angeles.* Princeton: Princeton University Press, 2008.

LaFeber, Walter. *The Clash: U.S.–Japanese Relations throughout History.* New York: W. W. Norton, 1997.

Lamport, Felicia. *Scrap Irony.* Boston: Houghton Mifflin, 1961.

Lancaster, Clay. *The Japanese Influence in America.* New York: W. H. Rawls, 1963.

LeFanu, Mark. *Mizoguchi and Japan.* London: British Film Institute, 2005.

Leff, Leonard J., and Jerold Simmons. *The Dame in the Kimono: Hollywood, Censorship, and the Production Code.* Lexington: University Press of Kentucky, 2001.

Lipton, Lawrence. *The Holy Barbarians.* New York: Julian Messner, 1959.

Loayza, Matt. "'A Curative and Creative Force': The Exchange of Persons Program and Eisenhower's Inter-American Policies, 1953–1961." *Diplomatic History* 37, no. 5 (November 2013): 946–70.

Lyford, Amy. *Isamu Noguchi's Modernism: Negotiating Race, Labor, and Nation, 1930–1950.* Berkeley: University of California Press, 2013.

Maltis, Elena. *The Solitary Explorer: Thomas Merton's Transforming Journey.* San Francisco: Harper & Row, 1980.

Masatsugu, Michael Kenji. "'Beyond This World of Transiency and Impermanence': Japanese Americans, Dharma Bums, and the Making of American Buddhism in the Early Cold War Years." *Pacific Historical Review* 77, no. 3 (2008): 423–51.

———. Reorienting the Pure Land: Japanese Americans, the Beats, and the Making of American Buddhism." PhD diss., University of California, Irvine, 2004.

Matsuda, Takeshi. *Soft Power and Its Perils: U.S. Cultural Policy in Early Postwar Japan and Permanent Dependency.* Washington DC: Woodrow Wilson Center Press, 2007.

Matusow, Allen J. *The Unraveling of America: A History of Liberalism in the 1960s.* New York: Harper & Row, 1984.

May, Elaine Tyler. "Explosive Issues: Sex, Women, and the Bomb." In *Recasting America*, edited by Lary May, 154–70. Chicago: University of Chicago Press, 1989.

May, Lary, ed. *Recasting America: Culture and Politics in the Age of Cold War*. Chicago: University of Chicago Press, 1989.

Mayer, Michael F. *Foreign Films on American Screens*. New York: Arco, 1965.

McAlister, Melani. *Epic Encounters: Culture, Media, and U.S. Interests in the Middle East since 1945*. Berkeley: University of California Press, 2005.

McClintock, Anne. *Imperial Leather: Race, Gender, and Sexuality in the Colonial Contest*. New York: Routledge, 1995.

McDonald, Keiko. *Mizoguchi*. Boston: Twayne, 1984.

McHugh, Ursula. "Made in Japan." *Industrial Design* 6, no. 5 (1959): 54–69.

McMahan, David L. *The Making of Buddhist Modernism*. New York: Oxford University Press, 2008.

McNeil, Peter. "Myths of Moderism: Japanese Architecture, Interior Design, and the West, c1920–1940." *Journal of Design History* 5, no. 4 (1992): 281–94.

Meech-Pekarik, Julia. *Frank Lloyd Wright and the Art of Japan: The Architect's Other Passion*. New York: Harry N. Abrams, 2001.

Merton, Thomas. *The Seven Story Mountain*. New York: Harcourt, Brace, 1948.

———. *Zen and the Birds of Appetite*. New York: New Directions, 1968.

Mikhailova, Yulia. "Apocalypse in Fantasy and Reality: Japanese Pop Culture in Contemporary Russia." In *In Godzilla's Footsteps*, edited by William M. Tsutsui and Michiko Ito, 181–200. New York: Palgrave Macmillan, 2006.

Min, Myungkee. "Japanese/American Architecture: A Century of Cultural Exchange." PhD diss., University of Washington, 1999.

Mori, Osamu. *Typical Japanese Gardens*. Tokyo: Shibata, 1962.

Morita, Akio. *Made in Japan: Akio Morita and Sony*. New York: E. P. Dutton, 1986.

Morton, Ray. *King Kong: The History of a Movie Icon from Fay Wray to Peter Jackson*. New York: Applause Theater and Cinema Books, 2005.

Morton, Ruth. *The Home and Its Furnishings*. New York: McGraw-Hill, 1953.

Napier, Susan. "When Godzilla Speaks." In *In Godzilla's Footsteps*, edited by William M. Tsutsui and Michiko Ito, 9–20. New York: Palgrave Macmillan, 2006.

Nelson, George. *Problems of Design*. New York: Whitney Library of Design, 1957, 1974.

Nicholls, David. *John Cage*. Urbana: University of Illinois Press, 2007.

Nute, Kevin H. "Frank Lloyd Wright and *Japanese Homes*: The Japanese House Dissected." *Japan Forum* 6, no. 1 (1994): 73–88.

Nye, Joseph. *Bound to Lead: The Changing Nature of American Power*. New York: Basic Books, 1990.

Oda, Meredith. *Gateway to the Pacific: Japanese Americans, Japan, and the Remaking of Transpacific San Francisco*. Chicago: University of Chicago Press, forthcoming.

———. "Rebuilding Japantown: Japanese Americans in Transpacific San Francisco during the Cold War." *Pacific Historical Review* 83, no.1 (2014): 57–91.

Ogawa, Dennis. *From Japs to Japanese: The Evolution of Japanese American Stereotypes.* Berkeley: McCutchan, 1971.

Ohi, Minobu. *History of Ikebana.* Translated by Seiko Aoyoma. Tokyo: Shufunotomo, 1962.

Okubo, Mine. *Citizen 13660.* New York: Columbia University Press, 1946.

O'Neill, William. *Coming Apart: An Informal History of America in the 1960s.* Chicago: Quadrangle Books, 1971.

Partner, Simon. *Assembled in Japan: Electrical Goods and the Making of the Japanese Consumer.* Berkeley: University of California Press, 1999.

Perez, Louis. *On Becoming Cuban: Identity, Nationalism, and Culture.* Chapel Hill: University of North Carolina Press, 1999.

Perry, Lewis. *Intellectual Life in America: A History.* New York: Franklin Watts, 1984.

Philips, Alastair, and Julian Stringer. *Japanese Cinema: Texts and Contexts.* New York: Routledge, 2007.

Podhoretz, Norman. "The Know-Nothing Bohemians." In *The Beats*, edited by Seymour Krim, 111–24. *The Beats.* Greenwich CT: Fawcett, 1960.

Polner, Murray, ed. *No Victory Parades: The Return of the Vietnam Veteran.* New York: Holt, Rinehart and Winston, 1971.

Prince, Stephen. *The Warrior's Camera: The Cinema of Akira Kurosawa.* Princeton: Princeton University Press, 1991.

———. "Zen and Selfhood: Patterns of Eastern Thought in Kurosawa's Films." In *Perspectives on Kurosawa*, edited by James Goodwin, 225–35. New York: Macmillan, 1994.

Prothero, Stephen. *Big Sky Mind: Buddhism and the Beat Generation.* New York: Riverhead Books, 1995.

Ragone, August. *Eiji Tsuburaya: Master of Monsters.* San Francisco: Chronicle Books, 2007.

Ranchan, Som P. *An Adventure in Vedanta: J. D. Salinger's* The Glass Family. Delhi: Ajanta Publications, 1989.

Reischauer, Edwin O., and Michael Auslin. *Japan Society: Celebrating a Century, 1907–2007.* New York: Japan Society, 2007.

Riesman, David, Nathan Glazer, and Reuel Denney. *The Lonely Crowd.* New Haven: Yale University Press, 1961.

Reps, Paul, and Nyogen Senzaki. *Zen Flesh, Zen Bones: A Collection of Zen and Pre-Zen Writings.* Rutland VT: Tuttle, 1957, 1985.

Richie, Donald. *The Films of Akira Kurosawa.* Berkeley: University of California Press, 1965, 1998.

——— *A Hundred Years of Japanese Film.* New York: Kodansha International, 2001.

———. "The Later Films of Yasujiro Ozu." *Film Quarterly* 13, no. 1 (1959): 18–25.

———. "A Personal Record." *Film Quarterly* 14, no. 1 (Autumn 1960): 20–30.

Richie, Donald, and Joseph I. Anderson. *The Japanese Film: Art and Industry*. Rutland VT: Charles E. Tuttle, 1959.

———. "Traditional Theater and the Film of Japan." *Film Quarterly* 12, no. 1 (1958): 2–9.

Rigney, Francis. *The Real Bohemia: A Sociological and Psychological Study of the "Beats."* New York: Basic Books, 1961.

Robinson, Greg. *After Camp: Portraits in Midcentury Japanese Life and Politics.* Berkeley: University of California Press, 2012.

Rodman, Selden. *Conversations with Artists*. New York: Devin-Adair, 1957.

Rose, Kenneth D. *One Nation Underground: The Fallout Shelter in American Culture.* New York: New York University Press, 2001.

Salinger, J. D. *The Catcher in the Rye*. New York: Little, Brown, 1951, 2001.

———. *Franny and Zooey*. New York: Bantam Books, 1964.

———. *Nine Stories*. Boston: Little, Brown, 1953, 1981.

———. *Raise High the Roof Beam, Carpenters; and, Seymour: An Introduction.* New York: Little, Brown, 1963, 1987.

Sand, Jordan. *House and Home in Modern Japan: Architecture, Domestic Space, and Bourgeois Culture, 1880–1930.* Cambridge: Harvard University Press, 2003.

Sasaki, Shigetsu. *Holding the Lotus to the Rock: The Autobiography of Sokei-an, America's First Zen Master.* Edited by Michael Hotz. New York: Four Walls Eight Windows, 2002.

Sato, Tadao. *Kenji Mizoguchi and the Art of Japanese Cinema*. Translated by Brij Tankha. New York: Berg, 2008.

Sbardellati, John. *J. Edgar Hoover Goes to the Movies: The FBI and the Origins of Hollywood's Cold War.* Ithaca: Cornell University Press, 2012.

Schaller, Michael. *Altered States: The United States and Japan since the Occupation*. New York: Oxford University Press, 1997.

Schlichtmann, Klaus. *Japan in the World: Shidehara Kijuro, Pacifism, and the Abolition of War.* Lanham MD: Roman & Littlefield, 2009.

Schulman, Bruce. *The Seventies: The Great Shift in American Culture, Society, and Politics*. New York: Free Press, 2001.

Schwantes, Robert S. *Japanese and Americans: A Century of Cultural Relations.* New York: Harper & Brothers, 1955.

Scott-Smith, Giles. *Networks of Empire: The U.S. State Department's Foreign Leader Program in the Netherlands, France, and Britain, 1950–70.* Brussels: P.I.E. Peter Lang, 2008.

Second Vatican Council. "Declaration on the Relation of the Church to Non-Christian Religions." In *Ecumenical Movement: An Anthology*, edited by Michael Kinnamon and Brian Cope. Geneva: WCC Publications, 1997.

Segrave, Kerry. *Drive-in Theaters: A History from Their Inception in 1933*. Jefferson NC: McFarland, 1992.

Sharf, Robert H. "The Zen of Japanese Nationalism." *History of Religions* 33, no. 1 (1993): 1–43.

Shibusawa, Naoko. *America's Geisha Ally: Reimagining the Japanese Enemy.* Cambridge: Harvard University Press, 2006.

Shimizu, Sayuri. *Creating People of Plenty: The United States and Japan's Economic Alternatives, 1950–1960*. Kent OH: Kent State University Press, 2001.

———. "Lost in Translation and Morphed in Transit: Godzilla in Cold War America." In *In Godzilla's Footsteps*, edited by William M. Tsutsui and Michiko Ito, 51–63. New York: Palgrave Macmillan, 2006.

Shorter, Edward. *A History of Psychiatry: From the Era of the Asylum to the Age of Prozac*. New York: John Wiley, 1997.

Shultis, Christopher. *Silencing the Sounded Self: John Cage and the American Experimental Tradition*. Boston: Northeastern University Press, 1998.

Shukert, Elfrieda Berthiaume, and Barbara Smith Scibetta. *War Brides of World War II*. New York: Penguin Books, 1989.

Smith, Terry. *Making the Modern: Industry, Art, and Design in America*. Chicago: University of Chicago Press, 1993.

Snyder, Gary. "Note on Religious Tendencies." In *The Beats*, edited by Seymour Krim, 147–48. Greenwich CT: Fawcett, 1960.

———. "Spring *Sesshin* at Shokoku-ji." *Chicago Review* 12, no. 2 (Summer 1958): 41–49.

Sparnon, Norman. *Japanese Flower Arrangement: Classical and Modern*. Rutland VT: Charles E. Tuttle, 1960.

Stewart, David B. *The Making of a Modern Japanese Architecture: 1868 to the Present*. New York: Kodansha, 1987.

Stirling, Isabel. *Zen Pioneer: The Life and Works of Ruth Fuller Sasaki*. Berkeley: Shoemaker & Hoard, 2006.

Stone, Judy. "Akira Kurosawa." In *Akira Kurosawa Interviews*, edited by Bert Cardullo, 159–65. Jackson: University of Mississippi Press, 2008.

Suzuki, Daisetz Teitaro. *Essence of Buddhism.* Kyoto: Hozoken, 1948.

———. *Living by Zen*. Compiled by Christmas Humphries. London: Rider, 1982.

———. *Zen and Japanese Culture*. New York: Pantheon, 1959.

———. *Zen Buddhism and Its Influence on Japanese Culture*. New York: Pantheon, 1936, 1979.

———. *Zen Buddhism: Selected Writings of D. T. Suzuki*. Edited by William Barrett. Garden City NY: Doubleday, 1956.

———. "Zen in the Modern World." *Japan Quarterly* 5, no. 4 (1958): 452–61.

Swaine Thomas, Dorothy. *The Salvage*. Berkeley: University of California Press, 1952.

Swaine Thomas, Dorothy, and Richard Nishimoto. *The Spoilage*. Berkeley: University of California Press, 1946.

Takaki, Ron. *Strangers from a Different Shore: A History of Asian Americans*. Boston: Little, Brown, 1998.

Thoreau, Henry David. *Walden and Selected Essays*. New York: Hendricks House, 1854, 1947.

Tobey, Mark. "Japanese Traditions in American Art." In *Sounds of the Inner Eye*, edited by Wulf Herzogenrath and Andreas Kreul, 156-57. Bremen: Kunsthalle Bremen, 2002. Originally published in *College Art Journal*, 1958.

Tsutsui, William M. *Godzilla on My Mind: Fifty Years of the King of the Monsters*. New York: Palgrave Macmillan, 2004.

Tsutsui, William M., and Michiko Ito, eds. *In Godzilla's Footsteps: Japanese Pop Culture Icons on the Global Stage*. New York: Palgrave Macmillan, 2006.

Tweed, Thomas A. "Nightstand Buddhists and Other Creatures: Sympathizers, Adherents, and the Study of Religion." In *American Buddhism*, edited by Duncan Ryuken Williams and Christopher S. Queen, 71–90. Richmond, Surrey: Curzon Press, 1999.

Tyler, Parker. "*Rashomon* as Modern Art." In *Rashomon*, edited by Donald Richie, 149–58. New Brunswick NJ: Rutgers University Press, 1987.

Uyehara, Allie. *Ten Keys to Japanese Flower Arrangements*. New York: Vantage, 1975.

van de Wetering, Jan Willem. *The Empty Mirror: Experiences in a Japanese Zen Monastery*. Boston: Houghton Mifflin, 1973.

Verhoeven, Martin J. "Americanizing the Buddha: Paul Carus and the Transformation of Asian Thought." In *Faces of Buddhism in America*, edited by Charles Prebish and Kenneth Tanaka, 207–27. Berkeley: University of California Press, 1998.

Victoria, Brian Daizen. "A Zen Nazi in Wartime Japan: Count Dürckheim and His Sources—D. T. Suzuki, Yasutani Haku'un, and Eugen Herrigel." *Asia-Pacific Journal: Japan Focus* 12, no. 3, pt. 2 (2014).

———. "Zen as a Cult of Death in the Wartime Writings of D. T. Suzuki." *Asia-Pacific Journal: Japan Focus* 11, no. 30, pt. 4 (2013).

Wagnleitner, Reinhold. *Coca-colonization and the Cold War: The Cultural Mission of the United States in Austria after the Second World War*. Chapel Hill: University of North Carolina Press, 1994.

Wagnleitner, Reinhold, and Elaine Tyler May, eds. *Here, There, and Everywhere: The Foreign Politics of American Popular Culture*. Hanover: University Press of New England, 2000.

Wagstaff, Christopher. "Italian Genre Films in the World Market." In *Hollywood and Europe: Economics, Culture, National Identity, 1945–95*, edited by Geoffrey Nowell-Smith and Steven Ricci, 74–84. London: British Film Institute, 1998.

Walker, Nancy A. *Shaping Our Mother's World: American Women's Magazines*. Jackson: University Press of Mississippi, 2000.

———, ed. *Women's Magazines, 1940–1960: Gender Roles and the Popular Press*. Boston: Bedford St. Martin's, 1998.

Warner Mettler, Meghan. "Gimcracks, Dollar Blouses, and Transistors: American Reactions to Imported Japanese Products: 1945–1964." *Pacific Historical Review* 79, no. 2 (2010): 202–30.

Waswo, Ann. *Housing in Postwar Japan: A Social History*. New York: Routledge Curzon, 2002.

Watts, Alan. "Beat Zen, Square Zen & Zen." *Chicago Review* 12, no. 2 (Summer 1958): 3–11.

———. *Beat Zen, Square Zen & Zen*. San Francisco: City Lights Books, 1959.

———. *In My Own Way: An Autobiography, 1915–1965*. New York: Pantheon Books, 1972.

———. *The Spirit of Zen: A Way of Life, Work, and Art in the Far East*. 3rd ed. New York: Grove Press, 1958.

———. *This Is IT And Other Essays on Zen and Spiritual Experience*. New York: Pantheon Books, 1958.

———. *The Way of Zen*. New York: Pantheon Books, 1957.

———. *Zen and the Beat Way*. Adapted and edited by David Cellars and Mark Watts. Boston: Charles E. Tuttle, 1997.

Webb, Lida. *An Easy Guide to Japanese Flower Arrangement Styles*. New York: Hearthside Press, 1963.

Wehr, Wesley. "Mark Tobey: A Dialogue between Painting and Music." In *Sounds of the Inner Eye*, edited by Wulf Herzogenrath and Andreas Kreul, 25–37. Bremen: Kunsthalle Bremen, 2002.

Wight, Frederick S. *Morris Graves*. Berkeley: University of California Press, 1956.

Wilinsky, Barbara. *Sure Seaters: The Emergence of Art House Cinema*. Minneapolis: University of Minnesota Press, 2001.

Willkie, Wendell L. *One World*. New York: Simon & Schuster, 1943.

Wilson Ross, Nancy, ed. *The World of Zen: An East-West Anthology*. New York: Random House, 1960.

Winther-Tamaki, Bert. *Art in the Encounter of Nations: Japanese and American Artists in the Early Postwar Years*. Honolulu: University of Hawai'i Press, 2001.

Wu, Ellen. *The Color of Success: Asian Americans and the Origins of the Model Minority*. Princeton: Princeton University Press, 2014.

Wuthnow, Robert. *The Restructuring of American Religion: Society and Faith since World War II*. Princeton: Princeton University Press, 1988.

Yamada, Shoji. *Shots in the Dark: Japan, Zen, and the West*. Translated by Earl Hartman. Chicago: University of Chicago Press, 2009.

Yamazaki, Sanae. *We Loved Every Minute; or, Life in "Western" Japan*. Tokyo: Pacific Stars and Stripes, 1958.

Yampolsky, Philip. "Kyoto, Zen, Snyder." In *Gary Snyder: Dimensions of a Life*, edited by Jon Halper, 60–69. San Francisco: Sierra Club Books, 1991.

Yano, Christine R. "Monsterizing the Japanese Cute: Pink Globalization and Its Critics Abroad." In *In Godzilla's Footsteps*, ed. William M. Tsutsui and Michiko Ito, 153–66. New York: Palgrave Macmillan, 2006.

Yashiroda, Kan, ed. *Handbook on Dwarfed Potted Trees*. Brooklyn NY: Brooklyn Botanic Garden, 1959, 1975.

Yoo, David K. *Growing Up Nisei: Race, Generation, and Culture among Japanese Americans of California, 1924–49*. Urbana: University of Illinois Press, 2000.

Yoshihara, Mari. *Embracing the East: White Women and American Orientalism*. New York: Oxford University Press, 2003.

Yoshihito, Takada, and James M. Vardaman Jr. *Talking about Buddhism Q&A*. Tokyo: Bilingual Books, 1997, 2008.

Yoshimoto, Mitsuhiro. *Kurosawa: Film Studies and Japanese Cinema*. Chapel Hill: Duke University Press, 2000.

Yoshimura, Yuji, and Giovanna M. Halford. *The Japanese Art of Miniature Trees and Landscapes: Their Creation, Care, and Enjoyment*. Rutland VT: Charles E. Tuttle, 1957.

INDEX

Page numbers appearing in italic refer to illustrations.

The Architecture of Japan (Drexler), 105

Arkoff, Sam, 193

art forms, Japanese: feminization of, 14; Japanese Americans and, 36, 41–42; Japanese film and, 60–61, 65; modernism and, 32–33; revision of Japanese, over time, 15; overview in America of, 9–11. *See also specific art forms*

art house theaters, 48–49, 52, 54, 57, 66, 224n45

artists and Zen Buddhism, 132–33, 145–51

"Asiatic," term of, 70

assimilation, 38, 41, 116

Auslander, Leora, 120

avant-garde ikebana, 71, 84, 85–87, 98

Avery, George S., 9, 90, 114, 115

Akiyuki, Nosaka, 27

Ball, Leo R., 88

Barrett, William, 161, 164

Barry, Dave, 182

Basho, 83

Battle in Outer Space (Honda), 196, 202

Battle of the Planets, 210–11

Bauhaus school of design, 33, 104

beams, exposed, 101, 102, 103, 107

The Beast from 20,000 Fathoms (Lourie), 191

Beats: about, 17, 161, 168–70; and Jack Kerouac, 171–78. *See also* Beat Zen

Beat Zen: background and overview of, 17, 158, 167–70, 178–79; Jack Kerouac and, 167, 171–78, 241–42n47, 242n49

"Beat Zen, Square Zen, and Zen" (Watts), 158, 175, 177

Belshore, Mr. and Mrs. Harry, 113

Benedict, Ruth, 7

Ben-Gurion, David, 162

Bestor, Theodore C., 201

Better Homes & Gardens, 77, 99–100

B grade movies, 190–91, 193, 197, 203. *See also* movies, Japanese monster; *specific B movies*

Bingham, Robert, 58

Bird, Isabella, 8

Bird with Possessions (Graves), 149

Blakey, Art, 54

Bonsai Clubs of America, 91

bonsai cultivation, 87–98, 89; American interest in, 88–92; Americanization of, 94–97; characteristics and values of, 92–93; demographics of, 34, 92, 94–95, 230n46; instruction in, 90–91; overview of, 71, 87–88, 97–98; today, 208–9

Bonsai for Americans (Hull), 91

bonsai scenes, 96–97

Bonsai Society of Greater New York, 91

Boss, Joyce, 201

Bourdieu, Pierre, 29–30

Bradbury, Ray, 164, 240n26

Brensen, Vera, 131–32

Bronstein, Daniel, 142

Brooklyn Botanic Garden (BBG): bonsai and, 88, 89–92, 94, 96, 209; Japanese gardens and, 111–12, 113–15, 119

Brooks, Charlotte, 40

Buddha, term of, 134

Buddha (Nagata), 66

Buddhism, 134, 207–8. *See also* Zen Buddhism

"Buddhism Now and Zen" (Lamport), 158–59

A Buddhist Bible (Goddard), 171

Buddhist Churches of America (BCA), 178

Buddhist Society of America, 136

Burr, Raymond, 198, 200, 202

Kennan, George, 26
Kerouac, Jack, 139, 167, 169, 171–78, 241–42n47, 242n49
Kikuchi, Charles, 116
King Brothers, 200
King Kong, 193
King Kong vs. Godzilla, 199, 202
King Kong vs. Gojira, 194
Kinugasa, Teinosuke, 45–46, 60
Klein, Christian, 5–6, 21
Knight, Arthur, 59, 61, 202
koans, 135, 150, 153, 163, 166, 172
Kobayashi, Masaki, 68
Kobayashi, Norio, 93, 94
Koehn, Alfred, 89
Koestler, Arthur, 16–17
Kokusai Bunka Shinkokai (KBS), 24
Kondoo, Akihisa, 152
Korean War, 185
Kramer, Eric Mark, 190
Kurashige, Scott, 40
Kurosawa, Akira, 45, 55–59, 67, 68, 209, 221n15
Kushi, Michio, 123
Kyo, Machiko, 56, 58, 59, 63
Kyoto Imperial Palace garden, *111*

Lamport, Felicia, 158–59
Lancaster, Clay, 104
Leary, Timothy, 208
Lebovich, Donatienne, 139
Le Corbusier, 104
Lee, Robert Tyler, 108
The Lesson of Japanese Architecture (Harada), 10
Levine, Joseph, 193, 198
Liberator, 177
Licht, Mrs. H., 126–27

Life magazine, 3, 31, 62, 106
The Life of Buddha, 171
Lipton, Lawrence, 172, 174
Little Carnegie Theater, 52
The Lonely Crowd (Riesman), 32
Look magazine, 30
The Lotus and the Robot (Koestler), 16–17
Lourie, Eugene, 191
lowbrows, 30, 31, 66
lower middlebrows, 30, 31, 33–35, 71
Lucky Dragon No. 5, 28, 191–92
Lynes, Russell, 30

MacArthur, Douglas, 26
MacArthur, Douglas, II, 78
MacArthur, Jean, 74
Machine Age Noise (Graves), 148
MacLow, Jackson, 145
Made-in-Japan merchandise, 183–88, 204. *See also* products, Japanese
"Made in Occupied Japan" label, 184–85
Mademoiselle, 157, 165–66
magazines and newspapers: class distinction and, 120–21; spreading of Japanese culture by, 9–11. *See also specific magazines and newspapers*
The Magnificent Seven (Sturges), 67
Mahayanism, 172, 241n47
Mandel Brothers department store, 126
manga comic books, 212–13
manga films, 213
marketing of monster movies, 200, 202
Marshall Plan, 20
masculinity: bonsai cultivation and, 92; image of Japan and, 13, 14–15; Zen and, 140, 156, 179
materialism, 156, 168–69
McAlister, Melani, 5–6

IN THE STUDIES IN PACIFIC WORLDS SERIES:

*How to Reach Japan by Subway: America's Fascination
with Japanese Culture, 1945–1965*
Meghan Warner Mettler

*Hawaiian by Birth: Missionary Children, Bicultural
Identity, and U.S. Colonialism in the Pacific*
Joy Schulz

To order or obtain more information on these or other University
of Nebraska Press titles, visit nebraskapress.unl.edu.

www.ingramcontent.com/pod-product-compliance
Lightning Source LLC
Chambersburg PA
CBHW020335100426
42812CB00029B/3130/J